Ecohumanism

April 2002

For Ana — love,
copyeditor, inspirer —
par excellence!
Gracias por todo —
Love,
Bob

Volume 15 of *Humanism Today*

Ecohumanism

edited by

Robert B. Tapp

in cooperation with the
North American Committe for Humanism

 Prometheus Books

59 John Glenn Drive
Amherst, New York 14228-2197

Published 2002 by Prometheus Books

Inquiries should be addressed to
Prometheus Books
59 John Glenn Drive
Amherst, New York 14228–2197
VOICE: 716–691–0133, ext. 207
FAX: 716–564–2711
WWW.PROMETHEUSBOOKS.COM

06 05 04 03 02   5 4 3 2 1

ISSN 1058–5966
ISBN 1–57392–937–9

Printed in the United States of America on acid-free paper

For Information on Leadership Training and other programs, please contact:

THE HUMANIST INSTITUTE
2 West 64th Street
New York, NY 10023

CONTENTS

ACKNOWLEDGMENTS

Grateful acknowledgment goes to the authors for their willingness to revise their essays on a tight schedule. This editor has allowed some capitalizations of ecohumanism and humanism where it seemed necessary to convey authors' intentions. Canadian/British spellings have also been preserved when appropriate. Thanks also to Paul Kurtz for facilitating the publication by Prometheus Books of this series; to Editor-in-Chief Steven L. Mitchell for his wise suggestions; and to my wife, Ana Martinez, precision proofreader, continuing pillar, and *manantial de paciencia*.

Volumes of *Humanism Today* are published by The Humanist Institute, which was founded in 1982 by the North American Committee for Humanism (NACH) as an educational venture to train professional and lay leaders for existing humanist organizations. The guiding principle has been that studying together would enhance all forms of nontheistic humanism, whether they described themselves as religious or secular; Ethical Culturist, Unitarian Universalist, Humanistic Jew; rationalist or freethinker; agnostic or atheist.

More than eighty students have completed a three-year graduate level curriculum. The Institute's adjunct faculty has gathered annually to consider pressing topics, and this book grows out of the 2000 colloquium. The adjunct faculty will be reassembling in 2001 to re-assess the role of traditional humanisms and to articulate viable positions for the new millennium.

Robert B. Tapp

PREFACE

Why ecohumanism? Just because ecofeminism, ecophilosophy, ecopragmatism, and similar compounds have appeared among recent titles? In part, Yes. But there is a stronger issue to be confronted. Many critics have denounced humanistic views of nature as too anthropocentric, too speciesist, even as too sexist—and these charges deserve to be assessed. There may be times when we need to use newer words to describe older matters in fresh ways.

Ecology is a fairly new term in the popular vocabulary and only slightly older in technical vocabularies. Yet it is clear that by Charles Darwin's time, something very like our "ecology" was coming into being. A central element in Darwin's evolution was the interaction of environments and species. Almost equally important, for Darwin, were the ways in which the "good" of one species negated the "good" of some other species. One famous passage is worth quoting as a reminder of this:

11

> We behold the face of nature bright with gladness, we often see
> superabundance of food; we do not see or we forget, that the
> birds which are idly singing round us mostly live on insects or
> seeds, and are thus constantly destroying life; or we forget how
> largely these songsters, or their eggs, or their nestlings, are de-
> stroyed by birds and beasts of prey; we do not always bear in
> mind, that, though food may be now superabundant, it is not so
> at all seasons of each recurring year.[1]

Of central import for Darwin, and so controversial that he long delayed proclaiming this, was the central assertion that humans were
one species among many in a process that not only had evolved but
was continuing to evolve.

There can be no doubt that Darwin was the founder of modern
ecology. Several other aspects of Darwin's thinking need to be remembered as we try to give some meaning to our new term. For
one thing, his biology was sufficiently different from the previous
sciences with their mathematically-stated predictions that Darwin
could describe the "laws of nature" as essentially human conven-
tions—not as fixed patterns "out there." When Darwin adopted
Herbert Spencer's phrase "Survival of the Fittest," he was clearly
aware of the metaphorical nature of that statement—and his parallel term "Natural Selection" should only be seen as a gentler label-
ing. Even what was fit for one species at one point in time in one
ecological niche might well prove "unfitting" in some other time or
some other niche.

The most important thing to recall about Darwin's impact, especially in the present moment, is the kind of qualified optimism it
reflected. Clearly, there was no "plan" or "purpose" or "designer"
that could be adduced from close natural study. In fact, it is quite
appropriate to use Stephen Jay Gould's term "glorious accident"
to explain whatever is.[2] In Darwin's own words, in the final lines
of *Origin*, which almost read as poetry:

Thus, from the war of nature, from famine and death, the most exalted object which we are capable of conceiving, namely, the production of the higher animals, directly follows. There is grandeur in this view of life, with its several powers, having been originally breathed by the Creator[3] into a few forms or into one; and that, whilst this planet has gone cycling on according to the fixed law of gravity, from so simple a beginning endless forms most beautiful and most wonderful have been, and are being evolved.

When the young Darwin took his famous voyage on the *H. M. S. Beagle*, he carried with him a well-thumbed copy of William Paley's *Evidences*. A central argument of that text had been that the human eye was far too complex to have come about simply by chance. By the time Darwin was writing *Origin*, however, it had become quite clear that various organs of perception in various species came about precisely in that matter, that is to say, adaptively.

Those who call themselves Humanist are beset today from many sides. They are charged with speciesism by some who contend that they favor the human species over all other species. On other fronts, they are accused of ignoring the divinely-endowed designs and beauties of nature. From the postmodern French and their disseminators, humanists are accused of clinging to some kind of "grand narrative" from the Enlightenment that is no longer defensible (nor would any other narrative, from this perspective, be any more defensible). And from fundamentalists and that large part of the public who have unwittingly learned their religion from the televangelists, the agnosticism/atheism/nontheism of modern humanists is incomprehensible.

The present volume tries to put these matters in a more accurate and contemporary light. The contributors are all practicing humanists in the naturalistic traditions of pragmatic philosophizing associated with John Dewey. Most are members of the Adjunct Faculty of The Humanist Institute. Readers will nevertheless note the wide range of positions taken by the authors. In the larger EuroAmerican climate of thought these days, ecology evokes responses that range from tree-hugging to technology-trusting. All of the contributors to this volume would place themselves somewhere between these two untenable extremes. Contemporary humanism has consistently stressed scientific modes of knowing as superior to any resorts to tradition or authority or intuition or impulse. The humanist trajectory, after all, during the Renaissance embraced a world that had been obscured by the Christian degradations of the Hellenistic outlook—a world of flesh but not devils, of a nature more accessible and appealing than any supernature. Humanism also draws upon the revival of a reason employed to understand this natural world that characterized the Enlightenment. Those streams—Hellenism, Enlightenment, Renaissance—flowed together in varied ways in the ensuing centuries, enhanced on the one hand by the movement of the sciences from the far-out reaches of astronomy to the close-in reaches of biology, and on the other hand by a deepening awareness of reasoning as an embodied activity rather than a detached one. Furthermore, modern humanists have been fully aware of the importance of values which stem from a variety of experiential and extra-scientific sources but achieve their full strengths only when tested by empirical, scientific results and close philosophical scrutiny.

So we must keep in mind three historical human qualities in situating modern humanists—reasoning, empiricizing, and valuing. It is the third strand of valuing that makes the humanistic position frankly anthropocentric. In the absence of any plausible divinities or forces of cosmic wisdom, judgments can only be made by humans; created and critiqued and remade in the light of future human experiences.

Our Abrahamic Western religious traditions (Judaism, Christianity, Islam) are presently rethinking their relationships to "nature" in the light of a newly perceived ecological crisis. This crisis was precipitated by a widely read essay of Lynn White[4] and an equally popular book by Rachel Carson[5] in the mid 1960s. White contended that the Biblical doctrine of "dominion" had directly served to justify any and all depredations of the natural world, and that religions were to blame for this. Coming from that rather rare type of academic who traveled in religious circles, this was a hard pill to swallow.

From a Humanist position, however, White's impact was one more case of evidence trumping ideology. The global impacts of human activities could no longer be ignored after the series of devastating wars that plagued the past century. Nor could the competitions of the Cold War be allowed to obscure the potentially destructive nature of unfettered industrialism—whether the profits accrued to stockholders (Western style) or to the state (Russian style). When the military or industrial operation was nuclear-based, the longevity effect of the pollutants projected almost indefinitely into the future.

If ecology is the study of interactions of organisms and environments, the bringing of value positions into this knowledge has variously been called conservationism, environmentalism, ecologism. The frequent tendency of those who have taken these positions has been to regard human activities as intrusive, destructive, malicious, undesirable. Many partisans of "wilderness" have gone far beyond defending wilderness areas as set-asides for contemplation and recreation, and have come to regard humans as lice endangering the welfare of the planet (a view that ignores the right-to-life of lice!). In somewhat parallel ways, the "population explosion" alarms appearing in the 1960s tended to be based on views of humans as intruders into a paradise. The biblical allusions were clear, even to the foretelling of apocalyptic doom.[6]

The positions of humanists, being tempered on the one hand by a commitment to knowledge from the sciences and on the other to the recognition that such knowledge was always tentative, shared a different perspective. Human life in the cosmos was the prime good, and the advancement of this life rather than mere preservation was always the goal. Thus the very early commitment within humanist circles to family planning, for instance. Not to hold down a population that would soon "overburden" the resources of earth but to produce children who would be wanted by parents who would be able to care for them effectively; and to give women choices in life other than becoming breeding instruments. (Or, for that matter, some men from achieving their status simply by their success as studs).

The reform traditions of humanists, freethinkers, liberal Protestants and Jews, and nineteenth century political liberalism interacted and grew together. The increase of human freedoms would increase human creativities. Institutions and ideas should be evaluated in these terms.

Universal education, the liberation of former slaves as well as women, the collective rights of all laborers as against the individual rights of factory owners, the expansion of democracy on the assumption that the government could be used to enhance the common life; the promotion of negotiations and rule of law rather than violence in settling disputes, the insistence upon international community based on the universality of human dignity—all of these were well established goals by the end of the 19th century.

By and large, the humanists were successful in maintaining their commitments to these goals throughout the bloody 20th century and its setbacks. The original dream of international order was never quite lost, despite the global wars and global totalitarianisms of the first half of that 20th century and the enormously expensive rivalries of a Cold War for most of the second half of its century.

As humanists moved into the 21st century, these values and lessons moved with them. The new element was the scientific certitude of the risks to future generations that present human activities might entail. Not just "risks to the planet," but risks to the human enterprise itself. The exhaustion of fossil fuels before alternatives could be developed and employed; the greenhouse effect and consequent old warming; the lethal potentials of commitment to nuclear fission power; the rise of fundamentalisms which represent a regression into religious/national chauvinisms, and the rejection of science as well as other forms of intellectuality that inevitably accompany fundamentalisms—all of these have been concerns within the humanist agenda, and all of these become factors in the description of any ecohumanism.

As the chapters of the present volume well illustrate, this broader inclusion for the human enterprise is a qualifier to any environmentalism that simply focuses upon the nonhuman world. While the authors emphasize different aspects of the human enterprise, it will be quite clear to close readers that they share quite completely the need for an approach to environmental issues that retains its primary focus upon the human impacts of human activities.

Readers, of course, will have to judge how much this persistent focus of the humanists reflects their nontheistic orientation. More traditional readers will miss references to various gods and various divine intentions and provisions. From the standpoint of the authors, the various actions and values that have historically been alleged to be divinely ordered have not only been and inconsistent but have, in the main, detracted from our human flourishing rather than enhancing it. Less traditional readers, it is hoped, will be moved to explore this nontheistic approach to human problems and will find fresh ideas herein.

Careful readers, whether or not they agree with the nontheistic positions of the authors, will sense the enormous need for better communication of ecological problems and values. The nonverbal, the aesthetic, the experiential—these are the dimensions and modes of communication that are also needed, and these are the areas in which not only humanists but many other intellectuals in the modern Euroamerican scene have been remiss.[7] The rise of anti-intellectual fundamentalisms should have made clear that modernism and its values were failing to make contact with many of our fellow-citizens. And the U.S. elections in 2000, where half of the eligible voters chose not to vote, and almost half of those who did vote were willing to vote for a candidate who clearly stated his doubts about evolution, that bedrock of any modern science, should leave no doubts that ecohumanism is a quite necessary enterprise for the future.

The sequence of chapters in this volume is based upon the shared emphases of ecohumanism—the combining of scientific knowledge with human/social values. Given their common commitments to a nontheistic humanism and their continuing conversations within the Institute, it should be no surprise that there are some overlaps of emphases. Rather than edit these out, I have tried to retain the full integrity of individual positions in order that readers who have not yet shared these conversations will be able to sense the full extent of intellectual and valuational community in this representational group of humanist leaders.

The beginning chapters set forth the view of sciences and technology that has been central to the humanist heritage. Here becomes evident the contrasts with many traditional religious views as well as with many widespread feelings about spirituality that, on the surface, have little to do with religion but nonetheless verge upon the anti-intellectual. The chapters by Radest, Rosenberg, Regal, Page, Kami, Gibbons, and Schafer make an excellent start in this direction.

Nontheistic humanists vary among themselves in relation to such labels as atheist and agnostic. Yet they share a commitment to certain emerging values and the human traditions that brought forth these values that moves well beyond any simple philosophical negativism or nihilism. For humanists, the centrality of this value matrix comes first, and philosophical stances are judges by their attention to and nurturing of these values. For this reason, past fashions such as existentialism, Marxism-Leninism, absolute idealism have had little appeal. In the present moment, much that passes as postmodernism suffers from this same undercutting of humanist values. To understand better that side of humanism, read next the chapters by Swomley and Larue.

The strong concern with knowledge from the sciences that we have been emphasizing comes from an historic reliance on "reason." Since this philosophic tool has so often been misunderstood as cold, rigid, aggressive-masculine-phallic, most modern humanists find that semantic shifts to "reasoning," or "intelligence" make more sense. In particular, the rise of the social sciences has produced humanistically important knowledge about the human parts of the ecosystem. Read Werner, Sarles, and Bullough from this perspective.

The humanist message is heard only faintly in much of the world. Even in the United States, many have never discovered it or explored its possibilities. This is partly due to the historic religiosities of the citizens. Rather like the free market, the separation of churches and the state in the United States has, ironically, forced the religions into better marketing. But the unawareness of humanistic alternatives is also the result of overly-verbal and unexciting presentations. Humanists spend much time analyzing their shortcomings in these areas of the symbolic and the aesthetic. Read Wintermute, Brewer, and Gilbert on this.

Many humanists speak as though the eighteenth century Enlightenment was the fount of their ideas. We need also to remind ourselves of those other times and places when human values were made central, and Madigan's chapter on the ancient Cynics does just this.

If humanism is indeed committed to the continual critique and improvement of human values, this must involve making good on the claim to respect all persons and knowledge. The various environmental movements of our time need to be studied. If ecohumanism is indeed a valid and defensible position, that claim should only be made in a comparative context. In somewhat differing ways, the final chapters by Oelberg and Tapp suggest ways to pursue that agenda.

Robert B. Tapp

Notes

1. *Origin of Species*, 6th ed.

2. See Wim Kayzer, ed. *A Glorious Accident: Understanding Our Place in the Cosmic Puzzle* (New York: Freeman, 1997).

3. The term appears infrequently in Darwin's writings, and its import is variously assessed. Certainly the concerns of Emma Darwin's Unitarianism and the more orthodoxly-Christian public are factors.

4. "The historic roots of our ecologic crisis," *Science* 155 (March 10, 1967), pp. 1203-7.

5. *Silent Spring* (Boston: Houghton Mifflin, 1962).

6. Biblical scholars and the public use some of these terms in quite different ways. Technically, an apocalypse uncovers and reveals something hidden, and often does so in highly cryptic and symbolic terms. The final book of the Christian Bible (Revelation/Apocalypse (Greek *apokalypsis*) of St. John) pur-

ports to reveal the way that the present age will end (the *eschaton*). But referring to some of these calamitous predictions more correctly as "eschatological" would not be readily understood outside the scholarly world.

7. Andrew Greeley, the provocative sociologist/priest, argues quite convincingly that Roman Catholicism's success is due to the fact that it has "better stories" (Mary, saints, angelic helpers, and the like). Similar explanations would work well in other parts of the world for Islam, Hinduism, Buddhism. But the larger problem is not the attractiveness of stories but their human meanings and consequences. Do they foster autonomy or dependence, maturity or infantilism, realism or fantasy, reasoning or emotionalizing, chauvinism or universalism? Can a science-based ecohumanism produce compelling narratives and stories? Before saying No too quickly, look again at the multinational successes of Jacob Bronowski, Isaac Asimov, Kurt Vonnegut, Carl Sagan, Arthur Clarke, Steve Allen, Gene Roddenberry.

OF ROACHES, RATS, AND RATTLESNAKES

IMAGING THE WORLD—THE THIRD VOICE

Howard B. Radest

From the Tradition

When nature assigned us [head and heart] the same habitation, she gave us over it a divided empire. To you ([head] she allotted the field of science, to me [heart] that of morals. When the circle is to be squared, or the orbit of a comet to be traced; when the arch of greatest strength or the solid of least resistance is to be investigated, take you the problem . . . . In like manner in denying to you the feelings of sympathy, of benevolence, of gratitude, of justice, of love, of friendship, she has excluded you from their control. To these she has adapted the mechanism of the heart. Morals were too essential to the happiness of man to be risked on the uncertain combinations of the head. She laid the foundation therefore in sentiment, not in science . . . .

Thomas Jefferson[1]

Science was false by being unpoetical. It assumed to explain a reptile or mollusk, and isolated it--which is hunting for life in graveyards. Reptile or mollusk or man—or angel—only exists in system, in relation. The metaphysician, the poet, only sees each animal form as an inevitable step in the path of creating mind. The Indian, the hunter, the boy with his pets, have sweeter knowledge of these than the savant. We use semblances of logic until experience puts us in possession of real logic. The poet knows the missing link by the joy it gives. The poet gives us eminent experiences

23

only—a god stepping from peak to peak, not planting his foot but on a mountain.

Science does not know its debt to imagination . . . .

Ralph Waldo Emerson[2]

. . . For all art is a process of making the world a different place in which to live, and involves a phase of protest and of compensatory response . . . .

. . . a genuinely esthetic object is not exclusively consummatory but is causally productive as well. A consummatory object that is not also instrumental turns in time to the dust and ashes of boredom . . . .

John Dewey[3]

A Three-Legged Stool . . . But Only Two Legs!

Something there is, despite moral fervor and scientific conclusion, that seems to block us from doing the things we know—or say we know—must be done and ought to be done. For some of us this is only to be expected, a Calvinist reprise of original sin and human willfulness; for others, an example of human blindness; and for still others, a further instance of the power of ego and of greed over good sense. The radical, despairing of the processes of civility, takes to the high seas to sink ships and block pollution or takes to the forests to pound nails in trees to defeat ax and saw. The moralist grows more condemnatory and preachy. The scientist musters yet more information and prediction, in hopes that the sheer weight of fact and fear will carry the day.

Perhaps little of this is wasted motion although at times it feels like it is. Certainly, it is laudable to guard against new environmental disasters and to repair old ones. And it would be a strange humanist indeed who denied the beneficence of moral conscience, organized intelligence, and prophetic outrage. Yet, the insufficiency of all of this energy and knowledge is evident enough.[4] We run very fast to stay in the same place—and we are at best only in the same place. With hope in our hearts or illusion in our minds, we go on doing more of the same. Yet, neither hope nor sentimentality serves. Nor is surrender a live option unless race suicide is a live option.

It is in this frame of mind that I turn to my roots to seek out a newly coined *ecohumanism*. I know that we humanists are accused of indifference to the world. We are said to be trapped by our adoration of the "human" into a disdain for the rest of existence. But the passages from Jefferson, Emerson, and Dewey which introduce this essay deny the charge and, announcing our history, confirm the legitimacy of a humanist claim to a voice in the environmental struggle. Inspired by these, I venture a reference to the classical, renaissance, and transcendental humanisms that modernism all too easily forgets. Thus, the proposition that the good and the true -- both amply and worthily present in the circles of ecology—lack that third voice which these other humanisms insist upon, the voice that sings of the beauty of beings, things, and places. These other roots of humanism are for us correctives to an enlightenment project that has lost its passion and become merely routine.[5] In a sense too , this essay continues my own project.[6] It explores further the relationship between ethics and aesthetics, now using *ecohumanism* as its exemplar. It explores the possibilities of a livable world using a reconceived relationship between the good, the true and the beautiful as its method. Again I find may way with Emerson, "We call the Beautiful the highest, because it appears to us the golden mean, escaping the dowdiness of the good and the heartlessness of the true."[7] Thus, my attempt at an *ecohumanism*!

Science and Sentiment

Spinoza, in his *Ethics*, reminds us that a "passion" can only be changed by replacing it with another and more powerful passion. And, our experience reminds us daily of his wisdom. Thus, a look at our habits, *our* habits and not those of some villainous other. Does the smoker do more than wince or grow deaf as he hears another warning about lung cancer or heart disease? Does the believer become an atheist or the atheist a believer when nodding to the arguments about, and benefits of, God's non-being or being? Does the democrat desert equality in face of human inadequacy? The facts and predictions of science instruct us, of course, but do not change us. The likelihood is denial, rationalization and not rationality. So we say, global warming is "only" a theory; the experts really don't agree; God or nature or science—take your pick—will provide.

We are double-minded. Typically then, we react to our resistance with a propaganda of fear and crisis as if to shock ourselves out of denial. Fear and crisis are superimposed on fact and virtue by the "good" and "desperate" people, the species, wilderness, and ocean preservers, the lovers of the earth. The rest of us join their effort to "sell" ecology, a bit shamefaced to be sure at the mismatch between conviction and conduct. But this propaganda only works over a short time and with limited, even at times contrary, effect. I am after all a stubborn creature who forgets quickly when it suits me to forget. Habit easily and happily overpowers me. Yet more likely, habit is supported by need and greed and so it is, if anything, strengthened by the retreat that fear and crisis invite. Fear, after all, stirs the coward in me more often than the hero.

Thus, I escape to my privileged position: the warning isn't really for me. Tomorrow isn't here yet. Besides, things look pretty good right now, particularly to me and those around me, members of the ravenous middle-class of industrialized societies. I've got mine, let "them" get theirs, or, failing that, let the future take care of itself. Conveniently forgetting fortune of place and time, I murmur to myself, let "them" earn it as I did—whatever "it" or "them" is in mind. I think of the attack on the poor here and abroad—the massive conversion of "foreign" aid to military ends and of community concern to so-called welfare "reform" is its tell-tale. The sciences cease to liberate and come to function as technique, replacements for a theology of predestination and the inexorable workings of sin and grace.

More problematically, as in the struggle to save the Brazilian rain forest or the California redwoods or the fishing grounds off the coast of Seattle or Cape Cod, we ignore the sacrifice that we expect, even demand of others—always of others. It is *their* moral duty.. Thus, we privileged few compound our advantage over the deprived of the earth. A bit of guilt, perhaps, adds a tone of regret for some of us. But we utter scarcely a word of compensation or justice. So the "good" people, who support the motley array of ecological causes, join the exploiters, unwittingly perhaps, as if justice were one battle and a livable world, another.

Nor should any of this surprise us. Crisis expects a "crisis response," which is always short-lived and self-protective. Anxiety, fear's neighbor, issues in blindness and finally numbness. The radical becomes merely boring and, knowing that, only shouts louder, grows more narrowly sectarian, even violent, in desperation. The propaganda becomes more strident. Or else, the over-powering need for an enemy turns the process of reason on its head. Ecology becomes an advocate's game and a defender's strategy, and not an invitation to a deeper penetration of our common condition in the midst of the things and beings of the world. Once again freedom and equality divorce. We choose up sides. An enemy, even an invented enemy, gives meaning to effort and crusade always legitimates the nomination of its victims as appropriately and deservedly victims. Ironically, the logic of scientific argument— e.g. that we are one species in one world—is transmuted into the least logical of outcomes.

More softly, crisis and fear turn us toward sentimentality. We are instructed by the propaganda—its messages are mere simulacra of picture and poem—to fall in love with the cuddly puppy, the baby seal, the magnificent whale, the sleek porpoise, the most ancient of redwoods. Surely this is a worthy love-affair—there are worse attractions for us to succumb to. And yet sentimentality is fleeting. Our affections are forgetful, always fickle. Like teen-age loves, they are deep, to be sure, but inevitably brief. We grow easily fatigued. Distractions take their toll. In the next moment, something else strikes our fancy so that our causes deteriorate. They too become fads.

And even for those few who remain steady in their sentiments there is a certain blindness. The puppy, the seal, the porpoise, the redwood: is a livable earth then to be designed by our taste and to our taste? What then of the flea and the poison sumac, the rattler and the asp, the warthog and the hyena...that endless array of beings that do not suit us, threaten us, even harm us? And is this "unpleasantness" of nature "tooth and claw"—the bloody side of evolution we choose to forget—to find its replacement in the zoo-caged, zoo-fed tiger and crocodile, in nature tamed and shaped to our ends, our enjoyments? Eco-system, we say in reply. But that is only abstract, indeed a way of masking the rich contradictory complexion of the world around us. We scarcely take its meaning. I am an instance of this ignorance; we are all an instance. Dedicated to "saving the environment," I rush at rapid speed in a heavy car on over-crowded roads to the protest meeting. There, I find endlessly duplicated documents for the increase of wisdom and the destruction of forests!

And ultimately, crisis and fear turn truth toward falsehood. We are, we are told, a "scientific" culture so that every puzzlement is a problem and every problem has its solution. But, it is magic that rules and not science. The turn of a switch is our incantation. Or, we grow nostalgic for Eden, invoking a world innocent and loving that never was. Again, the propaganda: a Native American weeps beside a polluted river. I am taught to forget that we humans were polluters and destroyers long before this day, to forget that the only salvation of buffalo and tree and plain and river until we oh-so-fecund moderns arrived on the scene was the fault of small numbers and not the virtue of "natural" peoples. [8]

The propaganda, once known for what it is, is a scarcely conscious acknowledgment that sentimentality is not sentiment and that utility is not science. To be sure, it half-heartedly points a direction not yet taken. To reject the propaganda of the "good" people then, is not to deny the uses of science or the virtues of sentiment or even the limited benefit of the "message". Alternatively, however, a deeper view of science and sentiment needs to emerge. It tells us that they are joined in their history and in their activity.[9] But for this to happen—as it does for a Leonardo, an Einstein—the mere instrumentalism that so infects us must be itself transformed and environed. Inquiry, in other words, is also a form of caring.

An Ironic Interlude

I try to imagine what could have been. I turn from the languages of ecology and eco-system to the tangibility of a livable world. This, taken seriously, should move us to perceive differently, to feel differently, to care differently, to live differently. Indeed, it should move us to a greater inclusiveness of things and beings, taking the human animal's pride of place and power as an invitation to lead in the creation of shared realities and ever renewing connections, a kind of democracy of existence itself. Against this stand our habits of analysis and reduction. How easily I use the language of objectivity to hide my mistakes. The cultures of tradition and enlightenment alike, place us in the modern world. We do not place ourselves. Thus habits penetrate our consciousness and not just our behavior, habits of ego and blindness, of postponement and indifference.

There is, in other words, a radical misfit between our intention and our perception, between desire and practice. Intention—serious and honest as it may be—is emptied of content by the one, of conduct by the other. Technicism rules, and ruling shapes us without benefit of a more generous intelligence—Emerson's little understood struggle for the distinction between "Reason and reason," the warning that rationalism is not necessarily rationality. Does this mean the surrender of the truths of analysis—and there are truths? Does this require the dismissal of fact or prediction or technique? Is objectivity to become mere myth; is doubt only a pose? That, in a mood of post-modern wildness or existential despair, is a sometime conclusion. *To the con-*

trary, that we are brought to this moment when the master-question of a livable world can be uttered is itself testimony to the beneficence of analysis and reduction. But the failure to address a livable world in such a way as to make it happen and not just seem to happen is also testimony to the need for re-perception.

We lack the metaphor and story of a livable world, indeed hold passion at bay with the scientism embedded in the language of "ecology" and "environmentalism." How tediously misleading is the language we use—as if to insist that passion is unworthy. This is doubly ironic since it was metaphor which put the theme of a livable world before us. Poetry inspired by intelligence caught us in the rhythmic alarm of "silent spring" and the prophetic image of "spaceship earth." In the mind's eye there appeared an earth bare and naked and dead, beings and things holding fast to a globe caught mindlessly in the currents of space and having only each other. For a moment—only a moment—analysis and reduction, captured by an image, seized us. And yet, in our romance with utility, metaphor was quickly lost and perception fragmented. Poetry yielded to truth—or what was taken as truth—and in this surrender, truth itself lost its power.

I know this sounds a romanticism that is alien to the children of the Enlightenment, alien to the laboratory, and alien to parliaments and the administration of clerks. But it is just that awareness of the apartness of a livable world from our lived-in world that poses the question of an *ecohumanism*. There are, of course, ways of overcoming alienation that do not demand a radical shift of culture. Denial is one, retreat to the safety of tribal enclaves is another and technicism is a third. Yet, it is this radicalism of culture that, it seems to me, offers the therapy for apartness. Without it we do not overcome that existential alienation that severs us from the world that is our habitation. It remains only an object to us—for use, for manipulation, for amusement. We are not of the world and it is not of us. In the modern mood, a line is drawn, a line which identifies us as modern, enlightened, and separated. And that will not do!

In seeking to overcome our culture, it would be sad and mistaken, however, to turn backward. I think of the temptations of a Scriptural image: the dominion of man over all that swims and crawls and walks upon the earth. It would be better no doubt to take its other image: stewardship of God's creation. Yet, whether it be dominion or stewardship, Scripture asks us still to bow the knee before a power not our own, and even more troubling, a power not of this world. Thus, Scripture is already compromised, already alienating, and so already inadequate to the task of a livable world. Else, why claim with Paul that we are "in the world, but not of it." But the opposing temptation, the Enlightenment image of inevitable progress served by a utilitarian science, fares little better. If it avoids subservience, it yet misleads in its disdain for the integrity of being, in its willingness to make use of the world and what is in it as mere object. Thus, the humanist error, the humanist alienation. We are still Cartesians—other beings have no souls. Thus, too, the humanist subservience to an inertia of objects.

Scripture and Enlightenment—though both deny it in anger and dismay—are siblings, the one taking its reality in the oppositions of the other. Yet, each in their own way, also points the direction for us. So neither is simply to be dismissed. Each tells a story of the world, interprets being and world. Once upon a time, each of these moved us beyond alienation to forms of piety and placement. And now, instructed by them but liberated from them as well, they suggest the possibility of a "natural piety" as George Santayana called it. They teach us to remember that there once was a lively union of self and cosmos—in this, the passion of the mystic and the reformer alike. Both made truth and goodness the content of an epic poetry, the one in an eternal destiny, the other in an ever renewing history.[10] But today, both Scripture and Enlightenment are become mere shells of worn-out theologies in their tedious rehearsal of faded passions deteriorated into mere routines.

Sometimes, we seem even to celebrate this deterioration—a kind of *Schadenfreude*—Scripture calling for a return to faith, Enlightenment boasting the virtues of disenchantment. Both thereby despair of the present. Yet, I am still a child of Enlighten-ment—aren't we all—so I praise the modern escape from illusion. Who would really desire or praise the falsehood, the mirage, sacri-ficing self and integrity to sentimentality with another face. Is our need so desperate that our salvation requires us to construct a world of lies? Of course not. Yet that is what the praise of disen-chantment threatens; that is what the call for a return to faith in-vites. Both, looking backward, ask for a time that no longer is and so both, looking backward, seek re-enchantment by nostalgia.

We gain the present by grasping, not echoing, the past. At the same time, it is the form of the past, and so the consequent liveli-ness of its content, that instructs the present. And what might we say of this form—that it was above all personal, and as such felt, acted upon, sung and celebrated. The revolutionary and the prophet made common cause in the joyousness of a proclaimed gospel. Thus, the "psalms of praise" and the "rights of man." With joy came practice and with practice came knowledge. And all of this, entangled, evoked its stories, its interpretations and meanings and, too, its drive toward a future dimly perceived yet genuinely be-lieved in and cared for. So sentimentality yields to sentiment and sentiment energizes perception and conduct.

Vision and Virtue

In these wanderings, I find the clue to an *ecohumanism*, the answer to those who accuse humanism of mere anthropocentrism. I con-fess—*pace* my secularist friends—that in this task I join both mod-ernist and traditionalist. I too need to own up to my sins against the world—the arrogance of dominion and technicism. But then, a humanist should not be surprised that, sharing a common condi-tion, human beings should address the world in like-sounding puz-zlement.

It strikes me how easily we depersonalize others and ourselves. We learn to play the role of users, consumers, and manipulators; we convert the world into our object, even our plaything. In turn, we are captured by exteriority: even human being becomes an object. This double message has its history. In the traditions, we are "just passing through." Or, moving eastward, we are, as Hindu and Buddhist would have it, trapped in appearance and struggling for Nirvana. For the modernist, we are knowers and mechanics, apart from the world while working on it. Nature speaks to us only of what is and we think to attach the lessons she teaches freely, even arbitrarily, according to our will and purpose. Hence, kind of cosmic arrogance in a comedy acted out by pigmies who do not know enough to laugh at themselves. Everywhere, the connection between ourselves and our habitation is broken. On all sides alienation is again revealed.

In fact, the struggle of faith—in another world or in this one—is embedded in a culture that is unfriendly to the integrity of ends and means and meanings. We live in and by a culture that invites egoism. It is, further, a culture of separation which ignores the sensibilities of natural affiliation. So, we think to live in a made-up world, selecting its shape and content according to our style and preference. For the rest, the world is hidden away and we perfect techniques that reinforce the secrecy of the world. We are born and die in sterile rooms attached to machinery. Life in its beginnings and endings becomes an abstraction. We paint our faces and maneuver our bodies to keep the secret. We make other beings our pets, still others our prey, and still others our disgust. And all of this is culture's symptom.

The radicalization of culture asks us to reveal the hidden world. That was, for a time, the genius of Enlightenment. But here I must avoid the illusion of control which was its flaw, as if revelation could ever be absolute and a matter of an ever more elaborated mechanics. The world is a scene of accident and event. Intention and action are but minor moments. The world is masked and is always at least as mysterious as it is transparent. So, a certain angst attaches to our existence for the thing we would capture and use must elude us. Even when we succeed in revealing what is hidden, we learn too that revelation is partial, temporary, resisted. So we

learn the lesson of attachment without guarantee. But we are un-
prepared for, even blinded to this lesson. For the children of the
Enlightenment, mystery is only a problem. Nevertheless, the reconstruction of culture does not expect us to escape to mystifica-
tion and obscurantism. At the same time, mystery is an accompaniment of being. It is an illusion to suppose that ultimately it might
entirely vanish.[11] I notice here the distinction between that which
can be formulated and asked, and that which can only be felt or
guessed at, that which is not reducible to the canons of inquiry.

The thought comes unhappily to mind: is their time enough and
world enough, for reconstruction; is their knowledge enough for
reparation, even atonement? Once upon a time, Julian Huxley and
Teilhard de Chardin, each a humanist in his own way, announced
that we were "evolution become self-conscious." Again, the aura
of control! They promised too much, I think. I cannot escape the
thought that our confidence in progress, in the beneficence of nature or even in our ability to muddle through, may be merely pre-
tentious, enacting again the comedy without an audience. Of
course, becoming audience, I learn to laugh at myself, but how often do I become audience!

A gleeful stoicism is the wisest background for reconstruction,
joining me with that other humanist, Erasmus, in celebration of
folly. Chastened, I turn to what it is that the world requires of me
and not, as is my habit, what I require of it. With that, I am brought
to the aesthetic transaction already hinted at by the forms of
meaning attaching both to tradition and modernism. In our time,
that transaction appears as a comedic spectacle of cosmic egoism,
the play without an audience, and as the mystery that cannot be
penetrated while we go on thinking to penetrate it. Our history and
our images point the need to re-locate the human animal from star-
dom to company, from observer to partner, from user to dweller.
We are not God's surrogate on earth nor are we the Promethean
hero who wrests truth from earth.

Counter to our culture, the world as I experience it consists in felt connections of being. This invites an earth-metaphor. With it we discover/create a new ground of faith and knowledge and a new ground of celebration too, in poetry and music and ritual. An earth-metaphor locates us differently, connects our history with natural history through time past and time future. Evolution then is not only a theory of development and an inquiry into coming to be and passing away. It is at the same time, a story of the connections of species and stone and star. In and through an earth-metaphor we find our way to the moral geography by which we grasp our place in the world and the cognitive geography by which we inquire into that place and ourselves. But these are not separable from each other nor from the tonalities of experience that precede and transcend both judgment and cognition, indeed that shape and echo through both judgment and cognition. The absence of a culture hospitable to the task of an earth-metaphor suggests why it is that the efforts of the "good" people shaped by an unconfessed metaphor of separation so often fail in their task.

Absent in our culture, and those of the past too, is a realization of what is fitting and what is not in these new times, the usages which establish a sociable reality beneath the workings of consciousness and machinery. In short, absent is a culture coherent with an earth-metaphor. To be sure, what counts as fitting varies with place, time, and history—there is no single and universal sense of what is fitting. Yet the variations are not wildly disparate. At the very least, commonality of experience connects us: birth, death, love, hope, suffering, laughter, and all the rest. These are familiar enough and familiar everywhere.

Fittingness reformulates the moral puzzle of means and ends too. Of course, we argue—as moralist and pragmatist do—that these entail each other. But beyond a pragmatist's logic, these become each other in my presence, melt into each other, when historicized and aestheticized. I think it not unfair to imagine means, ends, and meanings as a flow between artist, brush, canvas, and perceiver, or the flow of athlete, bat and ball. The continuum of creation is tangible. And failure to integrate means, ends, and meanings is not simply ugly but issues in anti-moral outcomes, failed outcomes. So, just as a false note jars the ear or a inappropriate action breaks the drama of plot and character, so too disharmony is experienced when means does not fit its end or when end negates its means or when both together remain abstract, lacking the connection of meaning. Bit by bit, then the continuum of the beautiful and the good is exposed. Broken, we are clumsy.[12]

The sciences too are grasped through the aesthetic transaction.[13] Thus a demonstration, we say, is "elegant," a proof is "beautiful"—each a testimony to fittingness. Thus too the not-so-hidden axioms of inquiry: simplest is truest, form follows function, and so on. Ockham's "razor" is a counsel of art as much as of criticism. Failing to appreciate these embedded guides—the culture of science itself we might say—the outcome is surely tedious and often false. Without prolonging what is already clear enough, the good, the true and the beautiful stand or fall together. This is not to claim that they are simply interchangeable or that they are merely different words for a single identity. Beauty is not truth is not goodness! Yet, each becomes what it can be not only by the task it sets and the perception it directs —to know, to judge, to participate—but by the setting in which it lives, the setting inclusive of the others.

It is this confluence expressed as ethics, science and art, I think, that led John Dewey, reflecting on his master-text, *Experience and Nature*, to suggest that a better and more accurate title would have been "Experience and Culture." The world, after all, does not come to us except through the filter of culture. And culture is had before it is known. Only afterward is it parsed. Yet, pretending to become self-conscious in a disenchanted world, our culture claims the world is on the way to being known by us in all its dimensions. In this it ignores the fact that self-consciousness itself is culture driven and not simply an outcropping of biology. As such, self-consciousness is not fixed but itself in motion, itself elusive. Hence the ability to be of a culture and independent of it.

Experience-as-having is at root intuitive; the particular forms this having takes are shaped by history. But experience too escapes our efforts to capture and tame it. We are, in other words, embedded in a process-world, essentially felt and only partially known and knowable—in spite of our pretense. This could lead —and has led—to a despair of intelligence, a derogation of moral effort, and an anarchic romanticism where willfulness is mistaken for beauty. But we are not without resource when facing, as William James called it, "a blooming buzzing confusion." Responsiveness, shaped by and within symbolic acts, forms and reforms the world—becomes the genre of reconstruction. The illusion that cognition, description, and design are the methods of mastery is broken by the realization that culture escapes limitation, experience exceeds understanding and world exceeds experience. "The owl of Minerva," writes Hegel, "takes flight at the setting of the sun."

I realize that the invocation of the aesthetic transaction, of intuition, feeling, metaphor, and ritual, comes strangely to the ears of a disenchanted people.[14] Yet, even the fundamentalist—traditional or modern—is disenchanted, else why his or her dismay and anger and frantic effort to suppress the other. Seeking desperately to re-take the past—the 13th century or the 18th—he or she becomes a manipulator and user too, an instance of the very culture he or she thinks to reject. In that sense, the fundamentalist is a threat to reconstruction not because he or she is mistaken in idea and ideology but because he or she lacks a necessary generosity of spirit. Categories of intuition—of having—are there for all of us. Reflection, moving beyond the bounds of history, initiates experiments of the imagination in the silent deliberately lonely moments, even at least for some of us the mystic moments, when solitude opens into connection. This then is to re-perceive the true and the good not simply in their more abstract and airy formulations, which is our habit, but in the concreteness of challenge, response, and appreciation—and so the demand for a different, a personal effort.

An earth-metaphor directs us to the tangible, the various actual beings in the world, and to our presence with world of being and thing. So I move through the doorway opened by fittingness and angst, by appreciation of both the harmonics and precariousness of existence. I am not a role or bundle of roles but a person and as person I encounter the world in all its kaleidoscopic reality. It becomes my world as I become its being. In that way, the world is for me a presence before it is a presentation and as presence it is appreciated and responded-to before it is known. Or perhaps—heretical thought—knowledge needs a more generous meaning! The world is not passively there, only a given. It too, lives. So a cold stream at the foot of a waterfall or a mountain top made red by sunrise, or the cry of the wolf at night—so too the rat scurrying through the cellar, the mosquito poised to attack, the muscled cat in mid-leap . . . . Endless images that disappear into flatness once life is denied and autopsy replaces presence. In the encounter, then, I respond, appreciate, fear, regret, mobilizes all that vast emotional and perceptual armament with which the human animal is equipped.

In the encounter, the world does not remain the same. The human animal is active being and as such, transformative. So the world alters as I respond, becoming other not by magic or incantation and not by the maneuvers of technicism but by shifting of needs and perceptions in the between of the encounter. It is then a "lively connection" for me and, as I am in the world and of it, it is at least thus far a lively connection for it too. I am, strange thought, both world and self—again the continuum of the aesthetic transaction. Thus, a landscape or sunset or rainstorm is at least an event in nature and an event in experience. And how much more? The edge of mystery appears in that question to which the reply can be, variously, nothing or a great deal. But that choice is precisely the élan of experiment which is aesthetic too and not simply a monopoly of the laboratory.

So it is not overly foolish to see the aesthetic transaction as an essential category of an earth-metaphor—the relationships of place and time and person, none of which could be what they are apart from each other. No doubt, a dead earth could be too—pushed and pulled by gravitation, circling the sun, ultimately disappearing into the ice of space or the fire of an exploding star. But it would not be the earth in which beings live and encounter happens. It would, quite literally, be a different earth. If discovered by some future being, it would not be the earth in which we respond. It would lack consciousness, the awareness which is our part in existence, as much our gift to existence as its gift to us. To suggest yet another metaphor, this sense of being suggests a partnership in which our presence would be noted by its absence. But our presence is not unique. Consciousness, responsiveness, relationship, connection is not our monopoly. Being is more broadly distributed. So, on a dead earth, emptiness would, as it were, come into being, replace being.

To be sure, we are a cosmic triviality and we know it. That interesting bit of self-awareness may indeed be the privilege of human being. So, our absence could go unnoticed. But knowing this, we become not merely trivial. We are also contributory—nature with us is not nature without us. At the least, our absence would likely entail that *noticing itself would be diminished, a vanished capacity of the world.* Thus, the sense of the comic which emerges when we take ourselves too seriously and the tragic when we catch the import of that failure. We witness, in short, the dual obligation that emerges from participation—humility which corrects pride, and duty which announces place. With this shift toward an earth-metaphor, we notice too how the aesthetic transaction embeds moral judgment and cognition, how much truth, goodness and beauty depend on each other.

Appreciation

Let me try to draw the import of an earth-metaphor for *ecohumanism*. I leave aside the activities already in place which evoke our loyalty and response—the sciences that expose emerging realities as we turn world into garbage heap, the ethics and politics of resistance, and all the rest. As I said in the beginning, these are neither to be dismissed nor disparaged. And yet, as I have also said, there is an insufficiency in these, an insufficiency of imagination much more than of inquiry and morality. It is this that has moved me to explore the shaping powers of culture, the inadequacy of our manipulative ethos—historic and worldwide—and the possibilities of the aesthetic transaction. And it is this sense of things that has moved me to risk the charge of mysticism and intuitionism from my rationalist companions. For the task of a livable world—a living world—merely doing more of what we are doing will not serve. A shift of perception, as it were, is called for.[15] Hence notions like fittingness, presence, participation, connection.

Cultural transformation is not merely a matter of problem solving. It demands a different sense of place, of time, of purpose, of consciousness itself. As such, it is an elusive process beyond control, certainly beyond human control. Here traditionalist and the children of the Enlightenment separate. The former populate that beyond with the gods, and the latter do not. But for both of them, there are no assurances. A dead earth is always possible despite faith or effort or fortune. So the appropriateness of acceptance, of acknowledging what is and what is not in our power. But this is not helplessness or passivity, or at least it need not be. Along with the work of science and politics, the aesthetic transaction calls for aesthetic effort, for the arts in the most generous sense of the term. Living itself is embedded in the aesthetic transaction. Sadly, aesthetic nurture as a biographical and developmental essential is neglected, even sneered at. Symptomatically, the arts are the least likely place for attention and support these days and not just in the halls of Congress. They are treated like everything else as merely instrumental, in this instance to pleasure, recreation, all the things we do when we are not seriously engaged in the work of the world. In reaction, the arts become less art and more wildness. Despair and frustration join with consumerism to reduce art to commodity.

It is not incidental, by way of counter example, that the great causes of the world emerge from the aesthetic transaction. Martin Luther nails his Theses to the church door and initiates the drama of reformation. Medieval Christianity does not connect with world and person through the learned writings of church fathers or the powers and properties of popes and clerics, but through the spires of the cathedral, the hymns of praise, and the stories of redemptive love. Nor is it incidental that democratic revolution is recalled in its passion by songs of liberation and comradeship and by the literature of pamphlet and proclamation—a literature that evokes more than it explains. In our time, I have only to recall the symbolic effect of "We Shall Overcome"—which echoes still long after civil rights marches and demonstration—or the silences transcending the furors of partisanship evoked by the Vietnam Memorial. The cynic in us may see in these mere epiphenomena of other agendas, economic and political. But that is to miss their strength, their ability to mobilize energies and to transcend the "realism" of economics and politics. It is revealing too that as the aesthetic transaction becomes routine, mere rite rather than ritual—a propaganda in short—clerisy replaces prophesy, terror replaces the rights of man, and revolution becomes bureaucracy. The potency of the aesthetic transaction becomes all the more visible when it is absent.

The aesthetic transaction, however, is not available on demand. Its roots are hidden in that edge of mystery that attends being, its appearance often seems fortuitous. Yet, its conditions are not hidden. The cathedral invites the Bach cantata; the barricade invites the legend. The invitation is visible, a certain hospitality to expression, to experiment. The responsive metaphor is the token of that hospitality—as the open door and welcome mat are symbols of invitation. So humanism must search out its metaphor if an *ecohumanism* is not merely to be an echo, another cliché, and ineffective. Hence, the suggestion of an earth-metaphor and its reasons.

What is it that such a metaphor offers? It re-perceives world and self as being and not as utility. As such it calls for apprehension and appreciation before it allows for inquiry and action and the measurement of outcomes. It re-perceives our efforts, asking what is it that they serve and do not serve and are these fitting, adequate to the harmonics of being in the world and with the world. In these processes, the metaphor is not gentle at all, not innocuous. It becomes the acid of culture, eating away at what does not fit, revealing what is immune to its erosion. As such, it outlines the culture in front of us long before it becomes possibility. And too, there is always the possibility of a warfare of metaphors—dominion and technicism resist and are surely strong enough to enter the lists. At the same time, the earth-metaphor is not an alien language. It is born within the symbols and meanings of present and past—mother earth, for example or nature's bounty or stewardship or progress. But then it rejects imitation and moves on. Cultures, as we know, do not appear like Athena, full grown from the head of Zeus. They too have their histories, their roots. So in the aesthetic transaction, the present and the past are not dismissed but transformed.

An earth-metaphor asks for a re-perception of place, an inclusiveness of place. Of course, any aesthetic transaction entails foreground and background. But this differs from that radical selectivity which ignores the flow between, which reduces both foreground and background to arid and flat dimension. Selectivity in the name of so-called realism leaves gaps in the tapestry of experience as it were without recognizing that they are gaps. So the designed nature of the 18th century English garden or the caged fascination of the zoological garden become its metaphor—an Enlightenment metaphor—and do not fit with the soft-edged and inclusive earth-metaphor any more than with the hard-edged technical solution to this or that problem—smog, or oil spill or what have you. More personally, much as I love the puppy who greets me when I return home, so too I must love the rat and the cockroach and the asp and the virus. And in destroying any of these—destruction is always an accompaniment of being—I deny myself the satisfactions of conquest and know the regrets of necessity. The metaphor, then, intends a more generous perception of belonging and a more demanding relationship to world and being.

Finally, the metaphor carries with it a sense of the uniqueness of being. Just as we grasp the aesthetic value of the original as original, we recognize the lesser values of the imitation. So, to an inclusiveness of place is joined an appreciation of individuals. But individuality is not restricted to human being alone. It is yet another mode of re-perception: beings are but they not only are. Fittingness implies their legitimate, even necessary, presence, the contribution of each one that is alike the gift of stone and saint. Of course, differentiations of being exist but the perceptions of inclusiveness are their context. So mere dismissal or mere indifference to being is already to cross the moral threshold into the immoral. The aesthetic transaction carries its moral imperative within it.

A Footnote: *Ecohumanism* and Faith

I have tried to dig beneath program and policy, to reach to the *idea* of an *ecohumanism* rooted in a sense of a livable world and radical in its demand for a replacement of culture itself. As I see it, it is the aesthetic transaction and not the judgment of the moralist or the power of the politician that opens the doorway to revolution. Nor should the children of the Enlightenment be surprised at this. After all, it was not just the philosophes and the pamphleteers who made a revolution. The sociability of the salon, the sound of opera and theater, the story tellers and the poets paved the way for the "rights of man" long before the Bastille. Our failure to grasp our own story may help explain why it is that despite effort and knowledge, so much of what we try to do does not succeed. Intuitively, we know what an *ecohumanism* would demand of us and this we fear. It would require the transformation of culture and life pattern and we are not sure at all that we are ready to pay the price. It is no accident then that denial, rejection, and negation appear in conduct if not in consciousness. It is no accident that abstraction afflicts morality and inquiry. We pretend to do the right thing. But we are comfortable with things pretty much as they are. It is a rare soul that invites discomfort.

Turning for a moment to the strategy and tactics of an *ecohumanism* then, it is also clear that fear and crisis, the horrific event like Chernobyl, Three Mile Island or the Alaskan oil spill only temporarily command our attention. Even the smog alerts of Los Angeles lose their dramatic effect and become one more bit of routine. In turn, we are well trained to pay only brief attention to events. They come packed for us in "sound-bites." We shift attention quickly so that experience is incoherent without our recognizing the fact. And besides, except for tourism or perhaps the loss of some minor investment, there is scarcely much that I feel unless I am an Alaskan fisherman or a Pennsylvania resident or a California commuter. So, no matter how correct the warning may be and how clearly oil spill and nuclear accident and smog alert are omens of tomorrow, I remain comfortable with perhaps a twinge, merely a twinge, of worry.

What then does this tell us about a strategy for the earth-metaphor? I hesitate, particularly when we are so deeply secularized. And yet, if I take the thought of an earth-metaphor seriously, then I am in the presence of a religious consciousness. To be sure, this is not a theological consciousness which is something else entirely. *Ecohumanism* does not rely on the being or non-being of the gods or on the elaboration of their careers and purposes. By a religious consciousness, I mean the willingness to make the imaginative experiments asked for by the aesthetic transaction and to trust the world and myself enough to accept its risks. I mean too, the religious dimensions of care, obligation, and appreciation: care so that what is supposed to matter really does; obligation so that the duty act upon experiment is fulfilled; and appreciation so that both duty and care are felt as worthwhile and worthy.

To put this in less exalted terms, the failures which an *ecohumanism* seeks to remedy are not the fault of our knowledge, our ethics or even of our politics. Rather, they are failures of presence, of personal connection. It is not enough to sign petitions, support organizations, lobby legislatures, to recycle waste. The task of an *ecohumanism* no doubt includes these as it does the advancement

of inquiry and the elaboration of policy. But unless these are embedded in the idea-become-personal—the religionist calls this
epiphany; the secularist might substitute passionate attachment—neither inquiry nor policy can suffice.

Ultimately, of course, there is   danger which becomes all the
more awesome as it is felt personally, as it is felt to be life-
threatening. And yet, unavoidably, in all experiment there is failure. For this not to trap us in fragmentation, despair or illusion, a
religious consciousness is necessary. Failure and success are interpreted, given meanings. In the aesthetic transaction—presence, response, connection, engagement—self and other and world are felt
as continuous. Within a religious consciousness, I care, appreciate,
and celebrate this continuity. I am grateful for its possibility. I am
carried over the gulf of failure to renewed effort. These historically
have been the gift of the religious consciousness. All too often it
has been attached to ideas we cannot believe or to structures we
cannot trust. But then a new culture evokes new ideas and new
structures. So it is that faith is not a matter of metaphysics but of
courage and confidence—not in assurances which cannot be believed but in meanings which permit failure without surrender.

Notes

1.   Thomas Jefferson, "The Head and The Heart," letter to Maria Cosway,
The Portable Thomas Jefferson, ed. Merril D. Peterson (New York: Penguin
Books, 1975), pp. 408-409.

2.   Ralph Waldo Emerson, "Poetry and Imagination" (1872), in *the American Transcendentalists (Their Prose and Poetry)*, ed. Perry Miller (Garden City,
New York: Doubleday Anchor Books, 1957), pp. 195-217, pp. 200-201.

3.   John Dewey, "Experience, Nature and Art," from Chapter 9, *Experience and Nature* (1929), in *The Philosophy of John Dewey* (Two Volumes), ed.
John J. McDermott (Chicago: University of Chicago Press, 1981), I, pp. 307,
308.

4.   As a recent article noted,
The list of victories in conservationists' never-ending struggle to keep the modern
economy from destroying and degrading the natural world grows longer all the
time. But while green forces are winning battles . . . many of their generals and

strategists say the war is being lost. Despite gains, for instance, humans continue to appropriate an ever-growing proportion of the wild landscape to their use. Largely because of this, wild species are going extinct at 100 to 1000 times the natural "background" rate. One in eight plant species is rated as imperiled. By some analyses, one in three could be extinct or doomed to extinction in 50 years. [William K. Stevens, "Conservationists Win Battles but Fear War Is Lost," *New York Times*, 11 January, 2000].

5.   Those who have followed my peregrinations these past years will recognize themes announced at the Humanist Institute Faculty Colloquiums and published in *The Devil and Secular Humanism* (1990); *Humanism With A Human Face* (1996) and *From Clinic to Classroom* (2000) all from Praeger Publishers, Greenwood, Westport, Connecticut.

6.   See "Companionship (A Metaphor for Humanism)," *Humanism Today* 4 (1988); "Intimacy: Humanism With A Human Face: Notes For A Humanist Psychology," 6 (1991); "Reason and Enchantment: A Humanist Speaks to a Postmodern World," 8 (1993); "Creating A Humanist Narrative," 10 (1996); "One World At A Time," 13 (2000).

7.   Ralph Waldo Emerson, "The Transcendentalist" (1842), in *Selected Essays*, ed. Larzer Ziff (New York: Penguin Books, 1982).

8.   Michael Kenney, "Exploring The Myth of 'The Ecological Indian,'" *Boston Globe*, 16 July, 1999, p. C10.

9.   For example, Richard D. Klausner on the occasion of the 1999 Lasker Awards writes,
   If we are to continue to support the type of beautiful science we celebrate today and enable the expression of the creativity of scientists we honor today, it will take more than well-disposed appropriations committees, even more than vocal advocates; it will take a society that truly values the science and the scientists much as Renaissance Florence valued it art and its artists. It will take a society that sees it own historical narrative as, in part, the narrative of science. ["Successfully Sharing Our Stories of Science," *The Scientist*, 13:2 (18 January, 1999), p. 13].

10.   I think here, for example, of Dante's *Divine Comedy* and Condorcet's *Outline of Human Progress*.

11.   See my discussion of "horizon" as a humanist metaphor in "One World At A Time," *Humanism Today* 13 (2000).

12.   Steven Fesmire in, "Morality As Art: Dewey, Metaphor, and Moral Imagination," makes the point, He writes:
   In a poignant passage in *Love's Knowledge*, [Martha] Nussbaum sums up this attitude when she observes that moral knowledge entails "seeing a complex, concrete reality in a highly lucid and richly responsive way; it is taking in what is

there, with imagination and feeling." The great moral vice is not failure to
universalize maxims or calculate pleasurable consequences; it is obtuseness.
Morality requires refined sensitivity and immersion in events. It is a matter of
artistry. "A responsible action . . . is a highly context-specific and nuanced and
responsive thing whose rightness could not be captured in a description that fell
short of the artistic.". . . Artists exemplify this receptiveness fused with
orchestrating power. They disclose and create relations that otherwise go
unnoticed. The moral artist, like the prototypical artist must have an amplified
receptivity to the potential of the present. *Transactions of the Charles S. Peirce
Society*, 35 no. 3, (Summer 1999): 527-550, 541 (reference is to Martha
Nussbaum, *Love's Knowledge* (Oxford University Press, 1990), pp. 152, 154).

13. Edward Rothstein, "Examining the Patterns of Life in Fractals," *New
York Times*, 9 October, 1999:

The Greeks, too, had such touchstones. . . . A design is found within the natural
world, and that design in turn shapes the world that is found. A design is a theory,
a theory a design. This is also the case in contemporary science, which . . . seems
to rely more and more on artistic metaphors that invoke design and pattern. In
"The Artful Universe," (Oxford, 1995), the astronomer John D. Barrow argues
that "the arts and the sciences flow from a single source; they are informed by the
same reality; and their insights are linked in ways that make them look less and
less like alternatives." The geneticist Enrico Coen. . . . uses painting as a
metaphor to describe how organisms generate themselves. Beautiful natural
patterns—spirals, butterfly wings, rippling waves—and their mathematical
origins are explored in Philip Ball's "The Self-Made Tapestry: Pattern Formation
in Nature" (Oxford, 1998) . . . . This attention to the close relationships between
the arts and sciences is not new. . . . Two hundred years ago, the philosopher
Immanuel Kant suggested that in attempting to understand the natural world
human beings treat it as if it were specifically constructed for contemplation . . . .
Kant argued that man treats nature "after the analogy of art."

14. Symptomatically, Craig A. Lambert, Deputy Editor of *Harvard Magazine* writes (Editorial, September/October 1999):

In American Universities, beauty has been in exile. Despite it centrality in human
experience, the concept of beauty has virtually disappeared from scholarly
discourse. . . . Criticized as an elitist concept, an ethnocentric creation of white
European males, beauty has been stigmatized as sexist, racist, and unfair.
Attention to beauty, some say, may distract us from the world's injustices . . .
Throats however are being cleared. Aesthetics is returning to the academy.
Beauty is rearing its beautiful head.

15. I know that Thomas Kuhn in *The Structure of Scientific Revolutions*
(Chicago: University of Chicago Press, 1970) introduces the notion of a "paradigm shift" which has become almost a cliché of discourse. And this certainly is
a close relative of the direction I'm moving in. But a paradigm shift is still too
closely tied to the cognitive for my purposes. I know too that notions like the
Gaia hypothesis were around for a while although we don't hear much about
them lately. But that hypothesis pretends to descriptive status and tries to pretend that it is a metaphor.

ECOHUMANISM

Andreas Rosenberg

Social-Democrats and National-Socialists in politics; Greek Orthodox and Roman Catholics in religion—and now Ecohumanists!
How do such patched, tongue-twisting labels come into being? Are
the Social-Democrats just Socialists with a new paint job, or have
some of the most militant attributes of Socialism such as the dictatorship of the proletariat been removed to make Socialism more
palatable? In a more dry and precise language we can say that the
formation of a new combined class such as Social-Democrats from
Socialists and Democrats is a reclassification of the population and
reassessment of the attributes that are defining the classes in question. There is a class we label Socialists for all individuals whose
defining attributes are maybe belief in the class structure of society,
the reality of human exploitation, and the problem of the ownership of the tools of production. Democrats is the label for a class of
individuals whose attributes are a belief in the blessings of the
popular vote and a government by elected officials. None of the attributes in either class contradicts each other. The attributes characterizing the two classes are not mutually exclusive. We can find individuals who are characterized by attributes of both the Socialist
and Democrat classes. The population can thus be conveniently divided into individuals with only socialist attributes and individuals
with only democrat attributes as well as those carrying both groups
of the attributes. It is the last group of people we declare to constitute a new class, Social-Democrats. Members of this third class

each carry attributes from the other two classes. Fine, but remember that if we had not removed the attribute "The dictatorship of the proletariat" from the row of Socialist attributes, the new class would be in deep trouble. This problem is more clearly apparent if we try to combine classes with attributes like "ticketed passenger-stowaway," "protestant-catholic," "vegetarian-meateater." There is no possibility of defining stowaways with tickets or vegetarians eating meat. The attributes contradict each other and being in one class excludes one from being in the other class. The rules for formation of combined classes and concepts are quite well defined in formal logic. If we want to define a new class C from the overlap of two previously defined classes A and B, we have to be sure that the attributes in classes A and B do not contradict each other.

The question before us is: What are the attributes that define somebody as a member of the class labeled Humanists and another as the member of the class labeled Ecologists? We further ask if the nature of the attributes characterizing these two classes is such that a class of Ecohumanists can be established.

The labels Ecologist or Humanist each represent a series of unique attributes. These attributes when combined provide a general definition for what characterizes a member of that class. In the case of the two classes we are talking about the labels represent world-views, narratives concerned with the meaning, goal, and justification of human existence. Such narratives are not produced magically or arbitrarily by rubbing some oriental lamp nor do they describe a world where "twas brillig and the slithy toves did gyre and gimble in the wabe."[1]

The narratives provide answers to the questions that humanity has been asking over and over. Why, whereto and how? Explain to us our situation and our choices. Consequently, as the situation changes for the people, the questions tend to change and the narratives have to change or be exchanged for new ones. The new narrative is often an antithesis to the previous one.

From whence did the narrative we label humanism come and what change gave birth to it?

It was a reaction to and replacement of the previously dominating religious-monarchial worldview championed at its bloom by Christian gentlemen claiming conquered lands for their worldly sovereign but with each conquest being clearly authorized by their celestial monarch. The world appeared to them as a creation by higher powers who acted as some kind of advanced interior decorators placing sinners and saints in attractive groups according to the decorators' whims. Each individual's place in such a display was, according to the most fanatic of these gentlemen, preordained by the decorators. The human figures had very little to say about the play but to suffer and accept their lot, hoping to reap their rewards in afterlife.

This monarchial-religious story, either told in the Christian or Moslem version, had in turn previously replaced a multitude of beginnings of worldviews produced by tribes, ranging from dictatorship of shamans to experiments in democracy. The monarchial setup was very effective in the conquest of arable land, and its hierarchical structure favored slavery and allowed its different forms to dominate the production of goods. In fact, religious monarchies were essential for the perpetuation of slavery—the most efficient tool available to landowners prior to industrialization. When the territorial conquest of arable lands as power basis for states was replaced by industrial production, the efficiency of monarchy was not so clear anymore. The monarchial-religious system had difficulties in combining industrial slavery with machine power, despite valiant efforts by Carnegie, Pullman, and other "Nation builders." The steam engines and steel constructions epitomized by the Corliss machine and the Eiffel tower had no heavenly equivalents;

they represented the human power. The myth of Valhalla or Paradise did not fit well with smokestacks and belching Bessemer ovens.

Humanism appeared as an alternative narrative after the scientific and industrial progress had revealed the immense powers of humans acting together according to their own plans. No interior decorators of heavenly origin were necessary to realize these plans. Humans are the creators in possession of the blueprints. The quintessential motto of humanism "Humans are the measure for everything" was re-born. The corollary to it "humans are basically good" justified the belief that humans have the ability to create their own morals based on rational preferences. The moral laws of the Christian past, based on revelations, could be discarded. The Humanism that appeared was a celebration of the rational aspect of the human mind and in the beginning inextricably linked to the technological and artistic wave of modernism. Why build cathedrals? When we need a rectangular meeting space, let us build a box. Beauty perceived lies in its utility. Mondrian resolved the image of a tree into a few lines which allowed the rational mind to reconstruct the essence of the tree—to be sure, a more standardized and uniform tree than the real one.

Machines were the liberators of humanity. Humanity was on the verge of creating a new set of Gods, the Platonic concepts of Reason and Progress.

This ebullient narrative describing the triumphal progress of humanity crashed during the Great War. It sank into the mud of the bloody fields of Flanders. The replacement of Celestial blueprints with Human ones did not evidently change the conflicts humans had inherited. The efficiency of building sewing machines was easily transferred into building machine guns. Machines, besides liberating humans from toil, turned out to amplify human follies.

The consensus among the intellectuals was that the narrative of Humanism was seriously flawed and a replacement was desirable.

The ecology movement and the corresponding academic discipline that had been spawned by Darwinism appeared as a suitable replacement for Humanism. The major thesis of the ecology teachings was and still is that the Darwinian evolution dominates everything in the Biosphere we inhabit and the genus man despite his intellectual superiority is just another niche holder in a complex, interdependent system of utilization of the sun's energy. This interdependence puts natural limits to man's expansion.

Humans cannot and should not destroy their habitat and change their own role in a pyramid of organisms. Calvinism is here making its reappearance in another much greener coat. We are predestined to fill our role as the thinking ape. The iron cage that supposedly limited and enslaved the proletariat of the machine age is now replaced by the green bamboo cage of Ecology. The suggestion is that humanity should not tie its banner to machine age modernity but readjust its thinking to the schemes of Darwinism.

We have thus the attributes of the evolutionary theory describing the *Ecology* narrative and the banners of modernism providing the attributes for the class labeled *Humanism*. Are these attributes mutually exclusive or can we reclassify our population and form the class labeled *Ecohumanism*?

Let us first consider what is essential for ecology and cannot be removed from its list of attributes.

Ecology—the basis for ecology lies in the axiomatic nature of the basic laws of evolution which in this case are best called Darwin's laws because their role in ecology has changed from effort towards scientific description of phenomena to value judgments. The narrative of Darwinism describes the development of the Biosphere based on two basic concepts. The first concept is the random change in biological structures from generation to generation defining the essence of biosphere development as a generational process. The same structure is rebuilt time after time but the blueprints are changed slightly and randomly each time. The second concept defines competition for food and territory between the changed and unchanged forms as the instrument that chooses the better built organism for survival. The extreme and popular interpretation of competition in terms of either me or you is not present in the evolutionary model or Darwin's laws. It is the brainchild of Herbert Spencer and his colleagues who tried to make the mundane Darwinian story a little more theatrical and appealing so it could be applied to human behavior in the short time-span of a generation or two.

In evolution the most efficient pattern of organisms becomes dominating, although domination may involve competition, evolution mostly encourages organisms to utilize each other, whether it be through direct symbiosis or membership in the same food chain. The essential attribute for ecology is thus the belief in the restricted nature of the human role in the totality of biosphere.

Humanism, if we for a moment cast it free from the technology and utilitarianism of modernism, bases its narrative on the unlimited powers and possibilities of the human mind. Humans are the architects for all the blueprints of our future. The future has any form that appeals to us and ensures the survival of the species. Future represents a continuous expansion of human capabilities to rearrange the physical world. The last aspect is the quintessence of humanism. We move from Stonehenge to the Eiffel tower to a Space-station. The move to more and more organized and capable structures and constructions is unavoidable and represents the nature of the human mind. We could also rephrase the essential attribute of Humanism in terms of increase in information—maybe not knowledge in terms of Trivia Pursuit but increase in understanding and communicating all the possible causal patterns we detect in the Universe. Sharing with each other the details of all the models we use to picture the physical reality around us.

Our arrogant goal is to achieve total understanding, both of ourselves and the Universe.

A solitary human standing on a hill in Northern Sweden, overlooking the endless quiet forests and deep dark lakes, observes the firmament of cold, brilliant stars in combinations staggering the mind. He or she does not feel crushed into insignificance by this icy, beautiful eternity—nor huddle by a small fire in search of a cozy God to worship. The vast, passive Universe pales if mirrored in the human mind. We understand the moving of the tiniest orbs and, *by knowing it*, stretch out and acknowledge that both stars and the quiet forest are ours.

This *Humanism* can coexist with or discard the tools and methods of modernism because, right or wrong, they are but a creation of the human mind. When, however, it comes to its relations with ecology, we see from this short description that the labels describing humanism and ecology are not compatible. Humanism cannot accept limitations of the bamboo cage, the patterns of tribal coexistence and membership in a food chain. You may call these limitations heavenly rules or Nature with a capital letter. They do not fit into the dictum that the Human is the measure for everything.

At this moment in my arguments, I hear the rustling voices of thousands of ecologists. "Unfair, unfair, you cannot deny reality," they cry. Man (the genus) is an advanced relative to ape, totally dependent on the food chain and the integrity of the biosphere. Humanism, if the man/ape can at all comprehend, it may be but a nightly dream for such an inhabitant of the bamboo cage.

If this Darwinian model of reality is the most suitable to describe humanity, then the extreme scenario of ecology, most artistically presented in *The story of B* by Daniel Quinn,[2] is the best alternative for the future of humanity. Quinn unequivocally states that the only role for humans in the biosphere is to be members of a conglomerate of hunting and gathering tribes. Humanity moved away from this sound ecological niche about 10,000 years ago by starting large scale agriculture and division of labor present in centralized states. This was a terrible error that is now leading the biosphere towards catastrophe. The ecologically correct role for humans is at present best modeled by the tribes of Native Americans who accept their subordinate role in the complex interdependent system created and governed by evolution, a system we call Nature. If we accept Quinn's views as a logical extrapolation from the basic concepts of ecology, it would seem that humanity is standing at a fork in a road with two alternative ways to go. One governed by the ecological narrative, and the second governed by visions embedded in Humanism. Do we accept the ecological narrative and revert to our tribal role? As a scientist, I can ask at this point if is it at all feasible. My reservations are not tied to perceived economic or emotional difficulties—although as the Khmer Rouge experiment showed, they are formidable. I have doubts whether a return is at all physically possible in an ever-changing Universe. The evolution of the Biosphere continues, and the envisioned harmony of the tribes with nature is, as always, a temporary state. We cannot stop the continuous, ongoing experimentation by nature in the name of harmony. Think, for example, of but one tiny detail: the bodies of 6 billion humans represent 600 billion pounds of biomass, feeding media for bacteria and viruses to grow in. The future development of virus and bacteria proceeds with a speed proportional to their present population and the available biomass. What immense possibilities for viral adaptation! We can say with certainty that if we arrest our development and revert to tribal patterns, the viral and bacterial world will not stand still and soon the Virus Triumphant will emerge in many disguises of which the AIDS is but a harbinger. The humanity unchanged will either be destroyed or left in terms of scattered and isolated tribes.

Where does then the other road from the fork lead? This has been most clearly articulated by the amazing Jesuit Father Teilhard de Chardin.[3] He quite correctly points out that the evolution of the biosphere is not the beginning of development of the Universe nor does it represent an endpoint in development of our planet. He suggests that the formation of the planet Earth started with the development of lithosphere that lead to the formation of Biosphere that evolves according to the teachings of Darwin. It is only in the Biosphere that Darwinism has any justification. What is happening now is that we are entering a new phase replacing the biosphere, a phase he defines as the Noosphere. Thus from Litho to Bio to Noo. The developmental machine of random mutations will here be replaced by changes initiated by design. *A Designer Universe appears*. The power of altering the genetic code between generations, available to humans now, is not a horrible insult to some clean Godly principle. There is no difference between a random mutation in an organism occurring spontaneously or the same mutation produced by experiments in a laboratory. Random changes in organisms with unpredictable changes in the biosphere are continuously produced and let loose by nature. The devastation of Dutch elm disease was the end result of random mutation that took place sometime ago. Genetically modified wheat is not a different product from the native; it was once produced from something else by mutations. We have only cranked up the speed of mutations and, most importantly, the speed of testing their influence on the biosphere. Nature needed thousands of years to decide what was more efficient or better. The FDA needs only a few month or years. You may argue that my argument is frivolous and that the speed must lead to errors and maybe fatal errors. Errors are a part of evolution. The development of the biosphere and the human race follows rules described in Cybernetics. Change is always a correction for an error signal. The three little pigs learned to build stone houses to avoid nosy wolves. Legionnaires disease taught us to check our air-conditioners.

The point I am trying to make is that the evolution in Noo-sphere will be under the control of humans. The random nature of mutations is removed. We will change our food chains and interdependencies. We can create all possible molecules and not wait for Borges' 10,000 illiterate apes to type the formula for some drug and then let it grow in some tropical forest. In Noosphere, the humanity does not rely on the capacity of a single human mind; instead the minds are all connected, creating patterns and causal models of complexity and abstractness that single minds need not necessarily comprehend. The collective ability of the humanity defines the development of the Noosphere.

Which of the roads of the fork should humanity choose? One, leading to a return to tribal culture and uncertain future, the other to Brave New World and uncertainty. Uncertainty is our heritage, and speculation and exploration our hallmark.

For that reason, I think that humanism will declare the road to Noosphere to be the high road and move ahead despite the terrible, possible scenarios, beautifully depicted in books from every culture. Books such as *The Brave New World*[4], *Kallocain,*[5] and *Stern der Ungeborenen.*[6] The road to Noosphere has possibilities and alternatives, whereas the low road to the green cage will, with certainty, lead to darkness and extinction until the typing apes of Borges provide the planet with a new solution. So it is for us to choose between apex and ape—a difference of one letter—pointing to two incompatible and different worlds.

The straddling of these two alternatives preferred by an imaginary ecohumanist becomes more and more difficult. I can imagine a teepee with internet-access but not the production of internet in teepees. It will be the sound of drums instead in the twilight of humanity. But as the protagonist in *After Many a Summer Dies the Swan* remarks after observing the antics of humans regressing to their primitive state: "It wouldn't happen at once . . . . they look like they were having a pretty good time . . . ."[7]

At this point a valid criticism can be raised. Are you not extrapolating your presumed adversaries, the reborn cave dwellers and the fictitious futurists, to extremes. Maybe I am setting up a caricature of the ecologist and thus painting an unrealistic picture of the conflict.

True, but the aim of this essay is not to define the average environmentalist-ecologist and the modern consumer represented by a rational humanist; the aim is to dissect the main threads of the logic embedded in the structure of the two movements, the ecology and the humanism. The isolated reasoning may appear as extreme, but use of opposing extremes represents the basic mode of human thought. Thesis, defined clearly leads to formation of anti-thesis and later to synthesis. We may call this process Hegelian or cybernetic depending on our academic home, the humanistic tradition or science.

It is preposterous to assume that the evolution has stopped. What we see is the confrontation between endless new species of man. Remember that it is not only wings and limbs that evolve to explore new possibilities for survival, patterns of behavior serve the same purpose. The moral of my story is that ecology and humanism offer two different models for human development. The first model gives absolute priority to the biosphere in its Darwinian structure. The second model gives priority to humanity, not as an exponentially growing biomass but as the combined human intelligence acting in the post-Darwinian evolution.

The forced combination of the two powerful models into something like ecohumanism is not useful or productive. The expected synthesis can be recognized by abandoning the basic premises of both schools and replacing it with something new. But what? I do not think ecohumanism is it.

Notes

1. Lewis Carroll, *Through the Looking-Glass* (New York: Bantam Books, 1947).

2. Daniel Quinn, *The Story of B* (New York: Bantam Books, 1996).

3. Teilhard de Chardin, *The Phenomenon of Man* (New York: Harper and Row, 1959).

4. Aldous Huxley, *Brave New World* (New York: Doubleday, 1932).

5. Karin Boye, *Kallocain* (Stockholm: Albert Bonnier, 1940).

6. Franz Werfel, *Stern der Ungeborenen* (Stockholm: Bermann-Fischer, 1946).

7. Aldous Huxley, *After Many a Summer Dies the Swan* (New York: Avon, 1939).

ECOHUMANISM:
REFINING THE CONCEPT

Philip J. Regal

Terms and Their Implications

"Eco-" from the Greek *oikos,* meaning house in the sense of house-hold or estate, has historically implied the principles of order of the "habitat" or conditions by which one works and lives. In Xeno-phon's *Oeconomicus* for example, Socrates argued that there was a science to the principles for ordering or organizing complex living and working enterprises ranging from homes and country estates to maritime shipping and the social basis for viable political states.

"Ecology" implies the order of the house that is nature, the organic and physical habitat for life, including human life.

"Economics" in the modern sense derives from the term "political economy" which was the study of the order of the King's house in the 16th through 19th centuries. When kings declined in power but the nation state remained, political economy came to mean the rationality behind the arrangement of the machinery of power. The current use of "economics" broke off from the larger concept of political economy (as did demography and political science), notably during the 19th century, to mean the quantitative and mathematical treatment of the monetary and commercial aspects of the power base of the State and its elites.

"Ecology" and "economics" both imply a recognition of grand abstractions—a recognition of the fact that we and most of what is around us are interacting components in larger dynamic wholes. Individuals carve out identities, adapt, and exist within large cultural, economic, political, ecological, and ideological systems.

If knowledge of the human condition is a keystone of humanism, then it is important for humanists to understand the larger systems in which we exist—from the basic structures and histories of these systems to their changing dynamics. What are the large systems into which we are born and raised and how do they shape us? Are we rationally autonomous individuals as some philosophers and economic and political theorists have argued? If not, what would rational autonomy be?

"Ecohumanism" implies insight into patterns of connectedness among individuals and between individuals and institutions and with the non-human environment. In the larger ecological, sociological, and emotional contexts it is obviously true, as John Donne put it, that no man is an island. Expanding on Donne's metaphor let us ask—would it be rational to believe that one *is* an island? Humanism can scarcely avoid striving to understand one's relationships to larger biophysical and cultural systems, and yet believe that humanistic consciousness is fully rational.

The humanist commitment to the ethical and material quality of the human condition means that the earth must be regarded as home and habitat. People's lives on earth should not be passed off as merely stepping stones to salvation in some eternal beyond. If this home and habitat is to be kept in decent condition for human life and for ethical and material development then humanists are among those who accept that this will require intelligence and deeds and not merely prayer and good intentions, or facile notions that "progress" is automatic and will solve all problems.

"Ecohumanism" then, if only by the meanings imbedded in its roots, is a term with diverse potentials to wind its way through the environmental and political issues of our times and to identify turf for contemplation and action.

Interrelationships between Environmental Problems and Social Conditions

Twenty-first century civilization faces major challenges in dealing with disorders to the ecology of the environment on a global scale, that range from pollution, misuse and expansion of agricultural lands, population explosion, forced migrations, destruction of natural communities and loss of biodiversity, and so on.[1] Even fresh water is expected to grow dramatically more precious as population grows and industrialization spreads in the 21st century. Ecological disruptions are evident not only on local scales but even threaten the sustaining characteristics of the entire biosphere.

Ecological disruptions in turn have serious implications for the human condition. They can degrade the quality of life, damage health, disrupt economic/commercial policies, challenge democracy and freedom, and even provoke war and dash hopes for stable peace. One might keep in mind that many if not most wars in the last few centuries have been fought over trade and strategic resources ranging from oil to farmland.

Ecological disasters are already contributing to forced migrations both within (e.g. from the degraded country to city slums in Brazil) and between nations (e.g. African refugees from drought-suffering and degraded lands) and these will increase as ecological deterioration continues. Degraded land contributes to poverty which in turn contributes to poor education and political corruption, which then feed back on ecological degradation.[2] A strong case also can be made that poverty too often in turn has encouraged large families and contributed to overpopulation because poor people feel they need many children to help farm, to earn supplemental family income, and as their security in old age.[3] Thus there are complex feed-back loops between environmental problems, poverty, political corruption, economic problems, and sometimes overpopulation.

Some will argue that they and others live in comfort and perhaps even luxury. But this does not eliminate the fact that from a bird's-eye view human life on the planet is commonly a hopeless struggle and that the conditions for most species, including ourselves, are degrading at an alarming rate.

One dimension of these problems and their dim future prospects is their retrograde effects on the potential for intellectual enlightenment and ethical progress. Forces that breed massive economic degradation and desperation, shattered families and communities, political disempowerment, inferior education, and even addictive habits clearly have in effect encouraged ignorance and superstition. Humanists are typically opposed to circumstances and ideologies that in effect encourage the *spread* of ignorance, superstition, and denial.

"Humanism" could be defined in many ways. But humanists typically esteem the *right* to pursue truth and rationality *honestly.* I say "the right to pursue" and "honestly" because it has been clear to knowledgeable humanists that there has been no simple formula even for simply making meaningful progress toward truth and rationality that does not involve motivation, intellect, sincerity, keen observation, and fearless self-examination.[4]

Simple logic and superficially reasonable assumptions have commonly fed hubris, self-deception, rationalizations, egoism, wishful thinking, and have misled multitudes throughout history and into our own time. There have been good chess players and mathematicians among the dupes of every poisonous ideology and religion. The inquisitors and ideological tyrants believed themselves to be quite rational according to what they thought to be true, but in retrospect the flaws in their thinking have become obvious. One recalls George Bernard Shaw, "The man who listens to Reason is lost: Reason enslaves all those whose minds are not strong enough to master her."[5] Yet a passion for truth, a disciplined critical reasoning, and skepticism of fanaticism have often enough, throughout history, led to more secure judgments and proved their worth.[6]

Ecological problems can cause political frictions and become national security issues, and these in turn can by several means detract governments and societies from humanistic concerns.

A literature has begun to develop in the professional journals on national security and foreign policy that documents a growing recognition that environmental problems create security risks. There have even been efforts in this literature to construct conceptual models of the contributions of various types of environmental deterioration to increases in the frequencies and types of political and military conflicts.[7]

Environmental deterioration has been leading to progressively greater conflicts over water and other limited and/or shared resources. It can lead to migrations within and across national borders. The loss of the quality of farmland will lead evermore to increases in food scarcity. All these can in turn increase social and economic needs, social tensions and dissatisfactions, political instability, and military challenges.

One should add to this dismal list the fact that popularly proposed techno-fixes such as biotechnology are in fact extremely expensive and risky economic investments, and expensive high-tech programs can also carry political risks. By their nature they tend to encourage the building of strong alliances between strategic elites, investors, bureaucrats, and elected officials and encourage concentrations of unaccountable political power. The notion of quick techno-fixes can be seductive and distract from the exploration of more realistic programs to solve problems that have complex economic, ecological, historical, and political causes. The development of powerful special interest groups that benefit from techno-fix agendas implies the development of aggressive self-interested perspectives, rhetoric, and campaigning that have little interest in the truth of circumstances or in the finding of alternative and more realistic solutions.

Investment in expensive hoped-for but too-often ineffective magic bullets can moreover increase the debt of a poor country and bring no ultimate solutions to its economic, social, and nutritional problems. In fact, increased debts commonly worsen environmental, economic, educational, and political problems. Much of the enormous Third World debt has accumulated due to misplaced enthusiasm for particular aid projects and loans for developments that failed.

One dimension of political frictions (and surely war) is that humanistic concerns are too commonly put aside when national (or merely political) security is thought to be at stake. Governments and media will give priority to economic priorities that can support military might and bureaucracy, to social psychology that can support societal order and mobilization, and to diplomatic efforts that emphasize strategic economic and military alliances.

For example, eighteen respected political scientists and economists met and corresponded at length to analyze the implications of educational development for emerging nations in the 1960s. Their analysis, *Education and Political Development*, was one part of a large project of the Committee on Comparative Politics of the

Social Science Research Council concerning the applications of lessons from older nations to emerging nations.[8] They struggled as they reminded themselves that political leaders and political theory tend to be very skeptical of broad popular education because this tends to contribute to political instability.

Leaders commonly much prefer narrow, technical educations for the population, since narrowly educated people are:

1. Less likely to understand how The System works and to question it.

2. Less likely to aspire to policy positions and to become frustrated when they cannot join the higher ranks of power.

3. Less likely to join revolutionary forces.

4. Less likely to add diversity and competition to the ranks of the elite.[9]

Development economists as well as political theorists and the politically powerful favor mathematics and natural sciences and education in crafts and occupational skills, rather than in those social sciences "which break up accepted attitudes,"[10] and which may even produce "large numbers of unproductive and destabilizing unemployables."[11]

The study team found that as a pragmatic matter they had to agree with many people in power that technically educated people are more easy to manage, and that technical-leaning educations would also be best for the social stability of developing nations in the short run. But they did confess their embarrassment at this anti-democratic conclusion; "we find ourselves in the astonishing position of casting the relationship between education and political development in essentially negative terms."[12]

In the end, as a practical matter, they recommended a 'mix' of technical and broadening educational programs. In effect, they recommended quotas on enlightenment and comprehension of the world.

One might add that there is a body of economic/political theory today that predicts that, "no state will rationally implement any policy that it considers to be a threat to order. . . . Economists, in considering policy implementation and recommendations, must focus their attentions on the constraints that the maintenance of order dictates."[13]

Globalization

Soon after the conquest of the Americas in the 1500s the entire planet was drawn into trade, debts, and other interactions and dependencies with Europe and a global economy and "world system" emerged. But today the term "globalization" that has been popular in schools of business, law, and management implies a new character or level of changes in the world system of global trade, communication, and intermingled political interests.

With the Thatcher and Reagan neo-liberal, so-called "free market," economic agendas reversals of anti-trust and other regulatory legislation began in the democratic countries. In the United States a highly effective political coalition had been forged between business interests and the religious right. Campaign financing levels escalated and lobbyist activity increased, which marked an increase in the political power of those with great financial resources and organizational skills. Rapid communication, information flow, and transportation allowed rapid transfers of huge amounts of money, and rapid shifts of the means of production to areas with weak environmental standards, low wages, and congenial or controlled work forces— thus keeping production costs low and profits high.

The idea was promoted that the old wine of trickle-down economics in the new bottle of globalization would not simply benefit economic and strategic elites, but would make a better world for everyone. Increasing profits would be invested to upgrade capital assets and would inspire technological, and management innovations. More jobs would be created and standards of living would be increased everywhere. Increasing profits would provide the wealth to finance the solutions to environmental problems and technological advances would provide simple solutions to difficult economic, environmental, and political problems. Doctrines of self-interest and competition would spur humanity to rise to its best.

In the new world order the increasing prosperity of those at the top would generate wealth that would *automatically* trickle down to all in an increasing cornucopian plenty and quality of life. The importance of the contributions of those humanistic religious and non-religious factions who had worked hard to help make a better world in the modern centuries was ignored—human rights advocates, labor leaders, liberal education advocates, conservationists, free-thinking intellectuals, scientists driven merely by a passion for truth, writers of conscience and with a critical eye.

Skeptical rationalist humanists should examine the grand promises of globalization enthusiasts as carefully as they have examined the enthusiastic claims about the Shroud of Turin, miracle cures for cancer, or astrological conjunctions.

Surely some good will come of globalization. There will be problems as well, and it is not clear if in the long run the upside will balance the downside.

Wealth does not always, automatically, trickle down freely. Wealthy countries where the people have been impoverished, such as the former Zaire, a classic modern kleptocracy, are familiar. Wealth can also be gambled away on bad business investments, can be used to corrupt politicians, to buy influence, to pay slick lob- byists, to support dictators and armed oppression. Wealth can be stashed away in secret bank accounts in the many tax havens around the world. There is no law of nature that dictates that wealth must trickle down freely and will automatically raise the conditions of even the average person, let alone of those at the bot- tom of the social hierarchy.

There is no law of nature that insures automatic and intelligent attention to humanitarian concerns even in the face of desires for cheap labor and political control, simply because wealth increases, and without vigorous humanitarian constituencies.

There is no law of nature that insures that environmental prob- lems will automatically receive proper attention even in the face of desires for reduced regulations simply because wealth increases, and without vigorous environmental constituencies.

It is shrewd business to externalize and reject paying the social and environmental costs of production. But if government accepts the bills for these costs, then these costs could eventually come back to business in the form of direct or indirect taxes. So it is easi- est simply to deny the responsibility of either business or govern- ment for such costs. In this sense, the a public consciousness of system interactions and interdependencies that I have suggested is rational, a public consciousness of that fact that no man is an is- land, can open a Pandora's box of ethical and practical problems for the enthusiasts of globalization.

Humanistic Concerns about the New World Order

A downside of the much-used term "globalization" is widely pre- dicted to be that as the power of multinational corporations and banks continues to spread, the independent powers of democratic nation states and citizen representation through traditional means in the domestic and international arenas will diminish.

This so-called new world order of globalization has implied the uses of technologies of rapid communication and transportation, and the accumulation and organization of huge amounts of money to increase the power of corporations, banks, and the megawealthy to influence politicians and bureaucrats, to buy and influence the media and public consciousness. The growing influence of corporations on governments and media has in turn implied a certain amount of disinformation, spin, distraction, and the selective and simplified presentations of information. Indeed, by the dawn of the Third Millennium citizens were turning evermore to NGOs (Non-Governmental Organizations) to gather and analyze information and to press for humanitarian and environmental interests.

Globalization forces have implied the ability of corporations to play off governments against one another— for example to weaken environmental regulations, weaken individual freedoms, weaken collective bargaining, redirect education from liberal arts emphasis to an emphasis on technical training and marketable job skills, to obtain laws and appointments to courts favorable to their interests, to obtain direct and indirect subsidies from public resources, to privatize publicly owned properties, to mobilize public and institutional support for projects favorable to the interests of powerful global players and their regional allies.

This downside of globalization implies in turn a range of obstacles to the mitigation of environmental problems and to the health, ethical, political, and societal problems that are enmeshed with them, as has been discussed.

Challenges for Liberal Education from Globalization

Globalization has serious implications for educational systems. This can be best explained by next outlining three important models that have played a role in agendas for education.

One model is expressed in the following quotation from Thomas Jefferson in his 1778 proposed *Bill for the More General Diffusion of Knowledge*. Jefferson argued that public education should prepare citizens to defend their freedoms from subtle efforts to concentrate power and to manipulate them. Public education should enlighten citizens about the ambitions of the powerful and the techniques by which people have been robbed of their freedoms.

> experience hath shewn that even under the best forms [of government], those entrusted with power have, in time, and by slow operations, perverted it into tyranny; and it is believed that the most effectual means of preventing this would be, to illuminate, as far as practicable, the minds of the people at large, and more especially to give them knowledge of those facts, which history exibiteth, that possessed thereby of the experience of other ages and countries, they may be enabled to know ambition under all its shapes, and prompt to exert their natural powers to defeat its purposes. . . .

This model can be distinguished for discussion from yet a second "liberal arts" philosophy that links education and citizenship, and that has long had a special significance for humanists. In this model, the public should be educated so that free citizens can make their own truly informed choices about personal growth, or about intelligent market participation, or so that they can form opinions on practical matters that come before voters. Education should challenge individuals and equip them with intellectual skills to join in the adventure of the human mind and of enlightened being. It should prepare citizens to be quality neighbors in thoughtfully ethical and nurturing democratic communities.

A third model for public education has focused on economics. Young citizens should be educated to suit them for the work force of laborers, clerks, and professionals.

View From the Political Top in the Economic Model: The economic strength and international competitiveness of a nation depends on the effectiveness of its work force and the ability of the population to supply firms with their human needs.

View From the Bottom in the Economic Model: Taxpayers should get direct services back from government and one service is the preparation of their children for careers.

Globalization finds the economic model in its best interest. Davis and Botkin,[14] for example, in a book that claims to summarize the views of a wide range of industrial leaders, argue from this last mindset that education in America was first controlled by family and church. Then government gained control of education. But government-led education has been slow to meet the fast-changing needs of an increasingly internationalized industry because of nationalistic priorities and because of bureaucracy. "It was built to serve an economy and society that no longer exist." Now business must lead the way and teach both grade school and college students to think in ways that will better suit them for the business world including a new Three Rs—children and young people must become used to Rewards as incentives, Relationships to business, and Rivalry as a healthy tonic. Tenure for teachers and professors protects obsolete values and perspectives and is an obstacle to making the needed changes, so it will have to go. The authors advance the argument that the elimination of tenure will not be damaging, but this is no more than an uninformed slogan that only superficially seems to make sense: "Those who deserve tenure do not need it, and those who need it don't deserve it." Business knows about such things, they insist. Humanists may well ponder what the elimination of tenure would imply for the traditions of free-thought and discussion.

These three types of models are all 'practical' and have all contributed to the shape of contemporary public education in democ-
racies. Yet the strongest political constituencies historically and in
our own time have been by far those that have desired the last
model. These perspectives eternally wrestle, like three oiled and intimately intertwined Grecian athletes painted on an ancient vase,
but the athlete who is usually on top is much bigger than the others, is clever, and has especially close ties with the referee. Business, industry, and banking have had powerful access to government and have effectively campaigned to have their needs met and
to have 'practical' defined to their advantage. Many parents have
joined business and have been convinced that their chief 'practical'
concern should be press institutions to educate their children for
the job market. Globalization is adding political and media muscle
to the top wrestler.

Thus, assuming that the dominant trends continue, the potential
use of nation states by citizens to secure citizen's rights and to facilitate the efforts of citizens to cultivate their individual and community potentials will continue to weaken in the 21st century. At
the same time, states will be evermore represent the interests of
corporations and banks when states exercise their powers over citizens and exercise their powers in relationships between states.

The "Ecology" of Educational Discourse—"Overeducation"

Educational systems do not exist and are not administered and
funded in a vacuum. They are parts of larger social systems, and if
only in this respect they have an "ecology." In this sense globalization represents the spread of economic/political perspectives, or
"ecological" principles, toward education that have developed
among the dominant "super-organisms" of the new world order.

The *Education and Political Development* study cited above reported that anti-liberal education attitudes among the powerful are more often discussed discretely than published openly. But economists/social scientists who develop policy positions for those in power do express opinions in succinct prose, albeit in technical language. Let us briefly survey some of this literature.

The 1960s and 1970s were years of social turmoil in the United States. Complex demographic, economic, political, and intellectual factors were at work. On the intellectual front, first came civil rights ideals and activism, the ending of censorship and explorations of sexuality, the start of a new women's movement. Then came the questioning of authority often associated with criticism of the Vietnam War. In this stormy climate, the term "overeducation" became a common buzzword at the higher levels of society.

Buzzwords have considerable power because they resonate with strong feelings, and yet they are commonly difficult to define meaningfully. This creates work for scholars who come aboard after buzzwords become common and try to better define the phenomena to which the buzzwords presumably refer. This was true again in the case of "overeducation." Thus a substantial technical literature had accumulated in the 1960s and especially the 1970s and much of it was reviewed in the early 1980s.

Harold Kaufman, Director of the Research Program in Science, Technology and Human Resources at the Polytechnic Institute of New York in Brooklyn wrote in his book *Professionals in Search of Work: Coping with the Stress of Job Loss and Underemployment* that overeducation was a fact and that it had reached "epidemic" proportions in both developed and developing countries. He did not conceal the political concerns. Not only is money lost training new employees when those who are unsatisfied with their positions in life take time off or move on, but educated people who cannot find satisfactory jobs have a "propensity toward political activism." They tend to blame "the system" for social problems.

Kaufman did not explore the possibility that a combination of education and difficult challenges might have helped to open their eyes to problems with "the system" and thus had actually made them more perceptive and useful citizens. Instead he simply assumed that tendencies toward political involvement are neurotic.

> With the fulfillment of their higher order needs blocked they may direct the anger resulting from their career frustrations against society. . . . A thwarted desire for job involvement could be redirected toward political involvement. We should, therefore, expect an increase in support for political activism and societal change concomitant with the increase in the number of underemployed professionals.[15]

Kaufman suggested a variety of possible responses by those in power, including that universities might increase the career orientation of education, and expose even liberal arts students "to the practical realities of work by means of cooperative education programs, internships, or similar experimental approaches that are attractive to both students and employers."

In any event, he warned repeatedly that one way or another the "epidemic" must be stopped.

> Indeed, it is the rapidly increasing numbers of educated workers who are likely to have the greatest influence on the shaping of future societies. Thus, if for no other reason than self-interest, national efforts must be devoted to helping assure proper utilization of professionals. Not to do so will lead to mass frustration of expectations and psychological deterioration among educated workers, which could, as past evidence indicates, contribute to political turmoil and conflict on a global scale.[16]

Russell Rumberger, Research Associate at the Institute for Research on Educational Finance and Governance at Stanford University did discuss the fact that there are serious problems with the term "overeducation." Yet it was clear in his book *Overeducation in the U.S. Labor Market* that "overeducation" had become an important word among the elite and while it could be questioned, it could not be ignored and social scientists would have to accommodate the desire to convert economic and political concerns into rational social policies.

Rumberger was persuaded to reject the argument that overeducation is the private concern of each overeducated individual. The negative effects of overeducation ultimately affect job performance. So it is the proper concern of firms and of governments, he maintained.

But what options exist for those in power? How, for that matter can one legitimate any claims that rationality directs educational policies? A discussion of economic costs and benefits in education may not encompass all legitimate social considerations, he noted, but it can set an agenda for negotiations that appear (at least) to be rational. Thus, Rumberger came back repeatedly to economic arguments in his analysis, even though he struggled openly with the flaws in them.

Rumberger suggested that jobs could in theory be redesigned to make them more satisfying to overeducated people. As a practical matter, though, employers are not apt to implement reforms that encourage individuality and reduce "the decision prerogatives of management ... or threaten their control over the work structure."[17] Workable options are thus few. One suggestion was that,

> The recurring movement of career education may be a way of getting students interested in jobs with specific skills that predominate at the middle levels of the job hierarchy, thus lessening the demand for higher levels of schooling and higher-status jobs. ... [G]overnment policy can do little more than promote the public's interest in particular levels or types of schooling.[18]

Personally, as a humanist, I would be very pleased and even comforted to be surrounded by well-educated neighbors and voters who understand how 'the system' works and who could help develop constructive suggestions for improving it and for enriching community life culturally. I find it difficult to use the word "overeducated." I am very pleased to know cultured and enlightened carpenters, clerks, and grade school teachers, as well as computer programmers and business executives, whose educations have given them the skills and incentives to fill their hearts and minds with the joy and personal riches that they have gained from sharing in the insights and creations of human intelligence, whatever their income level.

Even a narrow technical education can represent a misinformed investment decision. It would make no sense at all for multitudes of students to spend years learning primarily mathematics, chemistry, and physics so that they can become engineers when the job prospects are dim. 'Overeducation' might seem like a term with some meaning in this context, although 'mis-educated' would be better.

The suggestion that students should be encouraged to pursue narrow career tracks so that they will not become 'overeducated' makes no sense even in terms of job dissatisfaction. It is very difficult to predict job markets, and so the production of a generation of narrowly career-tracked college graduates would be (has been?) a recipe to increase widespread personal frustrations rather than an antidote.

Humanists should be skeptical when stereotypes of "overeducated" students are promoted and be aware of the ways in which these stereotypes can be inflated to lobby for educational policies that in truth aim primarily to serve political and economic motives, whether or not such policies are destined to backfire.

Globalization and The Internet

Against the disempowering aspects of globalization forces is the development of the internet, including the formation of internet interest networks and even virtual communities and subcultures. The internet can be a rapid, inexpensive, and effective vehicle for the spread of information and discourse on common issues for motivated individuals across the planet. It can be a way for motivated individuals to become semi-independent of mass media.

The potential of internet communications to empower citizens with humanistic and humanitarian interests raises an interesting question to ponder: What historically were the implications of the development of printing for the development of humanism? A meditation on the development of printing could lead to ideas for maximizing the potential of the internet as vehicle for advancing the principles of humanism. The internet can provide improved means for networking, the collection and sharing of information, thoughtful discussions of specific situations and general principles and the like.

The hard-won freedoms of the press, assembly, and privacy in certain countries were often led by humanists, and humanistic goals have surely benefited from these reforms. Today's humanists should develop policies toward the protection of internet freedoms and privacy with regard to both governmental and non-governmental powers.

Humanism and the World Condition

What does an awareness of "systems" and interdependent systems, of the interdependencies of human values and quality of life with the biosphere, economics, and politics, imply for humanism today? The issues are diverse.

At the personal level, and first of all, how does one keep one's head in such times of ideology, disinformation, poor media role models for thinking, a flood of escapist nonsense, and information overload? The idea of the *pursuit of rational autonomy* has long been a keystone for humanism and for claims to the dignity of humans. The premise has been that when people develop their rational skills they can find ways to run their own affairs without having to submit to a tyrannical government or church, that they can develop ethical systems that allow for mutual respect and the pursuit of human dignity, and can live free from the needless fears and mistakes of judgment that come with superstition and ignorance. How can rational autonomy be pursued in our own rapidly changing, increasingly complex, and politically contentious times? This is a subject that I discussed at length in *The Anatomy of Judgment*. A key objective must be to master the biological and social pitfalls that threaten good judgment, to understand how the mind works, to grasp that mind is not merely brain, and to master an understanding of the subtle biological quirks both of the brain and of the developmental habits and social forces that can undermine and mislead the pursuit of rational judgment.

At the personal level, how does one establish humanistic values when confronted at every turn by aggressive efforts on the one hand to persuade one of ideologies that are often little more than hedonism or forms of Social Darwinism or self-serving arguments spawned from special interest groups; or when one is confronted on the other hand with fears, hatreds, and disinformation in the name of God and His love? The first thing to remember is that humanists have faced similar obstacles before and managed to keep up their struggle to maintain a healthy, critical, and rationally disciplined skepticism about dogmas and seductive superficial arguments. They have lived in times and places where torture has been condoned, where the accused have not been allowed a proper defense, where slavery has prevailed, where women have been denied full human rights, where sexual minorities have been persecuted, where writings and speech have been censored, where children have been exploited and abused for labor, where education has been restricted, and they have resisted rationalizing such injustices. Indeed, humanists managed to find effective ways to oppose these and in the end have helped to build the great historical movements against them. The answer has had something to do with mixing determination and character, alert living, patience, morale, self-examination, and a disciplined cultivation of the mind in formulas that each individual must devise according to time, situation, and personality.

This is an age of miracles and wonder, as a bard wrote. Has human consciousness shifted now that for the first time in human history we can see our planet and weather patterns in satellite photos? I agree with those who believe that it has become more easy to think of the entire planet as a common home and environment for all of us, and that the photos have helped raise environmental consciousness, and the sense of a world community. At the same time, it seems possible that the photos make some people feel incredibly small and insignificant and seek significance in the irrational.

What do the problematic changes in global ecology and economics imply for humanism in the creative arts? The consolidation of ownership of the mass media has not been especially helpful. On the other hand useful readings and graphic arts can be found, especially in large cities. One especially optimistic aspect of our times has been made possible by relatively inexpensive cameras, thoughtful audiences, and creative predecessors. There has been a proliferation of small independent filmmakers around the world. Alongside the ubiquitous escapism on film and video, one finds artists who have used the enormous potential of images to capture and magnify fragments of humanity and illuminate the complexity and diversity of the human condition. We can all learn from stories, however modestly they are sometimes produced, of those around the world who face challenges creatively and prevail, and from those who cannot surmount their circumstances. Good films can help to break down the barriers of preconception, help us to understand that often we do have hopes and problems in common with humans who may superficially seem very different from ourselves, help us to see that we can relate to them. They can help us to better visualize foreign cultures, economic situations, ecological challenges—and thus open doors to improved understanding and communication. This in turn can help us to see larger systems or "ecological" patterns in global economics, human rights concerns, confrontations with technology, ecological challenges, and to see common grounds for working together.

It is clear in our times that vast frontiers wait to be explored in what different cultures can learn from each other.[19] We can surely learn in terms of our abilities to improve human relationships, to improve the quality of family and community life, to improve the ability of cultures to interact amiably, to improve the ability of people to manage their own affairs at the community and higher levels. The human family represents diverse experiments in finding solutions to the diverse problems of being human. We are social individuals. What ways have been found to balance our social needs and propensities with our egoistic needs and propensities? Social animality implies desires for love, community, bonding, communication, ethical structures (implicit rules) for social interactions, recognition and accommodation of non-destructive individual quirks. How have these needs been met in various cultural experiments, which include our own, and what can we learn from such experiments, that can inspire and discipline our thinking and humility?

As Western humanists deliberate evermore with people of other cultures and values about the fate of life on the planet and other common concerns, what will be the basis for communication, images, agreement, and joint action? Negotiation is best served by first understanding each other's perspectives. As only one example, consider overpopulation. Western humanists such as myself tend to be concerned about overpopulation. Yet Third World peoples tend to be extremely sensitive when this subject is brought up and can even get quite angry. There has been a history of blaming Third World problems simplistically on overpopulation and comfortably denying the contributions of centuries of development under colonialism and then neo-colonialism and the cold war, of Western-backed dictators, corrupt officials, and political factions, of arms peddling and the huge international debts this builds up, of poorly thought-through or implemented structural adjustments imposed by international banks, of cultural disruptions by misguided missionaries. I have found that if one is culturally sensitive to Third World history, perspectives, and concerns then one can go on and discuss overpopulation amiably and productively.

People within cultures can be diverse and practical as well as idealistic, ideological, and/or religious. How do diverse cultures balance practicalities in terms of ideals, ideologies, religious, and social beliefs? The growing intimacy of the global community and common global concerns presses the question: What is humanism from a "practical" point of view? Do the practical dimensions of humanism provide an adequate basis for negotiation with people of other cultures on matters of great common concern? What is the place of secularism in contemporary humanism? What is the relationship of contemporary humanism to historical humanism?

Historically (according to Abbagnano in the *Encyclopedia of Philosophy*) humanism was not anti-religious except in the sense that it 1) advocated intellectual freedom from authoritarian hierarchies and 2) sought to justify the capacity for people to seek their own destinies, 3) advocated that pleasure had a legitimate place in moral human life, 4) advocated that money had a legitimate place in the life of individuals and society, 5) pursued an interest in the original reasoning of philosophers such as Plato and Aristotle before they had been co-opted by Christian authorities.

Secularism is common, though not hegemonic, in humanism today. Some humanists are atheists and agnostics, while others may hold various supernatural beliefs but consider them to be a private matter. They prefer to make a separation between their civic roles based on rational discussion and scientific information, and a private inner world based on intuition and/or faith. In either case, humanists today commonly discourse among themselves in rational terms.

The secular terms of discourse among humanists are sometimes said to be an obstacle to working toward common social/ecological/global ends with religious cultures, especially those who have been persuaded that secular humanism is the work of their Devil. But these last believers are not a proper model or test case for pondering the issue. For that matter, they are unlikely in any event to be able to fully comprehend and discuss large-scale material problems within a scientific framework and work diligently toward material solutions.

Consider a different model or test case. Would even the most secular humanist find it impossible to discuss human problems and work toward solutions with Albert Einstein because he reportedly had a "deeply emotional conviction of the presence of a superior reasoning power,"[20] though he could not believe in a personal or punishing God? I find it difficult to see why differences of conviction on Einstein's religiosity would necessarily be a barrier to the pursuit of common humanistic goals with those humanists who are atheists or agnostics.

Working relationships toward common goals are possible when diverse parties want them to work and develop the interpersonal skills to make them work. Even tribes of warriors with profoundly different worldviews in the highlands of New Guinea who live side by side have found ways to interact, trade, mediate differences, and work together toward common goals. That their peace does sometimes collapse in misunderstandings, as can any human agreement, should not make the point any less valid.

The world *is* multicultural and faces serious crises and there are few resources and little time for anyone to have a meaningful impact on great problems that in one way or another affect us all. Humanists should hone their diplomatic skills and be proud of their traditions of respecting individual differences of opinion among people who want to communicate rationally, and gladly work with them toward decent lives and a healthy and nurturing biophysical environment.

Ideological Challenges for Humanism

Ecohumanist critical rationalist discourse will confront various ideologies from economic and political arenas that propose simple solutions to global problems.

The classical "liberal" or "free-market" (closer to "conservative" in U.S. politics) arguments are pervasive among classical economists and political scientists and throughout modern culture. They will argue that classical economic thinking *is* rationality. These will argue that secular humanism should be very much the same as economic freedom and that economic forces are best left alone to follow the alleged laws of nature, and that in this way "the" market and the moral calculus will work an impersonal magic to produce the greatest benefits for all, a best of all possible worlds.

Trickle-down ideologues will attempt to co-opt humanists along with everyone else. Can humanists thus avoid questioning the pseudoscientific assumptions imbedded in trickle-down and other such classical economic theories? These ideas have had a long association with pseudoscientific balance of nature arguments and with the pseudoscientific Social Darwinism of Bernard Mandeville and Herbert Spencer, years before Darwin published the *Origin*.[21] These ideas have been hotly contested both in their logic and in the realities of how they have been used to (mis)represent the world and to advocate public policies.[22]

Another ideological trend has been for scientists and economic powers to form alliances in advancing simple technological solutions to human problems. These promises have too commonly been utopian and fail to acknowledge fully that there can be downsides to particular technological programs as well as upsides. Thus society has not been braced to prepare for the downsides of technological introductions and can only live with the consequences or attempt to clean up after the fact, when possible. The enthusiastic overuse of pesticides and antibiotics would be examples. Some would point to diverse problems caused by the Green Revolution, that might have been avoided, or the restructuring of much of the United States for heavy reliance on automobiles and freeways.

Students of history should join with humanist skeptical inquirers and probe deeply when simple technological solutions to complex problems are being peddled by those who will profit by them. Historically informed humanists have good reasons for a healthy skepticism of utopian promises and idealisms of any sort, as they do for skepticism of arguments that ask one to overlook injustices in the real world around them because of some higher cause or in the expectation of some future paradise on earth or in the heavens.

Historian David Noble in *The Religion of Technology: The Divinity of Man and The Spirit of Invention*[23] gives fascinating evidence that the rhetoric of technological utopia has long implied enormous faith because so much of it has in fact come directly from its key proponents' religious theories about destiny and redemption. Indeed, believers have even long contemplated a future without the flawed corrupt human body. Humans could be replaced, for example, by computers without messy emotions or imperfect reasoning.[24]

The technological promises in our time now even include assurances that the salvation of humanity rests upon the genetic engineering of a new "post-human," a superman that will be the realization of all humanistic dreams, as Princeton professor of behavioral genetics Lee Silver has detailed in *Remaking Eden: How Genetic Engineering and Cloning Will Transform The American Family*.[25] The wisdom of the market place will build a mentally and physically superior "GenRich" class and they inevitably will choose not to breed with humans and will instead form a new species, the "post-humans." The new superior post-human species will naturally rule over the earth, including the inferior humans, and will bring order to the chaos in the world.

A historian colleague mused sarcastically, "Why should I bother trying to make a better world if my children and I are already inferior and we just have to wait for the marketplace and the genetic engineers to solve all our problems?"

Ideas can have enormous power. Hitler never did breed a superman, but his seductive and quasi-scientific promises of genetic utopia surely diverted Germany from contemplation of more realistic humanistic pursuits, and eventually shook the community of nations to its core. Whether or not the genetic engineers can ever conquer problems such as side-effects, and whether germ-line engineering of something as complex as supermen becomes actually possible, these promises are already part of an enormously expensive and politically powerful agenda. It is not simply the freedom of scientists to pursue research that is involved, but direct and indirect public funding and institutional development on a vast scale.

.ι this is public funding for science that might be spent else-where with quite interesting results in terms of the advance of human knowledge.

Thus the movement to genetically engineer humans by no means presents merely a freedom of science issue, as those who have a special interest in it commonly spin the matter, it is a public policy issue because of its tremendous financial and institutional costs to taxpayers, as well as its social implications.

When one considers the ideology that piggybacks on genetic engineering, this is surely a movement and public policy issue that humanists should study in depth, and consider the promotional claims with a critical eye.

And, suppose it would be technically and politically possible to actually genetically engineer supermen. What would the supermen be?[26] Do humanists agree that the wisdom of the marketplace should decide the future of humanity, or of post-humanity for that matter?[27] Optimism that the wisdom of the marketplace will produce in any respect a superior race seems naive at best.

Humanism has long taken an interest in human nature debates as a point of departure for deliberations on the advancement of the human condition. But theories of human nature quickly became the tools of ideologies to serve one political end or another. Thomas Hobbes, Bernard Mandeville, Herbert Spencer and others attempted to base elitist theories of political order on theories of human nature that they claimed were secular. Hobbes looked at a social species and proposed that the "basic particle" of human society is an anti-social, selfish, and predatory individual who requires absolute rulers, such as his own patrons, to prevent a war of all against all. Bernard Mandeville, arguably the father of so-called free-market capitalism argued that the vices of Hobbesian selfish individuals should instead be encouraged, since it is greed and competition, guided by the invisible hand of nature, that create the wealth and power of a state. Spencer who early in life began to advocate for "free-markets" did allow that humans can have a moral side, but he basically followed Mandeville in arguing that competition and the exploitation of the poor (who he saw as inferior) and domination of "primitive" peoples by his own country would result in the best of all possible worlds.

American "liberal" (and classical Marxist) rhetoric has too often relied upon a faith shared by Social Darwinists that there is a natural law of inevitable "progress." Progress once meant by definition the expansion of populations and cities, the spreading suburbs, the use of more and more machines, lots of things to buy, and so on. Today it is clear that the utopian visions of the past were too simple, and that science and technology must be much more carefully thought and used than they were in the past if they are to serve humanitarian values.

Contemporary sociobiology has been promoted as a solid, scientifically certain way of knowing what human nature "really" is. But it has not learned the lessons of history and it is not free of ideological blemishes from its roots in 19th century Social Darwinism. Legitimate Darwinian theory cannot be used as jury or judge to determine the "true nature" of something as complex and multi-faceted as human thought and behavior.

Darwinian theory cannot tell us with certainty that a man cheats on his wife "in truth" to increase his inclusive fitness (rather than, for example, out of boredom or to bond with someone he likes). It cannot tell us with certainty that a man aspires to be business leader "in truth" so that his high status will allow him to impregnate large numbers of women (rather than, for example, simply for the thrill and challenge of the game).

Darwinian theory cannot even tell us what the composition or other properties are of the simple threads that hold clumps of mussels together. It may be roughly speaking true that, "Individual mussels produce binding threads because it has proved over time to be in their individual self-interest." But it is a pointless and incorrect leap of logic to then claim that the threads are "really" in their essence[28] "self interest"—and it is absurd to believe that one has gotten as close to the core of the ontological status of the threads as a scientist needs to in order to understand the species and its dynamics. Rather, empirical studies are called for. And similarly, one cannot armchair what normal human behavior "really is."

Human Nature

What is clear about human nature and our evolution is that like all other primates, we are a social species and enormous needs for love and companionship seem to be wired into us such that they even survive into adulthood. It is clear that we have the physiological equipment and reflex neuromuscular patterns to react with anger, aggression, and violence when we or our families are threatened, or from frustration— but this is not to say that we use that equipment simply because we have it. The fact of the equipment is not logically the same thing as its engagement. It appears to take external circumstances to trigger the full responses, beyond youthful experimentation with one's feelings and capacities.

It is also clear that our brains have a remarkable capacity and unavoidable propensity for selective attention and imagination. These can be enormous gifts when employed wisely, but they can also lead to misunderstandings and are at the core of many human conflicts that may superficially appear to be evidence for the innate nastiness that authors have long argued characterizes our species.[29] Humanists may take hope from this fact, for it may be easier to devise conditions to lessen social tragedies caused by dreams and misunderstandings than if they were caused by relentless drive states, by a hunger for conflict as intense as thirst and hunger drives.

It is observable that humans can also have difficult childhoods that can lead to frustrations in life, and that they may learn poor skills for understanding one's feelings and resolving conflicts. This can be one of the tragedies when family structures are shattered by economic difficulties or rapid cultural changes—and ecological devastation can also usher in both. It is observable that emotional problems hamper the application of reason to challenges, just as failing to learn skills for negotiating, communicating, and resolving problems can increase serious conflicts in one's life. These are things for which improvement is possible if a person has the motivation and support.

Humans certainly have, in addition, genuine conflicts of interest that can cause frustration and make one feel threatened and in turn fuel anger, resentment, and conflict. But even here reason may play a constructive role. For genuine conflicts of interest can often be negotiated rationally and accommodations devised. Or as in the case of ecologically induced conflicts, some of these may be avoided if hard political decisions are made now.

But further, one should ask what, when all is considered, is a genuine interest? One hears that kids in street gangs will kill each other the latest fashion in tennis shoes. Only because of the kid's value system do the brand-name shoes may seem to be a more vital interest than they actually need to be for getting around or playing ball.

How often are interests that may seem vital not really so important as one has been led to imagine because of a particular value system? A Buddhist might say that they never are and that life's strivings, frustrations, and sorrows are unnecessary for an enlightened person. I would not go that far, but I believe that reason will reveal that many of the things people stress, and ruin their moods, and fight over are not fundamentally as important to them as they might believe.

Reasoned observation and critical thinking can help us to understand what is really important in life to us as individuals and social beings, and carefully reasoned systems of values should help to reduce anxiety and conflict in our personal lives and in the world.

Notes

1. An interesting introduction and new handle or device for thinking about the complexity of human impacts on the earth is the metaphor of "ecological footprints." Mathis Wackernagel and William Rees. *Our Ecological Footprint: Reducing Human Impact on The Earth* (Gabriola Island, BC: New Society Publishers, 1996).

2. Haiti is a notorious example of a country where these three factors have interacted and reinforced each other vigorously, along with overpopulation.

3. William W Murdoch, *The Poverty of Nations: The Political Economy of Hunger and Population* (Baltimore: Johns Hopkins University Press, 1980).

4. See also P. J. Regal, *The Anatomy of Judgment* (Minneapolis: University of Minnesota Press, 1990)

5. Man and Superman. The Revolutionist's Handbook.

6. Regal, Ibid.

7. Michael T. Klare, "Resource competition and world politics in the twenty-first century," *Current History* 99:641 (Dec 2000), pp. 403-407; Peter H. Gleick, "Water and Conflict: Fresh Water Resources and International Security," *International Security* 18 no.1 (1993), pp. 79-112; Thomas F. Homer-Dixon, "On the Threshold: Environmental Changes of Acute Conflict," *International Security* 16 no. 2 (1991), pp. 76-116; Norman Myers, "Environment and Security," *Foreign Policy* 74 (1989), pp. 23-41; David A Wirth, "Climate Chaos," *Foreign Policy* 74 (1989), pp. 3-22. .

8. James S. Coleman, *Education and Political Development* (Princeton: Princeton University Press, 1965).

9. Ibid., p. 523.

10. Ibid., p. 527.

11. Ibid., p. 533.

12. Ibid., pp. 538-539.

13. Kerry Schott, Policy, Power and Order: The Persistence of Economic Problems in Capitalist States (Princeton: Princeton University Press, 1984), p. 189.

14. Stan Davis & Jim Botkin, *The Monster Under the Bed* (New York: Simon & Schuster, 1994).

15. Harold G. Kaufman, Professionals in Search of Work: Coping with the Stress of Job Loss and Underemployment (New York: John Wiley and Sons, 1982), p. 283.

16. Ibid., p. 309.

17. Russell W. Rumberger, *Overeducation in the U.S. Labor Market* (New York: Praeger, 1981), p. 123.

18. Ibid., p. 127.

19. Philip J. Regal, "Evolutionary principles of adaptation: Implications for multiculturalism," in Robert B. Tapp, ed., *Multiculturalism: Humanist Perspectives* (Amherst, NY: Prometheus Books, 2000), pp. 105-119.

20. Quotation from George Seldes, *The Great Quotations* (Secaucus, NJ: Castle Books, 1966), p. 225.

21. Regal, *op. cit.*, 1990.

22. Some possible readings are Robert L. Heilbroner, *Behind the Veil of Economics: Essays in The Worldly Philosophy* (New York: Norton, 1988); T. W. Hutchison, *Knowledge and Ignorance in Economics* (Chicago: University of Chicago Press, 1977); T. W. Hutchison, *The Politics and Philosophy of Economics* (New York: New York University Press, 1984); Kenneth Lux, *Adam Smith's Mistake* (Boston: Shambhala, 1990); Andrew Bard Schmookler. *The Illusion of Choice: How The Market Economy Shapes Our Destiny* (Albany: SUNY Press, 1993); Richard F. Teichgraeber III, *'Free Trade' and Moral Philosophy: Rethinking The Sources of Adam Smith's Wealth of Nations* (Durham: Duke University Press, 1986).

23. Penguin Books, NY. 1999. Also of interest with regard to other aspects of ideology in the development of technology agendas is Ronald C. To-

bey, *The American Ideology of National Science, 1919-1930* (Pittsburgh: University of Pittsburgh Press, 1971).

24. What, I wonder, would the machines think about with their pure reason? Would they have any interest in the great works of art, music, and literature with which their creators explored their own messy human emotions, follies, and creative potentials? Would they have compassion? What would justice, in the larger sense, be without compassion?

25. (New York: Avon Books, 1998).

26. The reader may find amusing a project where paintings were made according to scientific surveys of what people like in paintings. The resulting "scientifically produced" paintings are typically bizarre and pointless and raise interesting general issues about what collective tastes can produce. JoAnn Wypijewski, *Painting by Numbers: Komar and Melamid's Scientific Guide to Art* (Berkeley: University of California Press, 1999.

27. Some possible readings are Jonathan Glover, *What Sort of People Should There Be?* (New York: Pelican Books, 1984). And more recently, R. C. Lewontin, *Biology as Ideology: The Doctrine of DNA* (New York: HarperPerennial, 1991); Ruth Hubbard and Elijah Wald, *Exploding The Gene Myth: How Genetic Information is Produced and Manipulated by Scientists, Physicians, Employers, Insurance Companies, Educators, and Law Enforcers* (Boston: Beacon Press, 1999); Richard Heinberg, *Cloning The Buddha: The Moral Impact of Biotechnology* (Wheaton, IL: Quest Books, 1999). An essential book for historical perspective is Lily E. Kay, *The Molecular Vision of Life* (New York: Oxford University Press, 1993). Also of interest historically is Lily E. Kay, *Who Wrote the Book of Life? A History of The Genetic Code* (Stanford: Stanford University Press, 2000.

28. Indeed essentialism and typological thinking are holdovers from Platonic and Aristotelian philosophies and have no ontological reality in modern science.

29. Regal, 1990.

THE AUTOBIOGRAPHY OF AN ECOHUMANIST

Don Page

Credentials

Later in the 1950s, as a graduate student in England, I marched in demonstrations with the Campaign for Nuclear Disarmament, and was persuaded by Bertrand Russell who, addressing the throngs that filled Trafalgar Square, argued that nuclear weapons were too dangerous to be trusted in the hands of imperfect human beings and their always imperfect organizations. My belief in the validity of Russell's argument was soon to be reinforced during the Cuban missile crisis. It is noteworthy that Robert MacNamara, the 1960s US Defence Secretary, today campaigns for complete worldwide abolition of nuclear weapons, as do many retired senior military officers from the US and Britain who have previously borne responsibility for possibly having to use these weapons.

Professionally, I had the good luck in the middle and late 1950s to work at Britain's Imperial College of Science & Technology in one of the three or four top groups in the world who were exploring the engineering applications of the then-new transistors, and as a result of my own published studies was invited to write a chapter of the first standard engineering handbook on the use of semiconductor devices, published by McGraw Hill—a heady experience for a young engineer. On returning to Canada in 1959, I joined the

95

core design team (of three) for the first Canadian satellite, Alouette I, which when launched by NASA in 1962 was the most complex space equipment hitherto put into orbit and made Canada the third country in space. The data gathered by Alouette was used to develop an understanding of the earth's ionosphere, making possible the building of reliable communications satellite systems.

In designing Alouette we were virtually obsessed with the objective of achieving a high degree of reliability in the satellite's electronics, since we were using large numbers of the still-new transistors and other semiconductor devices, the long-term stability of which, especially in the space environment, was unknown. We resorted to design strategies that incorporated a high degree of redundancy, and that took as little as possible for granted. The resulting spacecraft proved to be the most reliable piece of space hardware then produced (winning a NASA award)—eventually having to be switched off from the ground. This experience proved that a high degree of reliability can be designed into systems that are technologically self-contained; at the same time, it became even more obvious to me that guarantees of such reliability are meaningless when, as is more often the case in earth-based engineering systems, human beings are involved in the system's operation.

Through the 1960s, my professional life in government continued to be full and rewarding as I was given increasing responsibilities for guiding the work of others, while contributing as a part-time lecturer and research supervisor in Carleton University's electrical engineering department. As part of my government job I became a special advisor to Canadian technical delegations at NATO and the UN. Privately, because of Russell's influence on my thinking, I became a member of Britain's Rationalist Press Association, and began to receive the British Humanist magazine. As a result of this exposure to Humanism, in 1967 I helped to form the

Humanist Association of Ottawa and joined the first executive of the Humanist Association of Canada.

By the 1970s I was at the peak of a successful engineering career in Ottawa at the Department of Communications, responsible for a large research and development program in the field of radar technology that included several dozen in-house scientists, engineers and technicians, and contracts with engineering companies and university engineering departments. My overall mandate was to provide advanced radar expertise to those Canadian government departments which were prepared to provide the necessary long-term funding support. Inevitably, most of my funding came from the Canadian military, but I was also involved significantly with the Department of the Environment in the field of remote sensing from aircraft and satellites. My responsibilities also included cooperative projects and information exchanges with NASA, and with military R&D establishments in the United States, Britain and Australia.

Disillusion and Resolution

While enjoying this professional success, in the 1970s I was conscious of clouds gathering on my philosophical horizon. Like so many others, I had been moved by Rachel Carson's book *Silent Spring*, and this experience, coupled with the oil crisis of 1973, precipitated a process of personal transformation. By this time I had also become a strong opponent of nuclear power generation, primarily for the reason that no method appeared possible for disposing of the highly dangerous waste products, other than stuffing them in the ground and hoping for the best. (It is of interest to note that after the Three Mile Island accident, my professional association, the Institute of Electrical and Electronic Engineers, used this nuclear waste problem to urge the US government to stop further construction of nuclear power plants.)

My other major reason for opposing nuclear power generation arose from the same distrust of human institutions that motivated my objection to nuclear weapons—that is, the impossibility of ensuring against human error. Whatever the protestations of infallibility of the safety precautions that are designed into engineering systems, including nuclear systems, it has since been amply demonstrated that such precautions are easily short-circuited by human error, laziness or stupidity, as happened at Three Mile Island, Chernobyl and recently in Japan. The Challenger tragedy is another recent example where human error was the cause of catastrophic failure in a complex engineering system.

The 1973 oil crisis exposed another major environmental problem to which most people, including politicians, still appear oblivious. We had not yet heard about global warming, but the dependence of our Western lifestyle on fossil fuels strongly suggested that we were collectively heading for an unsustainable global level of overconsumption. At the time I was becoming increasingly disturbed about a world that had become dependent on burning the great quantities of carbon that were stored in the young earth over hundreds of millions of years. We now know the consequences in terms of global warming; it is one thing to burn or decompose the carbon compounds that exist within the earth's current biosphere, a natural phenomenon that has been going on throughout the later eons of earth's history, but it is quite another to burn, in a few short decades or centuries, the vast amounts of carbon (in the form of coal, natural gas and petroleum) that were stored beneath the ground in those earlier eons when much vegetation did not decompose or burn, so producing the oxygen-rich atmosphere in which subsequent life evolved. In 1973, it was becoming clear to many like myself that our modern reliance on fossil fuels was not only an insane waste of an irreplaceable resource but also an assault on the earth's ecological systems.

The nuclear industry used the oil crisis of 1973 to lobby many jurisdictions, including Canadian provincial governments, to plan and build many more nuclear power generating plants, and to push sales of these reactors abroad.(Such a sale by Canada gave India the fissionable material used in its first atomic bomb test.)The industry argued that nuclear power generation was "cleaner" than the use of fossil fuels, and dismissed the waste disposal as a problem that surely will be solved in time. (The folly of such "faith"—the religion of scientism—is discussed later.) As a result, the moratorium on building further nuclear power reactors that was enacted in the United States after the Three Mile Island accident went unheeded elsewhere. The province of Ontario, for example, which boasts the largest power generating utility in North America, continued expanding its nuclear facilities by building the largest nuclear plant in North America at Darlington on Lake Ontario. More recently, however, some of the chickens have come home to roost as the true cost of these nuclear plants is being revealed—their core systems have begun to deteriorate prematurely, and Ontario is now having to refurbish, and in some cases decommission, its power reactors many years short of their design life. To maintain supply, older fossil fuel generators are being reactivated. Today the nuclear power critics have been vindicated, and no new nuclear power generating plants are currently planned in Canada. Meanwhile, the quantity of highly dangerous spent fuel from the existing systems continues to mount, and the disposal problem remains unsolved. It is entirely possible that this problem will be an unwanted legacy to our descendants for millennia to come.

If burning fossil fuels and nuclear fission are both ecologically unacceptable methods for generating electricity, the primary energy on which modern societies are based, what then is to be done? The traditional alternative, hydroelectric generation, seems to have been taken as far as it can be, at least in the developed world. (In Canada, for example, plans to further harness the energy in northern rivers have been successfully opposed in recent years by the First Nations people whose culture would be adversely affected by the destruction of wildlife habitat caused by the large dams required.) The rational response to this dilemma must surely be to significantly reduce global energy consumption until more benign and sustainable energy sources become widely available. (In this regard, those futurists who promote the "faith" that fusion—as opposed to fission—energy will be our salvation in the near future are, in my opinion, also indulging in the religion of scientism).

By 1974, I had become convinced that our Western urban lifestyle was unsustainable, and that there seemed little hope of early acknowledgment of this fact by the major political elites, left or right—the small Green movement notwithstanding. Feeling driven to act on this conviction, in 1975 I sold my city house and moved to an old farmhouse on 150 acres of grassland and bush within commuting distance of my Ottawa job. I put a herd of beef breeding cows on the grass, using a grazing, cropping and manuring rotation system to avoid reliance on the use of chemicals. Within three years I was selling organic beef to friends and neighbours, while my best yearling calves were winning ribbons at the annual regional livestock fair. As well, since then a large organic garden has provided much of the family's fruit and vegetable needs, with the help of two large freezers and traditional bottling and pickling methods.

In these northern latitudes the major household energy use is for heating, a fact to which I paid some attention. I looked long and hard at solar heating and also at harnessing energy from windpower—concluding that, except for special small-scale purposes such as water heating, these were not a practical source for the sustained energy demands of the Canadian climate. With a large supply of trees available in the countryside, however, it was natural to install a wood-burning furnace of the newer, more efficient variety. In addition, and since we did not have the time or inclination to be tied entirely to wood heating, I replaced the existing oil-fired furnace with a ground-source heat pump to supply the main heating and air conditioning requirements—a move that halved our total energy consumption for the household. It should be noted that the decision to use wood for supplemental heating is not in conflict with the previously-discussed concern about burning fossil fuels (coal, gas and oil). At the current stage of earth's history, all living vegetation eventually decomposes or burns, in both cases producing greenhouse gases, but in quantities with which the ecosystem had reached a stable balance long before *Homo sapiens* came on the scene—a balance that is now being assaulted by our burning of the vast quantities of carbon stored in the earth's crust during the early stages of the planet's biological history.

Discussion

The change in lifestyle just described provided some relief from the sense of being a willing participant in our collective assault on the environment. It appears, however, that many (probably most) people are not concerned with these issues and, in any case, my particular solution is not available to large numbers. The larger solution must lie in large-scale energy conservation, applied across the whole of modern society. But with so little serious recognition of this, it appears that it may require a sustained catastrophic crisis—for example widespread flooding due to global warming (or, due to another current assault on the environment, a disastrous further thinning of the ozone layer)—to bring people and politicians to their senses, by which time it could prove to be too late. The problem is made even more urgent as living standards rise in the developing world—it is clear that the current high energy-consuming lifestyle of Western society cannot be extended to the rest of the world's people without making even more grave the consequences for the global environment.

Five years after moving to the country I terminated my professional engineering career by taking early retirement. The decision astonished many friends and colleagues as there was no apparent reason for leaving a successful and well-paid job. In reality, however, the decision followed naturally from my new lifestyle—notwithstanding my success in the world of high technology, I found the new low technology world more rewarding philosophically. It was good to leave behind the endless battles for funds to be used for the development of technological systems that are allocated a higher socio-political priority than the social programs needed to improve the lot of people. Moreover, although the engineering systems in which I was involved were not in themselves environmentally unfriendly, they were an integral part of a larger society that, I felt, is becoming increasingly unsustainable.

In the years since, other technologies have developed to the point of presenting further danger to human welfare. Perhaps the most frightening of these developments are in the field of biotechnology and genetic engineering. Like their nuclear predecessors, these technologies are promoted mainly by industrial corporations that, while claiming to be motivated by the need to solve human problems (e.g. feeding the world's hungry), make quiet deals with politicians to obtain trade and regulatory arrangements to circumvent the warnings of their many objective critics.

The Challenge of Scientism

One must surely wonder how it is that the great majority of people appear unconcerned about the degradation of the global ecosystem, signs of which are all around them, and in spite of the fact that there is no shortage of media attention to these signs. Indeed, it is this apparent lack of public concern that makes politicians vulnerable to the pressures from the corporate vested interests. As this is being written it is election season in both the United States and

Canada, and although the major political candidates pay lip service to the environment, it is evident that they know their priorities must lie elsewhere if they are to be elected. It would seem we are dealing here with a public denial process on a massive scale which, I submit, is due to the kind of thinking that arises from conventional religious faith.

There seems little point in trying to deal with the simplistic, fatalistic beliefs of the fundamentalist religious folk who assume that whatever happens is governed by God's plan as revealed in holy scriptures. Most people, however, are more liberal in their religious thinking, and have some sense of responsibility for the fate of the planet. This is the majority that will probably determine the future course of events. It is to be hoped that this majority can be aroused to the dangers facing them and their children. But there is, clearly, a widespread defence mechanism that needs to be overcome—an irrational assumption, that "science" will make things right in the long run. This assumption is, in reality, the religious faith of "scientism". The scientific and technological community—particularly within those parts that have been bought and paid for by corporate vested interests—has been complicit in implanting this religion in the public psyche. Effectively countering this widespread scientism is, I submit, the single most pressing humanist issue of our time.

Until now, our species has thrived on this planet because of its ability to adapt, technologically and sociologically. It now appears that the fecundity of humankind could prove to be its Achilles heel, with large populations creating environmental conditions to which we are unable to adapt quickly enough to avoid a new dark age of pestilence and violent competition for resources—or worse.

THE EXPONENTIAL SOCIETY

Michael J. Kami

Human beings walked on this earth for 100,000 years at a speed of 3 mph. They then rode a horse at 10 mph for some 3,500 years. The locomotive first chugged away in 1829, only 167 years ago, at the world-record speed of 30 mph. The 100 mph barrier was overcome by the year 1900. In 1933, a plane flew at 300 mph. Twenty-seven years later it reached 3,000 mph. Then, only 3 years later, the first manned space capsule exceeded 18,500 mph. This progression—compression of time and explosion of performance—represents the exponential curve of technological progress created by human beings.

The same curve and formula applies to our ability for destruction. For 50,000 years we used the bow and arrow, hurting one person at a time. Twenty-five hundred years ago, a catapult hurled heavy rocks, with damage to small groups of people. Some 400 years later the Chinese invented the gunpowder. It took another 500 years for it to be introduced in Europe. It was the year 1300. Powerful dynamite was invented in 1866 and the exponential curve took off vertically! By 1918, we could explode a single bomb with the equivalent power of 10 tons of TNT. In 1945, an A-bomb had the equivalent of 20,000 tons of TNT. In 1954, an H-bomb carried the power of 8 million tons of TNT. This increased to 60 million tons by 1961. Today, several nations have the potential for total, instantaneous destruction of our entire planet. That's another proof of the exponential curve of technological progress. Technology is blind and amoral. It depends on people for decisions for good or evil. We can use nuclear power to desalinize ocean waters and create oases of plenty in the midst of deserts. The same nuclear power can destroy civilizations and leave uninhabitable scorched earth for thousands of years ahead. Advances in medicine and chemistry can cure people and prolong life. They also can kill entire populations with lethal nerve gas and biological warfare.

Similar exponential curve of breakthroughs in the field of computers has changed the way we live, act and interrelate. For 4,000 years we made additions with an abacus at 2 seconds per calculation. In 1642, Pascal doubled this speed with his mechanical adding machine. It took 400 more years, to be able to calculate at 5,000 items per second. Then technology took off again. In 1955, computers whizzed at a million calculations per second. The billion mark (nanosecond) was reached in 1965, the trillion (picosecond) in 1985. Today, in year 2,000, Einstein's once theoretical limitation of speed of light will become a practical reality in the design of new electronic chips. Our world is in practical, not theoretical, transition from the Newtonian concept of certainty to the quantum theory concept of uncertainty and probability.

It is necessary to visualize the extraordinary changes, affecting our daily life and behavior in the field of communications. From millennia of tribal drums, to centuries of hand semaphores, to Morse's telegraph, to Bell's telephone, to radio, TV and global satellites and fiber optics networks. Soon optical cables spanning the earth will carry 100 million words per second and 250,000 simultaneous phone conversations in each of the lines, thinner than a single human hair! Similar breakthroughs occur in the field of medicine and genetic drugs, surgery and animal cloning. Chemistry yields new compounds in plastics and synthetic man-made materials. Nanotechnology produces working motors the size of an atom.

Hubbel telescope explores new vistas of deep universe and changes our perception of laws of the universe. Robots, ATM machines, plastic cards, PCs and computerized sensors change the way we think, perceive, live, act, and behave in this new society and new environment,

Progress in knowledge, technology, and global communications contracted our planet earth to a virtual, easily accessible *village*. Within that village, however, we have 6 billion people, living in 308 separate countries, speaking 4,823 different languages in 24 different time zones. They live in different climates, different cultures, and extreme conditions—from freedom to slavery, from great riches to abhorrent poverty, from happiness and hope to terror and despair. That's some village!

Why is it that the immense, exponential progress in technology and human knowledge did not bring better, saner, happier life to billions of people on this earth? Why is it that we still hate, we still persecute, we still kill our human brothers and sisters? Why is it that thinking men and women haven't really changed their basic instincts, their behavior and their deep, inner, secret, private thoughts in ten thousand or more years of progress and education. Why didn't the biped mammal, the *Homo sapiens,* the human species, manage any improvement in its still primeval, savage behavior?

Science gives us an answer. Microbiologists, specializing in cloning plants and animals, call it the *genetic imperative*. Human evolution, human behavior, like those of any other living organisms, depend completely and solely on their genes, their unique DNA pattern. These genes do change and adapt to new conditions. But it takes time. It takes an immense number of successive generations. Major changes and improvements may take hundreds of thousands of years, often millions of years. Patient nature has a lot of time. We don't.

Human genes follow the same basic imperative of any organism. It's absolutely identical, from the simplest cells, to bacteria, to plants, to animals, to intelligent beings. The imperative is *survival* and *procreation*. The genes for every cell are programmed to continuously seek and absorb nourishment, to resist any attack, to recreate themselves and to multiply. It's a built-in mechanism for survival at any cost. The basic genetic nature of a human being is exactly the same. Our inherited, internal DNA program continuously instructs every one of us: be absolutely selfish, take care of yourself, stash resources for survival, kill anything and anyone who even remotely threatens your natural activities. Resist change at all costs!

As human beings couldn't and didn't change *genetically* over the past ten thousand short years, a growing gap was created between two competing forces: the exponential progress of technology, product of the wonderful, immense and fast growing human brain cells, the intellect, and the basic, unchanged, genetic character of living creatures: their built-in natural mechanism for selfish survival. This is not a theoretical premise. This is not a blue-sky, unproved hypothesis. These are accepted, verified, valid scientific facts. Can we do anything about it? Yes, we can. We must!

Genetically, all of us are naturally driven to selfish pursuit of self-preservation. Why is dieting so difficult? Because billions of cells in our body continuously yell at us: feed me, feed me, feed me! Dieting is unnatural. But some of us do diet successfully. Why don't we share more of our own resources with others who may desperately need help? Because billions of cells in our body continuously yell: hoard, hoard, hoard. Giving and sharing is unnatural. But some of us give and share their possessions with others, often total strangers. Why do we hate, fight, destroy, kill whatever and whoever stands in our way? Because billions of cells in our body continuously yell: protect yourself, protect yourself, protect yourself. But some of us act unselfishly and altruistically and even sacrifice our own lives to save others.

Because the brain development of men and women progressed beyond instinct and automatic reflex to rational and emotional thought processes and self-analysis, we can, or at least should try, to *transcend our genetic imperative!* Such a task should become the primary objective of any thinking human being, in his or her effort to bridge the growing gap between the flat, unchanging genetic plateau and the exponential explosion of technology dramatically changing conditions on this earth.

What does such effort entail? What are the steps to move towards a better self and a better humanity? It's a personal and individual effort. It's not a group effort, because every person must transcend their own, unique and very strong genetic forces. Groups may help, they may provide a positive environment and nurturing support, but the true transformation rests entirely inside the body and the mind of each individual.

First step. It takes knowledge. Most of the *nice*, average people, are pathetically ignorant! During the past 10 years, the amount of information available to an average person, not a scientist or a genius, just a normal, average person, increased by a factor of 10,000! Are we really 10,000 times more knowledgeable than 10 years ago? How about 1,000 times? Perhaps only 100 times? Let's settle on a conservative factor of ten! How many of us can truthfully admit to ourselves that we are 10 times more knowledgeable today than a decade ago? To bridge the universal gap of genes to knowledge, individuals must increase their own knowledge. It takes a lot of work and a strict discipline. It means reading three newspapers a day. A local, a national, and an international paper, such as *The Times of London, Le Monde* or *Neue Zürcher Zeitung*. It means knowing how to find and access the many diverse and immense data bases available on the Internet. You can access for free 2,500 world newspapers if you type *mediainfo.com*. It means reading articles on many different subjects in at least 20 to 40 different magazines, on science, society, business, government, national and international issues, environment, education, demographics, psychographics, etc. etc. etc. It also means reading at least one latest major and serious non-fiction book a month. It means expanding our field of knowledge to other areas, so that we can become a multidisciplinary, multi-faceted, globally knowledgeable, up-to-date person. Age doesn't matter, position doesn't matter, geography doesn't matter. What matters is that the world desperately needs more and better *knowledgeable* people.

Second step. It takes focus and concentration. One must be selective. Which of the many gaps between the material progress and your personality bothers or affects you the most? Which gap do you want to bridge and why? Define it precisely in your mind. Be passionate about it! Is it personal or societal or in your business? Is it political, economic, social, or psychological? Is it local or national or international? Define it more and more precisely. Make a detailed and, if necessary, a long list. Only then, proceed to the next step.

Third step. It takes priorities to decide what to tackle first, even after you decided on a narrow category of endeavor. Priorities must be very clear and very specific. Priority one, two, three, four. Don't jump to much lower priority items or you'll stretch yourself so thin that nothing will be accomplished. Tackle only items of critical importance. Do it with a *critical mass* of effort, to really make a difference.

Fourth step. Important projects and actions take time. Allocate enough personal, professional, and business time to do what may be the most important task in your life. That means cutting out other endeavors, even pleasures, social activities, leisure. Time is the most precious commodity we have. Time is irreversible. We must control it strictly, allocate it wisely, and use it with a great deal of thought and care.

What are the key characteristics of a person who decides to change their genetic predisposition and to embark on the road to reduce the human gap of imperfection?

I propose to you the fourteen *"Cs."* These are the fourteen necessary traits of modern individual leadership, required to make you a person able to reach beyond your genetic imperative and to inspire others to follow your example.

1. Competence: be knowledgeable beyond expectations, stay continuously current.

2. Conviction: believe implicitly and without reservations in what you think, in what you say and in what you do.

3. Character: set an example of integrity and fairness.

4. Care: show genuine concern for people at all levels of life. Do it equally, impartially, without exceptions or reservations.

5. Courage: say and do what you think is right, not what is popular. Say and show openly what you really are, what you are doing and what you want to accomplish.

6. Composure: demonstrate emotional stability, remain cool, calm and collected under any circumstances. Keep your head, when all about you are losing theirs, as in Kipling's poem.

7. Clarity & Certainty: be precise, be solid, be unequivocal. Don't hedge, don't compromise your convictions. Stand firm and clear.

8. Creativity: be an example to others in your creative, advanced thought processes and ideas. Promote and pioneer innovative thinking and actions.

9. Communications: communicate, communicate, communicate. Continuously, constantly, comprehensibly. Good and precise communications are the bridges of progress and success

10. Change: be a pioneer, be a change agent. *Walk the talk*, be real, be with it, be genuine. Just do it!

11. Confidence: inspire confidence in those who are frightened, who hesitate, who are slow and timid. Be strong.

12. Culture: understand the changing cultures, changing times, changing aims and aspirations throughout the world. Establish your own new culture: embrace the best of the new and reject the worst of the old.

13. Continuity: make a plan for smooth, logical, flowing continuity of your actions and an orderly transition from old to new endeavors.

14. Cheer: show a good sense of humor. Take your objectives and endeavors very seriously, and yourself very lightly.

You may say that this is a pretty tall order. Yes, these are very difficult objectives and difficult tasks, in addition to all the normal and good things you're already doing in and with your life. Nobody can ever promise you that *transcending the genetic imperative* is going to be easy. It's probably the most difficult of any personal endeavors a human being can attempt. But it's necessary, it's important, it's urgent, it's essential, it's crucial. I believe, it's vital.

Every human being has extraordinary hidden potential Find it, deep inside of yourself, open it and use it! Use it for common good and inspire others with passion and perseverance! You'll then be able to proudly say: "I did make a difference!" and you did!

EMPTY BOWLS[1]

Kendyl L. Gibbons

Item 19 of the United Nations Millennium Summit Resolution states the intention of the leaders of all countries to reduce by half, by the year 2015, the proportion of the world's people who suffer from hunger. It is a goal that is at once historically breath-taking, and yet, in the context of today's knowledge, modestly feasible. Many of us grew up with the admonition to eat the food set before us, because remember, there are children starving—in Armenia, or China, or Africa, or whichever distant, afflicted place our parents chose to name. Some of us grew up hungry ourselves, or close enough to the edge to have a sense of its reality. And we cannot help being affected by the images of starvation, hollow-eyed mothers and emaciated children, that are beamed into our comfortable homes by satellite, or in the pages of glossy news magazines.

Hunger is a challenge older than human existence, for it is the common struggle of all animal species to find enough to eat in order to stay healthy and to rear the next generation. In unfavorable climates or ecological situations, any species can experience starvation, and for most of human history, homo sapiens has been no exception. Hunger, like war, disease, and mortality itself, was long seen as an inevitable product of both natural and social calamities; to not be hungry was good fortune, and cause for gratitude—and most likely, temporary.

We who are alive at this turning of the millennium are in a historically unique position; not only do we have the technology and the cooperation to know the state of food distribution and hunger with remarkable precision throughout the globe, but we also have the potential essentially to eliminate famine and starvation from present and future human experience. The U.N. national leaders summit resolution merely states a timetable and a target of measurable progress for a process that is already underway; the questions have to do with how long it will take, and what will be the costs in human suffering before we reach that once unimaginable goal, a world in which everyone is fed. There are many road blocks, both literal and figurative, that could slow the process down, and perhaps most of us are not in a position to carry agricultural expertise to areas where food sufficiency is an urgent hope rather than an accomplished reality. Yet we can contribute our awareness and our understanding; we can support the work that moves toward food sufficiency—not all of which is intuitive—and we can pay attention to what our own habits of consumption tell about the ways in which we honor both human need and food.

The Humanist tradition is known for its emphasis upon science, reason, and empirical evidence. Nowhere is this insistence more imperative than in dealing with such crucially tangible issues as world hunger. In an article entitled "Billions Served," which appeared in the April 2000 edition of the journal *Reason*, Ronald Bailey observes that:

> In the late 1960s, most experts were speaking of imminent global famines in which billions would perish. "The battle to feed all of humanity is over," biologist Paul Ehrlich famously wrote in his 1968 bestseller *The Population Bomb*. "In the 1970s and 1980s hundreds of millions of people will starve to death in spite of any crash programs embarked upon now." Ehrlich also said, "I have yet to meet anyone familiar with the situation who thinks India will be self-sufficient in food by 1971." He insisted that "India couldn't possibly feed two hundred million more people by 1980."

Yet the facts are these:

In Pakistan, wheat yields rose from 4.6 million tons in 1965 to 8.4 million tons in 1970. In India in the same period, they rose from 12.3 million tons to 20 million. And the yields continue to increase. Last year, India harvested a record 73.5 million tons of wheat, up 11.5 percent from 1998. Since Ehrlich's dire predictions in 1968, India's population has more than doubled, its wheat production has more than tripled, and its economy has grown nine-fold. Contrary to Ehrlich's bold pronouncements, hundreds of millions didn't die in massive famines. India fed far more that 200 million more people, and it was close enough to self-sufficiency in food production by 1971 that Ehrlich discreetly omitted his prediction about that from later editions of *The Population Bomb*. The last four decades have seen a "progress explosion" that has handily outmatched any "population explosion."

Despite occasional local famines caused by armed conflicts or political mischief, food is more abundant and cheaper today than ever before in history.

For the sake of our fellow human beings, whose suffering we may have the power to alleviate, we must be prepared to put both our preconceptions and our moral indignation on hold, so that we may examine with intelligent appraisal the actual historical record of what has best served to bring adequate food within the reach of the whole planet. Where old prophecy has proven wrong, we should seek new insights; where the data cast doubt upon prior calculations, we should welcome the data, and rethink our assumptions. For this purpose, it may be helpful to identify some categories for our thinking.

I used to contemplate hunger as a monolithic problem—people were either starving or fed—but I have learned that this is not exactly so. There are several levels to hunger. There is the question of absolute calories needed to sustain life; the sheer amount of any kind of food. But beyond that is the question of adequate nutrition; barely sufficient calories may not contain the various nutrients required for the complex functioning of the human body, and people can die of malnutrition even when they have, theoretically, enough calories. Beyond that is the issue of comfort; one can receive what technically constitutes adequate calories to sustain life, and enough nutrients that there are no active deficiencies, and still go to bed crying with hunger, and still be unable to concentrate on school or work or hopes of a better life. Finally there is the experience of abundance; of food not just as a means of surviving from one day to the next and silencing hunger, but as a source of enjoyment and pleasure, of cultural connection, of choice, novelty, celebration, and sharing with others. We, of course, are so accustomed to the abundance of American culture that we sometimes do not appreciate how many steps removed we are from the experience of want. When I lived in Naperville, we had a sister city in the Ukraine, and it happened more than a few times that visitors from there would be taken to one of our local grocery stores, where they burst into tears. These people were not starving or malnourished in any clinical sense, but they lived without the abundance that we take for granted. The challenge before us is not necessarily to supply an American diet to everyone in the world; in fact, the American diet leaves a lot to be desired in terms of health. But I believe it is not enough just to ensure adequate calories and nutrition. Everyone is not fed until everyone partakes, at least most of the time, in a sense of modest abundance; that food is one of the creative joys of human living; a sensual pleasure and a social bond.

On October 30, a few weeks following the Millennium Summit, the United Nations Economic and Social Council met to discuss the implementation of the resolution on eliminating hunger. Presentations were made by the leaders of the Food and Agriculture Organization, the International Fund for Agricultural Development, and the World Food Programme. Their observations contained striking examples both of progress made in this endeavor, and of challenges yet to be overcome. A few numbers stay with me. Five percent of the world's population eat almost 45 percent of all meat and fish. Eight hundred million people go hungry every day, including one out of three in sub-Saharan Africa, the hungriest area of the world. Losses in productivity from hunger and related health problems make hunger itself an economic handicap for communities and nations, though estimates of what it might cost to end hunger worldwide range from $2.6 to $6 billion more than present levels of assistance. Compared to some national and international budgets, this is not an impossible amount. Both the presenters and the representatives from member nations who responded stressed that what hungry people constantly ask for is not for food to be provided to them, but for the opportunity to grow food to feed themselves and their families. Essential to understanding and ending hunger is recognizing the central role of women. Women are responsible for finding food and water for their families, and they grow most of the food in the world, but they eat the least of it. Undernourished women give birth to low-birth-weight babies, and offer less nutrition when breast feeding, resulting in children susceptible to disease, less strong and less equipped to learn. When women are educated, when they can plan the number and timing of their children, and when they have economic options, such as either paid employment or land ownership and entrepreneurial opportunities, food sufficiency increases.

The world of our generation confronts the opportunity to end world hunger because of the convergence of three factors in the development of agriculture as a human enterprise. The first factor is our ability to leverage our labor, both with knowledge and with mechanical assistance. People around the world gathered much important information about effective farming practices that were preserved in folk wisdom and traditions, but today we know much more that trial and error could never teach. From effective methods of fertilization and controlling for weeds and insects, to crop rotation and breeding for high-production grains suitable to a particular area, knowledge enables farmers to reap greater benefits from their work. In the same way, engines and equipment designed for agricultural tasks serve to make the labor less back-breaking and mind-numbing, and to increase productivity, especially for women. What is often referred to as the "green revolution" of the 1960s and '70s began with the development of a strain of dwarf wheat that because it did not bend over like its taller cousins, was easier to cultivate and harvest, and was less subject to disease and being consumed by pests.

The second developmental factor has been the advance in our ability to store and transport food from areas of surplus to areas of want, and to preserve it over time. As lately as 1995, it was estimated that at least one-fourth of the Third World's annual farm production was lost to birds, rodents, insects and spoilage. The capacity to store and process harvests cuts such losses, and enables seasonal surpluses to be spread into dependable supplies. Infrastructure for transportation, such as roads and railroads, enables farmers to market their harvests more readily, allowing the food to reach those who need it, and the farmers to realize better prices for their crops.

The third factor that has brought us to the possibility of eliminating human hunger is, perhaps ironically, the interdependence of the global market. Especially for women, the opportunity to own land, to own dairy, meat and fiber producing animals, and to engage in cooperative ventures for their communities, has significantly changed the quality of their lives, and the food available to them and to their families. This is the understanding behind the work of the Heifer Project, which the sale of our empty bowls today will help to support. Besides the provision of an ecologically appropriate animal to one family, two other principles guide the project's operation. One is that individuals, again often women, must be trained in how to care for the animal or animals adequately.

Whether it is bees or chickens, goats or rabbits, the effort will only succeed if people have the necessary understanding of that creature's needs and habits. This means that participation requires at least minimal literacy, the achievement of which is a benefit in itself. Only when they are satisfied that participants know how to keep the animal properly will Heifer Project send them one. The second principle is that the first gift is only the beginning. When the animals reproduce, the participants are expected to pass along one or more of the offspring to others in the community, so that the project spreads, and becomes self-sustaining. By owning these animals and being able to market their produce, in the form of wool or honey or eggs or milk or meat, the families gain not only an economic foothold, but also the hope, self-confidence, and vision for the future that goes with success.

Given that we have the knowledge and the machines, the ability to store and transport food, and the stimulus of a global market, what is it that is still in the way of all the earth's people being fed? There are several major impasses. By far the greatest is entirely a human creation, and that is war. Whether it is military conflict between nations, or revolutionary or ethnic violence within a given country, war produces famine, malnutrition and starvation with dependable consistency. Especially when, as often happens, war displaces whole groups of people from their homes, it destroys whatever food sufficiency they might have achieved. The hungriest and most vulnerable people in the world are refugees.

A second issue, of course, is oppression, especially of women. In places where they have little opportunity for education or self-determination, women cannot help to break the chain of constant child-bearing, malnutrition, infant mortality, and food insufficiency. Where children receive adequate nutrition and can be expected to live to adulthood, and where reasonably reliable birth control methods are available, women almost always choose to limit the number of their children, so as to be able to provide better for those they have. This places less stress upon the capacity for food production, and makes food sufficiency easier to attain. For both genders, the more economic and political power people have, the more creative and forward-looking their hopes and plans. Participants at the UN Economic and Social Council discussion also emphasized the importance of microcredit programs in empowering small farmers and women in poor communities to make their own decisions about what crops, technologies and projects would best meet the needs of their families. Simple, sustainable and often relatively inexpensive changes in technology have led to considerable increases in farm production, and thus to both incomes and access to food. The opposite of this process of empowerment is a whole set of perverse economic incentives which destroy food sufficiency, including government corruption, astronomical international debt, the misappropriation of land, central planning attempts, the imposition of inappropriate technology, and the power of western consumption preferences such as for beef. It is when ownership, knowledge and decision-making are all in the hands of ordinary people who have the most to lose and the most to gain, that sustainable decisions and long-term progress are made.

At the same time, one of the obstacles to eliminating hunger remains despair. If we believe that it cannot be done; if we accept the verdict of history that periodic starvation always has been and always will be part of human experience, then we can hardly help but retreat behind the bulwark of our own prosperity and try to shut our eyes to the suffering of our brothers and sisters and their children. If we will not look, we cannot see; and if we do not see, we cannot act; and if we do not act, the world will continue turning, and I even believe that progress will come—but it will come slowly and painfully, and it will come without us, and our very humanity will starve within us, surrounded by our abundance. But if instead we will open our eyes and look, we shall see both the suffering and the hope; if we see, we will not be able to resist the one thing that we *can* do, whatever that one thing is; and when we act, not only will the change come, quicker and cleaner and more joyfully because it is shared, but our own humanity and our common humanity will be nourished, and the human community of which we are all a part will grow strong.

Once upon a time, in a day when starvation was a stark possibility anywhere and everywhere, a teacher said, "Blessed are those who hunger and thirst after righteousness, for they shall be filled." May those of us who seldom hunger for food, be such people as hunger and thirst after righteousness; and may we know in the profoundest depths of our being that so long as any child, any man or woman upon this globe still hungers for bread, that our hunger is not yet assuaged. In this season of generosity and joy, when we celebrate light in the darkness, and the human capacity for indomitable hope, let us carry in our hearts this new hope of the world that before long—indeed, very soon—we may rejoice in the knowledge that humanity's long hunger is over, and all—*all*—of our brothers and sisters are fed.

More than a century ago, at the cruel height of this nation's war between the states, the Unitarian poet Henry Wadsworth Longfellow wondered how it could be possible to celebrate Christmas in the awareness of the carnage that was taking place on the southern battlefields. He wrote of the Christmas bells, and the message of hope for a better future that he heard from them as he, too, hungered and thirsted for righteousness.

> I heard the bells on Christmas day
> Their old familiar carols play,
> And wild and sweet the words repeat
> Of peace on earth, good will to men.

I thought how, as the day had come,
The belfries of all Christendom
Had rolled along the unbroken song
Of peace on earth, good will to men.

And in despair I bowed my head
'There is no peace on earth,' I said,
'For hate is strong and mocks the song
Of peace on earth, good will to men.'

Then pealed the bells more loud and deep:
'God is not dead, nor doth He sleep;
The wrong shall fail, the right prevail
With peace on earth, good will to men.'

Till ringing, singing on its way
The world revolved from night to day,
A voice, a chime, a chant sublime
Of peace on earth, good will to men.

Then from each black, accursed mouth
The cannon thundered in the South,
And with the sound the carols drowned
Of peace on earth, good will to men.

It was as if an earthquake rent
The hearth-stones of a continent,
And made forlorn, the households born
Of peace on earth, good will to men.[2]

Notes

1.   This was a Christmas-season address at the First Unitarian Society of Minneapolis, 2000.

2.   Longfellow had just learned of the death of his son, a soldier in the Union army. Almost as poignant is the fact that the poem has been transformed into a Christmas carol, and most church hymnals omit the final three verses.

TIME IS NOT ON OUR SIDE

David Schafer

Prologue: The Humanist Landscape

In this essay I want to look at the way we humanists view the relation of humans to our surroundings—other animals and plants on Earth, Earth itself, and ultimately, the Cosmos. The Grand Humanist Narrative properly begins with the origin of the Cosmos, roughly 15 billion years ago, give or take a couple of billion. Our Solar System came into being much later, some 4.6 billion years ago—let's say 5 billion for simplicity. Our Sun is an unremarkable Type G2 star of the so-called "Main Sequence"; its present mass is 2 billion billion billion tons (that's 2 followed by 27 zeroes), but it is losing about five million tons of this mass every second, converting it into 400 trillion trillion (4 followed by 26 zeroes) watt-seconds (joules) of energy.[1]

This energy warms the Earth just enough to have created a critical range of temperatures at its surface that, a billion years or less after Earth was formed, permitted a highly ordered state of matter to appear ("life"), made from certain reactive compounds of carbon, oxygen, hydrogen, and a few other elements. While virtually every other place in the Cosmos is terrifyingly hostile to life, the amazing "fitness of the environment" on Earth allowed not only single-celled organisms but increasingly complex multicellular forms of plants and animals to evolve rapidly in the oceans over the next three billion years, until vertebrates began to appear, about 500 million years ago (mya), and later began to leave the ocean and walk on land. By 40-50 mya, early primates showed up; the earliest erect hominids had diverged from the apes by 7 mya; *Homo sapiens* was present 500,000 years ago (ya); and around 10,000 ya agriculture began. All this on Earth in under 5 billion years![2]

Astronomers calculate that in another 5 billion years, when our Sun has had a total lifetime of 10 billion years it will exhaust the hydrogen fuel at its core and will leave the Main Sequence to become a much hotter "red giant." It's halfway there! Worse yet, only about half of this time, or 2,500 billion years, remain until this depletion of the core hydrogen begins and the Sun will start to burn a higher proportion of helium, at a gradually increasing temperature. When this happens, Earth's temperature will rise slowly but steadily, until life on Earth will no longer resemble the life we have known, and temperatures will gradually become incompatible with human existence, and ultimately with life itself.

If we optimistically imagine that by the time this catastrophe occurs, our remote offspring will have learned to "slip the surly bonds of Earth" (and those of the sun as well) to survive indefinitely in space, they may achieve a reprieve of sorts, but ultimately even this may end, depending on an uncertain scenario. The two best-known alternatives offer no hope whatever of human survival. If we accept the concept, based on the second law of thermodynamics, of the freezing death by cold and uniform temperature of the ever-expanding universe, it will no longer be possible for life to exist, to reduce the local entropy of a "living" organism at the expense of its environment. Or, if the cosmos ends in a Big Crunch through gravitational attraction, inconceivably high temperatures not seen since the Big Bang will annihilate all that's made, perhaps to introduce a new universal cycle beginning with a new Big Bang. So, if either of these theories is correct, "time, that takes survey of all the world,/Must have a stop," and the day must come when all good things—including life—will come to an end.[3]

There is, however, a third projection of how the world might end, one that is much less well known, and considerably more optimistic. Theoretical physicist Freeman Dyson, one of the four founders of quantum electrodynamics, published in 1979 an article in *Reviews of Modern Physics* entitled "Time Without End: Physics and Biology in an Open Universe," in which he advanced an argument in a series of 137 equations that in a cosmos "infinite in all directions," in spite of (or because of?) thermodynamics, "life and intelligence are potentially immortal, with resources of knowledge and memory constantly growing as the temperature of the universe decreases and the reserves of free energy dwindle." This thesis, which formed the basis of his 1985 Gifford Lectures and won him the Templeton Prize for the year 2000, may not be universally accepted, but so far as I know it is the only scientific justification of any hope at all for the ultimate survival of humanity.

Yet even Dyson does not provide us with any guarantee—far from it. This is the best possible case—the rosiest possible scenario for an infinitely long series of precarious situations in any one of which we might collectively slip and fall into the abyss of eternity. So, for the Humanist, time is not on our side, and unless we are permanently lucky, sooner or later the likelihood is that we, and all life with us, will yield up forever the joys of existence in favor of total extinction.

But why should we rush it?

Humanism and "Ecohumanism"

For humanists, a prominent feature of the United States presidential election campaign of the year 2000 that somehow managed to escape the attention of most mainstream commentators was the near absence from the campaign dialogue of two words, "environment" and "humanism," and their congeners. Of course, nobody seriously expected a discussion of humanism, but the fact that the whole topic of the changing human environment also remained largely below the national radar seemed especially noteworthy, considering that one of the two major presidential candidates had, as a U.S. senator, authored the 1992 book *Earth in the Balance*, an impassioned if somewhat New Age-Christian plea for all of us to pay closer attention to the future of our planet, in the interest of the survival of humanity.[4]

Being immersed during the campaign in research for this essay on " ecohumanism," I was particularly struck by what looked like a silent conspiracy between the two major political parties, both reluctant to open a public debate about environmental issues admittedly controversial, yet at the same time vital and timely for a democratic electorate whose future and whose children's future could well be adversely affected by governmental policy miscalculations in what might be the disturbingly near future.

Humanism, on the other hand, has never been shy about raising these issues. I am referring here to that nontheistic humanism which, far from being preoccupied with the mere advancement of naked atheism, sees it as its primary mission to heal and unite humanity. As far back as Humanist Manifesto I (1933), for instance, the goal of humanism was described as "a free and universal society in which people voluntarily and intelligently co-operate for the common good."[5]

From this perspective, then, what do I understand by the novel expression " ecohumanism"? Quite simply, if we realize that what is ultimately at stake in the maintenance of the human environment is *the near-term survival, not just of every object we hold dear, but of humanity itself—possibly even life itself*—then "the environment" becomes for humanism the most urgent concern of all; ecology, the scientific study of the environment, finds its place among our most urgent priorities; and environmentalism, our recognition and expression of the human environment's importance to us, ranks among our most cherished values. Thus our neologism refers not to a particular *kind* of humanism, but a particular *aspect* of humanism, namely, humanism as it views the facts of ecology and the values of environmentalism, and formulates strategies in the light of those facts to implement those values.

It is my thesis in this essay that not only that modern humanism has been deeply concerned about the natural environment and its effects on the "common good" from the days of its conception in the early 30s, but that humanism is today one of the strongest defenders of the natural environment, and one of our best hopes for the future of the natural environment.

Dominion, *Stig*, Garden, Vista, Campground, Nest, Lifeboat

Ecohumanism is but one of many environmentalisms, with most of which it shares some values, and it can probably best be understood in the context of all the others. All forms of environmentalism, ecohumanism included, have evolved rapidly during the past century, against a background of environmental change, and increasing knowledge about environmental change, which has been not only fast and vast but accelerating, and which continues to accelerate. Thus, the very terms of environmental discourse are not at all what they were a hundred years, or even ten years, ago.

Contemporary ecohumanism can be fully understood, then, only when we take into account the changes in *all* forms of environmentalism during less than seventy years of existence of an organized Humanist movement. For this purpose I intend to focus in this essay on the Abrahamic tradition of environmentalism, and the secular-scientific Western traditions that have grown out of it and alongside it. Much of the original tradition was concerned with Earth as a gift of God, over which humans were granted essentially total dominion, which eventually came to be seen as a temporal reward for a role as caretakers (stewards, or guardians of the *stig*, or hall—literally, "sty," a word some might say increasingly characterizes the human environment). In this scheme the environment was important, initially, as the backdrop for human happiness on Earth. In later Christian and Muslim developments, it became the setting in which humans prepared for eternity, where they would be judged according to their behavior on (and toward) Earth and rewarded accordingly. The ultimate survival of humanity, or even of Earth, was not a prominent consideration.

The Abrahamic tradition grew up in an agricultural setting that was in the process of replacing a nomadic herding society. The domestication first of animals and then of plants, out of which came the agricultural revolution and the other technological advances (e.g., in metallurgy) which accompanied it, has been cursed by some environmentalists as the first great environmental catastrophe, giving rise to a sense of permanent control and ownership of portions of the land, and also to a startling growth of the human population. Here we have perhaps one of the earliest instances of technology's displaying its now infamous potential both to help and to harm human beings, who acquired an increase in security (of food supply, clothing, shelter) at the price of an increased dependency on, and degradation of, a particular area of soil.

This single observation highlights an essential feature of the complex relations between human beings, technology, and the environment. In the relative comfort of (much of) the developed world, it is all too easy to forget the truth of Thomas Hobbes' description (1651) of human beings in a state of nature: "No arts; no letters; no society; and which is worst of all, continual fear and danger of violent death; and the life of man, solitary, poor, nasty, brutish, and short." In such a state, and even today, for that matter, human beings have usually been happy to pay an often indeterminate price to avoid the miseries and terrors of starvation, disease, extreme cold, extreme heat, miscarriages, infant mortality, death in childbirth, fires, floods, hurricanes, tornadoes, earthquakes, landslides, volcanoes, and the miscellaneous dangers of obtaining clothing, food, and shelter in the jungles or on the oceans, to say nothing of arts, letters, and society—or even the pleasures of dining in a fine restaurant on imported fruits and wines. If we truly consider the alternatives, most of us today would prefer to live with bridges, potable water, vaccinations, refrigerators, and flush toilets—that is to say, with technology.[6]

But not everybody. There are some who, in the name of environmentalist purity, assert that no amount of real or imagined benefit to human beings is worth the price exacted by technological advance. This extreme view marks one of the fracture lines in the environmentalist movement. In fairness to this extreme view it must be said that nearly everyone can identify *some* limits to the amounts or types of technology that are compatible with long-run human interests. Just about every technology involves what engineers call "trade-offs" and doctors call "side effects"—the fact that you rarely get something for nothing, and the balance of good and bad effects is what really counts. In designing or buying an automobile, for example, everybody has to decide what is most important—initial cost, maintenance costs, operating costs (including petroleum depletion and emissions), safety, speed, comfort, durability; and almost all technology has a potentially harmful aspect. This is why, in the end, most environmental controversies can never be about absolutes, but about balancing consequences, about *where* to draw the line, and for what ends.

Balancing consequences, however, is attended—not to say plagued—by a very serious problem common to all consequential-ist utilitarian decisions: the problem of unanticipated, let alone un-intended, effects. The sad truth is that when changes are made in systems of any complexity, ecosystems being prime examples, the number of uncontrollable variables is likely to be so large that it is difficult in the extreme, not to say impossible, to have absolute confidence in any outcome. The best one can hope for in such situations is a high probability. This is yet another reason why ab-solutes are unworkable in environmental disputes, even though they may sometimes seem more attractive as a result of uncer-tainty.

Different environmentalisms have prominently identified very different ends as reasons to draw the technological line. For some environmentalists, "caring for the environment" means restoring the lost Garden of Eden, or perhaps, in Voltaire's very different under-standing, "cultivating our garden." For some, "appreciating the en-vironment" means climbing to a high promontory and surveying a majestic scene; while for others, it connotes pitching a tent near a stream and fishing for trout, with the recognition that "a good camper always leaves the campground better than she found it." For still others, earth is our Beloved Home, and "no wise animal fouls its own nest." And for some, earth is our finite and only hos-pitable refuge in a relentlessly hostile universe.

Among the values we can identify here are, in no special order: (1) a *duty* to something or other, whether to future human genera-tions, some higher authority, or some abstract principle; (2) *pres-ervation* of Nature and/or natural beauty; (3) *conservation* and *re-newal* of (finite) natural resources and, closely related to this, the elimination or reversal of *pollution* of such resources by waste products; (4) the human need for *recreational* facilities; and (5) designation of *sanctuaries* for plant and animal wildlife and *protec-*

tion of plant and animal species and complex habitats threatened with extinction. These ends are not always necessarily in conflict with each other, but are in conflict at times, when it then becomes necessary to set priorities among them. In my judgment ecohumanism will recognize validity in most, perhaps all, of these worthwhile purposes, but will surely not assign equal weight to all of them (nor, for that matter, would most other environmentalisms).

Ecohumanism and the Growth of Human Population

A common feature connects all the environmental concerns in the preceding list: Every one implies that it is desirable to maintain earth's resources indefinitely. As a nearly closed system, except primarily for radiation coming from the sun and radiation lost to space, earth cannot be sustained for many centuries in anything approaching a steady state unless its resources remain fundamentally in balance, despite human demands upon them. In the end, humans must use no more of essential materials than they can replace or find acceptable substitutes for, and must produce no more wastes than can be recycled. The rates at which human beings utilize resources and produce wastes both depend on the number of human beings on earth. As long as human population remained minuscule, the environment as a whole enjoyed near-immunity to human onslaught. The primary engine that has driven all these concerns, therefore, is the *size of the human population itself.*

Humanists have long recognized the importance of population control for management of earth's environment, in sharp contrast to conservative elements of the Abrahamic tradition, which have continued up to the present day to preach that God/Jahweh/Allah commands human beings to "multiply and inherit earth." Not to do so is to risk eternal punishment. Within this commandment, however, lies buried the implication that "God will provide."

That God might not continue to provide forever was, ironically, implied by the work of one of His own, the English curate Thomas Robert Malthus (1766-1834), in his *Essay on the Principle of Population* (1798), which purported to demonstrate, on the basis of a rather too simple mathematical model, that human population would inevitably outstrip food production, halting human progress, and inexorably leading to "poverty, misery, vice, selfishness, famine, disease, and war." Equally ironic, in retrospect, is the fact that Malthus' pessimism was devoutly opposed by two optimistic antecedents of modern humanism, the French *philosophe* M. de Caritat, Marquis de Condorcet (1743-1794), in his posthumously published (1975) *Esquisse d'un tableau historique des progrès de l'esprit humaine*; and English atheist William Godwin (1756-1836), in writings at about the same time and particularly later, in *Of Population* (1820). In essence, the position of both these authors was that not God, but human beings "would provide," and that "science and education would ensure a world of peace and plenty, 'where the benevolent, creative, and intellectual sides of human nature will have a chance to flourish.'" (These and other relevant quotations are taken from a review by conservative historian Gertrude Himmelfarb of *Progress, Poverty and Population* (1997) by John Avery, in which the reviewer, not surprisingly, defends the notion long fashionable among conservatives that under-population is a greater threat to civilization than is over-population).[7]

In the 20th century, earth's human population grew to the point where several reasonable demographic projections yielded at most one more doubling of the total in all, sometime around the year 2200, though one optimistic prediction (if that is what it was) suggested a peak around three times the present total. Arguments about whether "Malthus was right" are beside the point, since his mathematical model has long since been shown to have been far too simple; but the basic issue of earth's inability to accommodate so many people "comfortably" is not in serious doubt, since the total supply of available water, for example, is insufficient, with 1.5 billion people already lacking safe drinking water; and many other problems, such as pollution of the air and global warming, are also expected to move from severe to intolerable, well before earth's population reaches its peak.[8]

Ecohumanism, therefore, can do no less than to continue and intensify the efforts of past and present humanists, and many outside the humanist movement, to extend the effectiveness of birth control measures around the world. It is widely agreed by most futurist demographers that in the absence of such measures the human situation on Earth will become increasingly precarious.

Humanist Manifesto II and Ecohumanism

In attempting to delineate contemporary ecohumanism as precisely as I can, I have found no better starting point than a classical Humanist document, *Humanist Manifesto II* (1973).[9] Since there are many environmentalisms, and they have all been undergoing rapid change, it is not surprising that this document has been found wanting by some of its readers. I hope to demonstrate here that in at least one instance the lack of appreciation has been based on a simple misreading of it.

In a celebrated article in the [Unitarian Univeralist] *World* at the end of 1997, a respected Unitarian Universalist minister (described *as a Humanist!*) was quoted as saying of her newer church members, "Many, I think, are a little startled, if not put off, by the bloodless, passionless packaging in which humanism tradition-ally—perhaps not intentionally—has presented itself... In this moment of ecological crisis, religious humanism often sounds anthropocentric, pompous, downright dangerous." She then cited *Humanist Manifesto II* (I'll use the abbreviation *HMII* below) to prove the point: "We have virtually conquered the planet...[and]

stand at the dawn of a new age." "'Yikes!' thinks the new Unitarian Universalist," the minister went on. "New UUs seem to carry into our churches a certain wariness of humanism. [They] sense that they are not the measure of all things, and do not need to be."[10]

In the minister's defense I would have to agree that if the sentence, "We have virtually conquered the planet...," here quoted completely out of context, were truly representative of the argument of *HMII* some of her criticisms, at least, might be more understandable. While surely there is nothing objectionable about "[standing] at the dawn of a new age," the hyperbolic phrase "We have virtually conquered the planet" makes sense only in comparing recent and earlier times, and then only when the opening paragraph of *HMII*, from which the phrase is taken, is viewed, more accurately, not as a triumphalist remark, but as *a rhetorically concessive prologue to a series of dire warnings*, and therefore to be understood as "Maybe (this) BUT (that)." The correctness of this interpretation will, I think, be quite obvious if one reads the entire opening passage, where I have added italics for emphasis:

The next century *can* be and *should* be the humanistic century. Dramatic scientific, technological, and ever-accelerating social and political changes crowd our awareness. *We have virtually conquered the planet*, explored the moon, overcome the natural limits of travel and communication; *we stand at the dawn of a new age*, ready to move farther into space and *perhaps* inhabit other planets. Using technology *wisely*, we *can* control our environment, conquer poverty, markedly reduce disease, extend our life-span, significantly modify our behavior, alter the course of human evolution and cultural development, unlock vast new powers, and provide humankind with unparalleled opportunity for achieving an abundant and meaningful life." [*But* here's the problem (!):]

The future is, however, filled with dangers. In learning to apply the scientific method to nature and human life, *we have opened the door to ecological damage, over-population, dehumaniz-*

ing institutions, totalitarian repression, and nuclear and bio-chemical disaster. Faced with apocalyptic prophesies and doomsday scenarios, many flee in despair from reason and embrace irrational cults and theologies of withdrawal and retreat.

Traditional moral codes and newer irrational cults both fail to meet the *pressing needs* of today and tomorrow. False "theologies of hope" and messianic ideologies, substituting new dogmas for old, *cannot cope with existing world realities.* They separate rather than unite peoples.

Humanity, *to survive,* requires bold and daring measures. *We need to extend the uses of scientific method, not renounce them, to fuse reason with compassion in order to build constructive social and moral values.* Confronted by many possible futures, we must decide which to pursue. *The ultimate goal should be the fulfillment of the potential for growth in each human personality—not for the favored few, but for all of humankind. Only a shared world and global measures will suffice.*

Hear! Hear! The second paragraph of this quotation, especially, spells out some of the very environmental *dangers* the UU minister warned against, and seems to me, in fact, an excellent short introduction to ecohumanism, particularly for 1973, the year of its writing. The second and third paragraphs warn of further dangers in the form of irrational responses and withdrawal—reactions which, sadly, are not unknown in many UU churches and elsewhere in the human community today. And the final paragraph recommends sound humanist solutions.

I say this summary is "excellent. . . for 1973," but go on to emphasize that a great deal has happened since 1973 that must be included in an up-to-date analysis. As with any discussion of a major movement in the history of ideas, we must always take historical and social changes into consideration. Environmentalism in general and ecohumanism in particular have changed strikingly over the thirty-odd years since *HMII,* in considerable measure as a consequence of the same influences—new technologies, new information, new economic and political realities, which I want to adumbrate below.

Is Humanism Anthropocentric (. . . .)?

Before I proceed further, however, let me respond to two additional charges in the *World* article I cited above, two that address the basic nature of humanism in general, and ecohumanism in particular. Humanism was described there (still on the basis of the passage from *HMII* we examined above) as having "presented itself" in "bloodless, passionless packaging" and as "[sounding] anthropocentric, pompous," and "downright dangerous"!

First, about that "packaging." I submit that when we make allowances for the formal purposes of *HMII* and the styles characteristic of the authors and the times, there is plenty of implied "blood" and "passion" in the passage cited, if one reads it with sensitivity. *HMII* was not a poem or a polemic, but an attempt to write about a profoundly emotional matter in an objective and reasonable fashion. I submit that this was OK. More importantly for my present essay, the attempt to communicate objectively ("intersubjectively") and reasonably is *fundamental* to humanism and therefore to ecohumanism, which articulates its arguments through a rational exposition of Humanist values coupled with an understanding of our world and of ourselves based on scientific observations. More ideological forms of environmentalism often try merely to rouse us to depths or heights of righteous indignation, to excesses of pathos or ecstasy, without first engaging our minds in a rational consideration of facts and values. Humanism never needs to apologize for reasoned discourse about environmental or other realities.

As for the charge of "anthropocentricity," in my judgment this can be either true or false, depending on whether the anthropocentricity others are speaking of is "good" or "bad," by which I mean, roughly, "inclusive" or "exclusive." Humanism, especially as it has been co-evolving with ecological science in recent decades, is *inclusively anthropocentric*, in the sense that we see ourselves as "star stuff," in Carl Sagan's powerful phrase, and entirely a part of the material universe out of which we evolved, and in which we remain. Humanists practice a form of Schweitzer's "Reverence for Life," with a dual aspect—we are in awe of the processes of life shared by all living things; and we are concerned for the feelings of our fellow sentient beings, so far as we are able to know about them. In regard to the former, we are comparatively promiscuous, since there is good evidence that *all* plants and animals are ultimately our relatives, however distant. In respect to sentient beings, first, we have reason to believe that there is a huge gradient from the least to the most conscious of living things; and second, we recognize the absurdity of even attempting to imagine equal treatment for ants, zinnias, and Streptococci. The image comes to mind of the Jains, wearing veils over the face to strain out gnats, lest they be injured inadvertently. It is a possibly noble, but decidedly impractical thought.

Genetically, we are programmed by evolution to struggle to preserve our own species. Moreover, we appear to be the only species that cares about the future of our species, or the future of anything else, for that matter. We claim the right to defend ourselves against attack from predatory animal species, disease carried by animal vectors, and plant and animal toxins; and more than that, we claim the right to defend ourselves against hunger by killing and eating plants and animals, and against exposure by wearing clothing and building shelters using their tissues. While such claims are regarded as controversial in some quarters, I haven't chosen to explore them more deeply here, where my main purpose is to set forth some features of ecohumanism that distinguish it from other environmentalisms. I would answer those humanists who are Unitarian Universalists, and who may argue against these claims on the ground that they violate the UU principle of the "interdependent web of all existence, of which we are a part," with the comment that any biologist, or anyone else who has watched a few PBS programs on plants and animals in nature, will realize that a very large part of this "interdependent" web goes by the name of the "food chain." In this respect our genetic programming for survival resembles that of other species.

Moreover, the "*inter*dependence" is often distinctly unidirectional, as might be readily seen from comparing my dependence, say, on the sun with the sun's on me. Still, the recent development of ecological science has shown us that biological "ecosystems," whose boundaries are often ill-defined, frequently are functionally integrated to an astonishing extent, with tens of thousands of species co-existing in a fragile balance, in which removal of a single species may affect hundreds of others in ways that are known, and potentially far more in ways that are not. The growth of our knowledge of such interactions, e.g., through the protection and the study of *biodiversity*, could well have the most profound implications for the future of our own species, inasmuch as we are still pitifully ignorant of their detailed mechanisms. We are told that every year now species, many still undiscovered or microscopic, are becoming extinct by the thousands; but especially in this century, when we have new ways to interpret the DNA of even extinct species, we also have the exciting prospect of understanding for the first time all such species and their complex interactions in ecosystems, including the ecology of the dominant species on Earth, *Homo sapiens*.

It has been my impression that humanism has not (not yet, at any rate) come up with a single unifying rationale for all humanist values, including humanist inclusive anthropocentricity. If this is so, the implications for ecohumanism are obvious, and enormous.

To me it means that different humanists may disagree about the relative importance of different environmental values, though I would expect more agreement among them than between humanists and non-humanists. Speaking for myself, I find I value conscious life more than unconscious life, more complex organisms more than less complex organisms, and living organisms I know to exist more than living organisms I can only imagine. For me these preferences coalesce in the vertebrate brain—especially the human brain, which so far as I am aware is the most complex structure in the entire Cosmos, and the most complex we are likely ever to know. What is so great about complexity? The answer is that complexity in a functioning organism implies order, the opposite of chaos, of what physicists call "entropy" or disorder. It appears to me that the evolution of the natural universe through natural selection has, overall, tended to result in an ever-increasing order—not, to be sure, in a straight line, but on the average. There, in a nutshell, is my ultimate value system, and the rationale behind my ecohumanism.

"Preservation" versus "Conservation"

Early in the 20th century President Theodore Roosevelt, an enthusiastic outdoorsman, took the lead in protecting huge areas of the western United States from commercial exploitation. He did so under the influence of two strong pioneers in environmental protection, Gifford Pinchot (1865-1946) and John Muir (1838-1914). Ironically, these two practiced very different forms of environmentalism, and came to look upon each other as adversaries. The conflict between the two kinds of environmentalism they espoused has persisted to the present day, and we can learn from the conflict.[11]

Pinchot, who studied forestry in Germany, was the first American to become a professional forester, and became the first chief of the Forest Service, a branch of the U.S. Department of Agriculture.

Having witnessed the rampant exploitation of some forests in Europe, he strongly advocated the German-style *conservation* of forests and other natural resources through sound public management, believing that there were important advantages not only to humans but to maintenance of the environment itself in this policy of "wise use" (perhaps an antecedent version of the modern concept of "sustainable development").

John Muir, on the other hand, was much closer to Thoreau and the other Transcendentalists, whose attitude was a kind of worship of Nature for its own sake, rather than for any human use. From his point of view *any* modification of Nature was a form of violation, the only legitimate "use" being to *preserve* as much of Nature as possible in a wild state, where it might be appreciated but not altered. Muir was able to persuade Roosevelt to set aside 148 million acres of government land in the West for undisturbed National Parks. It is easy to understand why Muir's quasi-religious philosophy of *preservation* was frequently in direct opposition to Pinchot's of *conservation*, and adherents of the one viewpoint came to look upon proponents of the other not only as adversaries, but often as downright immoral.

"Deep ecology," a term coined in 1973 by the Norwegian Arne Naess, could be described as preservationism carried to its logical extreme; it is so passionately against any disturbance of Nature by humans that its position might be summarized as "Earth would be a very wonderful place if only there were no humans in it." Under the heading of deep ecology Mark Dowie quotes John Muir, "If a war of races should occur between the wild beasts and Lord Man, I would be tempted to sympathize with the bears." *Anthropocentrism* is replaced by *biocentrism*, even *naturocentrism*. American forester Aldo Leopold (1886-1948), anticipating deep ecology, asked his readers to "think like a mountain." Dowie, who is sympathetic to this impulse, nevertheless concludes, "It's all

very inspiring, but it's also puritanical, insulting, and in its contemporary absolutist form, it is futile."[12]

Where should ecohumanism come down in this controversy? In
principle the *preservation* concept may be opposed to "use" of
any kind, but a less absolutist version of it might well have much
appeal to humanists. Ecohumanism as I have outlined it above is
anti-ideological, essentially pragmatic; it abhors absolutes (but, I
must be careful to add, "not *absolutely*"). As I have implied above,
there is clearly a utilitarian argument for some form
of—presumably limited—preservation of ecosystems, for the mutual benefit of human and nonhuman species. Ecohumanism may, I
suspect, come to favor a "balance" between preservation and conservation.

In the '30s and '40s in elementary school I learned that much of
the world's helium came from holes in the ground in southeastern
Kansas. We were told that some day it would run out, and we
wanted to know what would happen then, but as I recall we never
got a truly satisfactory answer—just "conservation." When there
were gas and oil shortages during WWII, we learned that the earth's
fossil fuels were being used up at an alarming rate, and we wondered what would happen when they ran out. Same
thing—"conservation."

After the war we had to worry about strontium-90 in our milk,
caused by fall-out from far-away nuclear tests. Fortunately we also
had nuclear energy to help solve the problem of dwindling fossil
fuel stores, but some people became concerned about where we
would put the radioactive wastes, and others about the "thermal
pollution" of streams by water heated as it cooled the reactors. I
wasn't sure what to think about some of those things, but I defi-
nitely agreed that microwave towers on the tops of high hills
spoiled the beauty of the Kansas landscape. And everybody was

glad we had DDT to control insects, while we all practiced "conservation."

Ecohumanism and the "Beauty of the Environment"

Painters, poets, and ordinary people have found great beauty and inspiration in nature for thousands of years, as we do. Sociobiologist E. O. Wilson, in *Biophilia*, argued that humans are programmed to love nature, because that is where we came from. Possibly so, but a similar argument could account for an aversion to nature. Still, we all have gaped in awe at the grandeur of large vistas, and we are all able to find something to admire in an enormous variety of outdoor settings. Humanists yield to none in our appreciation of the esthetic qualities of our surroundings. It is an essential part of the quality of life, the joy of living that we find so important.[13]

At the same time I am impressed both by how much our tastes differ from one person to another, and also by how easily they can be retrained. Perhaps nothing shows this better than the way we who feel a microwave tower mars the view can adjust to the idea that acres of solar collectors or windmills are photogenic. In my judgment, what environmentalists call the "beauty of nature" is, and should be, in the I of the beholder. Much of it depends on what one is used to, or learns to become used to. I emphasize this because while ecohumanism must certainly value "beauty in nature," and anywhere beauty occurs, it does not, in general, assign the highest priority to natural beauty in making environmental decisions. Not only that, but when I say we value beauty "anywhere [it] occurs" I mean to emphasize that one corollary of humanism's "inclusive anthropocentricity" is that we insist on looking at any human activity or product as a *part of nature*. If we are an integral part of nature, then our houses and skyscrapers and landfills are as much a part of nature as a bird's nest or a beaver's dam. To ignore them as such is a form of sentimentality in appreciating "the beauty (and ugliness) of nature."

When I was a child, protected during the '30s (the "Depression Years") and '40s (the "War Years"), it seemed to me that most of us thought the world itself was basically safe and beautiful, and most of us felt we ought to help keep it that way, and believed that that shouldn't be too hard to do. Growing up mostly in Kansas I became almost addicted to a sky-induced euphoria. Sure, I thought pictures of the mountains were beautiful, but so were wheat fields. Like Francis Parkman in *The Oregon Trail*, I loved to watch storms approach from a great distance, gradually filling up the whole sky with dark clouds, bringing strong winds, thunder and lightning, hard rain and hail, and often a sudden drop of perhaps thirty or more degrees Fahrenheit in temperature. I learned to tell time to within a few minutes at night from the positions of the brighter stars. Ever since, I have felt hemmed in unless there was an open space I could go to, or a high building with an observation tower. In the '40s, after an automobile trip across the northeast United States to Maine and back home by way of Virginia and Tennessee, I was relieved and thrilled to return to the comparative flatness of the Kansas prairie. Some people who have heard this story refused to believe it.

Living in Calcutta in the mid '60s I was one of the very fortunate few to have a wide, flat roof from which to survey the congested, hard-working, feverish, frantic world below, struggling to achieve the status of a developed country—and the heavens above, especially the dramatic, tall post-monsoon clouds of October. There was a painful beauty in this juxtaposition. Finding beauty in our environment is the responsibility of each one of us. One person's beautiful is another person's ugly.

From Conservation to Environmentalism to Ecology

In 1962 a major change occurred almost all at once: what we had been calling "conservation" became "environmentalism," after an American marine biologist, Rachel Carson, whose 1951 book *The Sea Around Us* had been a great popular success, published a new book, S*ilent Spring*, that frightened the daylights out of nearly everybody with its vision of a dying planet, being destroyed by ubiquitous substances of our own making, formerly thought to be safe. A year later I took my wife and two small children to live in Calcutta, where malaria and filariasis were endemic, secure in the knowledge that both these terrible diseases were being effectively controlled by DDT—one of the principal substances indicted by Rachel Carson's new book. Nowadays, when DDT can no longer be used as it was then and malaria is rampant, I'm sure I'd be far less likely to make that move. I might even hesitate to visit Calcutta again, despite a recurrent urge to do so.[14]

Silent Spring is usually said to mark the beginning of the coming of age of the environmental movement, described by Mark Dowie as "an amalgam of resource conservation, wilderness preservation, public health reform, population control, ecology, energy conservation, anti-pollution regulation, and occupational health campaigns," which developed as the public and political leaders started to learn about the engineering "trade-offs" I mentioned earlier. Now not only did we lovers of Earth have to worry about the depletion of non-renewable resources, attacks on the beauty of the landscape, and avoiding the avoidable consequences of nuclear testing, but we also had to be concerned with a host of unintended, unforeseen, and undesirable consequences of the very technological advances we had long sought! Fortunately, though, we still had some perfectly safe, decidedly inert and nontoxic miracle compounds like the chlorofluorocarbons (CFCs) we all were using for the refrigerants that kept our foods safe to eat and our bodies comfortable during the fiercest heat of summer.[15]

The magnitude, diversity, and complexity of the many radical changes that took place during the 20th century in the human environment and in our knowledge of that environment, and the responses to both of these, have been set forth in some detail in several books, one of the best of which appeared only recently.[16] I can only hope to suggest here the scope of these changes after *Silent Spring* appeared, in a very brief chronological outline, primarily to introduce the complexity of the problems we are likely to face in the years to come:

1960s: Radicalization of the environment, linked to protests again the Vietnam war, "the establishment," industry, nuclear technology, technology in general, fear of thermonuclear war, major environmental accidents

1967: *Torrey Canyon* (tanker) oil spill near Cornwall, England—120,000 tons of oil into the English Channel

1968: Paul Ehrlich, *The Population Bomb*[17]

1970, April 22: First Earth Day—observed by 20 million Americans (to mixed reviews)

1972: Club of Rome, *Limits to Growth*[18]

1972: United Nations Conference on the Human Environment held in Stockholm (June), leading to founding of UN Environment Program (UNEP)

1974: F. Sherwood Rowland and Mario Molina propose that CFCs can do serious damage to earth's stratospheric ozone layer, which absorbs harmful X-rays from the sun

1976-1978: Love Canal district of Buffalo, NY—residential neighborhood built on a landfill (thousands of tons of toxic chemicals buried, 1947-52) showed alarming signs of serious soil and water toxicity and other hazards

1983: "Nuclear winter"—scientists predict devastating worldwide effects of a thermonuclear war on world climate

1983-1987: UN General Assembly created the Brundtland Commission (World Commission on Environment and Development)—explored the intimate link between economic development and adverse worldwide environmental change

1986: Chernobyl (Ukraine) nuclear reactor explodes; wide contamination

1987: Final Report of Brundtland Commission ("Our Common Future"), with emphasis on a new concept, worldwide "Sustainable Development"

1987: Montreal Protocol under UNEP to limit production of CFCs

1988: Start of concern about "greenhouse effect" and "global warming"

1988: Spread of quantitative environmental thinking; UCLA course in environmental problem solving, using approximation methods and familiarity with very large numbers (textbook, *Consider a Spherical Cow* by John Harte)[19]

1989: Exxon *Valdez* tanker—11 million gallons (34,000 tons) of crude oil spilled, Alaska

1992: Rio de Janeiro "Earth Summit" of UN Conference on Environment and Development ("UNCED")

1992: "World Scientists' Warning to Humanity"; multiplicity of threats to survival of humans and other living things

1994: UN Conference on Population and Development (Cairo); increased emphasis on concerns of women

Staggering Problems, Stammering Attempts to Solve Them

As the 20th century began to run out, certain themes increasingly dominated environmental dialogues: population pressures on surface and underground water, soil, foods; accidental and deliberate spread of chemical, nuclear, and biological pollution; finite capacity of lands, oceans, and the atmosphere to absorb change; attempts by the UN, its affiliates, and other supragovernmental and governmental organizations to facilitate and enforce negotiated agreements; attempts to limit widespread destruction of ecosystems (e.g., rain forests). A sense of urgency was found in many of these efforts, but the world was sharply divided along economic and cultural lines concerning which actions, if any, should be undertaken.

Fundamental to many of the debates were issues of the state of the sciences involved. Those who wished to go slow in instituting environmental controls often cited what they saw as inadequate scientific basis for action, while those on the other side felt either that the science was already adequate or else that humanity could not afford to wait for "completely adequate" science, because then it might be too late to prevent a catastrophe. Each side tended to challenge the other side's integrity, sometimes with justification.

The fundamental formula most of the world could agree upon in principle was the Brundtland Commission's "sustainable development." The problem was in the details. The richer developed nations with their industrial interests, generally the major per-capita consumers of resources and producers of wastes, felt they could not tolerate stringent controls, which they believed would imperil their standard of living and thus their stability. The poorer undeveloped (and often overpopulated) nations, wishing to attain a higher level of economic development, with its attendant higher levels of per-capita consumption and waste, pointed out how unfair it would be for them to have to bear the entire burden of environmental actions. Negotiators made serious, ingenious attempts to resolve these differences incrementally, so that no group would be overly disadvantaged.

Cultural divisions were of many sorts, as one would suppose from the history of world cultural misunderstandings. There are libraries filled with humor based on cultural differences ("In heaven the cooks are French and the police are English. In hell the cooks are English and the police are German.") Objects of disagreement ranged from a distrust of science as an instrument of the Haves (or, according to the issue, the Have-nots) to a total failure to appreciate why another group requires a particular commodity in order to survive (I recall that Bengalis cannot live without rice and mustard oil, so that attempts to supply them with wheat and ground-nut oil during one shortage led to something like an armed insurrection). Solutions deemed appropriate by one group were outrageous to another (as when French authorities, faced recently with a series of automobile fatalities when drivers took a curve much too fast and ploughed into a grove of trees, simply cut down the offending trees).

Mark Hertsgaard has recently traveled around the world collecting personal anecdotes about environmental attitudes in different cultures. Two in particular from China illustrate the level on which the environmental debate often founders. One was about the frequently heard question, when environmental issues were raised, "Is your stomach too full?" It was directed particularly at "Americans who talk about saving birds and monkeys while there are still many Chinese people who don't have enough to eat." Another common phrase, used to shrug off air pollution, was "I am used to it." The idea here is that worrying about the environment is a sign of weakness and a sheltered life, and that the correct response is to tough it out. The journalist Orville Schell offers the explanation that "a society that has for decades had to ignore so many unjust and irrational things in order to just get along...is one in which the capacity to avoid recognizing all sorts of problems, including environmental ones, has become essential to survival."[20]

Little wonder, then, that Paul Ehrlich, 1968 author of *The Population Bomb*, has turned his attention more recently to genetic and cultural determinants of human behavior, in a 530-page book which he concludes, in part, with these remarks:

> Our global civilization had better move rapidly to modify its cultural evolution and deal with its deteriorating environmental circumstances before it runs out of time. Whether the natures of most of us can be changed to establish better connections among diverse groups and to take more systematic control of our cultural evolution remains to be seen. . . . Our challenge is to learn to deal sensibly with both nature and our nature*s* [plural]—for all of us to learn to be both environmentalists and "people people." Utopian? Perhaps. I tend to be optimistic in thinking that we *can* do it but pessimistic about whether we *will* do it.[21]

Another who is even more pessimistic is Robert Kaplan, who has recently written that the environment is "*the* national-security issue of the early twenty-first century." In developing this thesis he draws heavily on a 1991 analysis by Thomas Fraser Homer-Dixon, head of the Peace and Conflict Studies Program, University

of Toronto. "Future wars...will often arise from scarcities of resources such as water, cropland, forests, and fish." Citing the National Academy of Sciences, "95 percent of the population increase
[from 5.5 billion to greater than 9 billion] will be in the poorest re-
gions of the world. . . ." We are slouching toward Armageddon. Or
are we? It is significant that the environmental problems Kaplan is
expecting will be due mainly to overpopulation and underproduc-
tion, especially of food. Massive as these may become, they are
the sort of problems we have had success with in the past, and appear to be manageable in the future, if we have the will to manage
them.[22]

Global Warming—A Paradigm?

An altogether different environmental problem, one we show no
signs of being able to solve as yet, is disposing of our excess waste
carbon dioxide. Since the summer of 1988, when NASA's Jim Hansen testified before a Senate committee in the middle of a drought,
the human race has been trying to figure out whether Earth's surface is in fact warming up; and if so, whether the warming is due to
the "greenhouse effect"; and if so, whether this effect is caused by
human activity (an "enhanced greenhouse effect"); and if so,
whether it is very dangerous to humans and other living things; and
if so, whether we can do something about it in time to prevent a catastrophe; and if so, what?[23]

Over the past twelve years the scientific data have been seemingly contradictory, leading some skeptics to doubt that any significant warming has taken place, and others, while accepting that
warming is a fact, to blame it on causes other than a human-induced
enhanced greenhouse effect, mediated by increased release of
"greenhouse gases" (GHGs). The difficulty is twofold: First, it is
extremely difficult to obtain heating values averaged for Earth over
time, space, and physically very different objects, such as air at

various altitudes, oceans at various depths, soil at different latitudes, etc. Second, it is equally difficult to correct these values for changes due to the normal cyclical variations, sunspots, volcanic activity (which can have both positive and negative effects).

A persistent disparity between temperature measurements at the surface and GHGs in the upper atmosphere has cast doubt in some minds of the reality of global warming. Within the past year, however, measurements have been made in the ocean depths and in ice cores from altitudes high in the Himalayas that have helped greatly to reconcile the discrepancies in earlier balance sheets, so that most global warming skeptics have now become convinced. A review of all the data by the National Research Council indicated that surface warming could rise by 1.5 to 6.0 degrees C by the end of this century—a *very* significant amount, when we realize that the last Ice Age, which ended about 10,000 years ago, was only about 6 deg C cooler than today, and the U. S. Midwest was covered with ice at that time. The IPCC (The UN's Intergovernmental Panel on Climate Change), the main clearing-house for this research, also estimated that by the end of the century the mean sea-level will rise by 15-95 cm—likewise a *very* significant amount! But what the longer-term effects of global warming may be, and what to do about them, remained in doubt.[24]

Nothing could better illustrate the controversy over global warming among the experts than the recent comments of Cambridge physicist Stephen Hawking and a speedy reply to Hawking from a German climatologist. The *Times* of London reported on September 30, 2000 that Hawking, in informal remarks preceding a lecture at the Royal Society of Edinburgh, said the following (indirect quotations):

1. He feared the human race would not survive for another thousand years.

2. An accident or global warming would wipe out life on Earth.

3. Only by settling on other planets could humanity guarantee its survival.

4. Space travel would not solve the problems of overpopulation, but without colonizing other planets, humans were presented with the possibility of becoming extinct.

The only direct quotation attributed to Hawking in the article was this: "I am afraid the atmosphere might get hotter and hotter until it will be like Venus with boiling sulphuric acid. I am worried about the greenhouse effect." There was no further explanation, and Hawking gave no supporting evidence, but his remarks, naturally, were widely reported in the world media.[25]

A few days later, on October 3, *Telopolis*, "the magazine of Net culture," reported the following reply to Hawking [in German, my translation]:[26]

CLIMATE INVESTIGATOR ANSWERS HAWKING:

NO EXTINCTION OF LIFE

The annihilation of life on the earth before the year 3000, as feared by Stephen Hawking, is highly improbable, in the opinion of a climate investigator. "Only if we were to burn up all the carbon reserves in the earth could we theoretically create a hot atmosphere similar to that on the planet Venus," said Manfred Stock of the Potsdam Institute for Research on Climatic Effects. "Nevertheless, I take the position that we should bring about a reduction in the release of greenhouse gases." ...In Stock's view...humanity will have essentially converted to alternative energy sources in about 50 years. The prospects for hydrogen automobiles and solar energy are excellent. In the first place, within the foreseeable future the consumption of fossil fuels will become uneconomical. "Nobody will pay more than ten marks for gasoline." Secondly, humanity will cut back on the release of greenhouse gases for environmental reasons.

"Still, we do have a few surprise effects in the Earth system
that are difficult to estimate," Stock said. It is uncertain what
would happen if the methane ice layer from the ocean floor
were to break down. It is possible that the warming that is already beginning might cause methane also to be liberated from
the oceans or from thawing permafrost soils, and that might
push the climate in the direction of Hawking's prophecy. But it
is dangerous "to paint such catastrophic scenarios on the wall."

Such was the debate, or a portion of it, between two European
scientists on the medium-term (1,000-year) effects of global
warming in early October. This was just over a month before 5,000
persons, both delegates and observers, met in The Hague for a
summit to discuss implementation of the UN Kyoto treaty on climate change (1997), when delegates from the rich nations of the
world had agreed to cut their GHG emissions by 5 percent, on the
average, below 1990 levels before 2008-2012. At that time many of
those delegates regarded a 5 percent cut as draconian, while the
Green parties found them far too small, demanding that emissions
eventually be reduced by 80 percent ("contraction") and be no
more for the rich than the poor ("convergence"). Everyone agreed
that the guiding principle of the discussions was to be "sustainable
development"—the enormous differences were in the *interpretation*
of this phrase.

In order to work out these enormous differences, several technical issues were placed on the table at the summit: First, the use of
market mechanisms by developed countries, that is, to trade emissions permits and to earn credits for investing to help poor countries reduce their emissions and for carrying out joint projects in
other developed countries. The rationale for such arrangements was
to permit cuts to be made wherever they were cheapest. Second, it
was proposed to give credit for carbon "sinks," new and growing
plants that absorb and hold atmospheric carbon, in reforested areas
and when deforestation is ended; such processes are not yet well
understood, however, and create anxiety because it is not known

how permanent their effects may be. A third mechanism was for economic sanctions to be imposed on nations that fail to meet their targets. And there were others. The importance of these details for us here is that they illustrate the kind of specialized technical issues that a pragmatic approach to environmental problem solving may raise, in contrast to an ideological approach, which is likely to be "all or nothing."

Even so, the Hague summit ended with no agreement, although a few hours before it ended an agreement seemed to be in sight. The *Economist* said they came "tantalizingly close to an accord." Britain's environment minister claimed that his French counterpart had been "too tired to understand the deal." There were also recriminations from other participants who felt some of the rest were trying to get away with something. The *Economist* wrote, "Green lobbyists swiftly declared that the earth was doomed." Paul Krugman wrote a column for the New York *Times* called "Sins of Emission." They will all meet again in six months, in Bonn. The Dutch environmental minister Jan Pronk, president of the summit, suggested that "we did not succeed . . . [but] looking back, I think it is better to say that perhaps we did not yet succeed." I suspect that future ecohumanist talks will look like this.[27]

Is Nothing Sacred?

Humanists are often asked *why* they do what they think they ought to do. It can't be fear of eternal punishment, or hope of eternal reward. Maybe nobody is even watching what they do. Sometimes what you think you should do is not the easy thing to do. So why do it? Ecohumanism will surely require sacrifices at times, and the humanist who wants to do the right thing about the environment will sometimes feel alone. What motivation will strengthen her resolve?

In 1972 James Lovelock, an atmospheric scientist and inventor who had made some crucial observations with an instrument he called an "electron capture detector" leading to the discoveries underlying Rachel Carson's *Silent Spring*, published a theory that Earth's biosphere was a kind of superorganism, made up of many lesser organisms that worked together in some sense. The "superorganism" idea was helped along by his colleague Lynn Margulis, ex-wife of Carl Sagan, and a creative microbiologist in her own right, who had earlier argued that multicellular animals like ourselves are superorganisms made up of eukaryotic cells which are in turn superorganisms that incorporate borrowed organelles from more primitive organisms. The superorganism concept was an old speculation, probably going back to primitive times, and certainly at least to Giordano Bruno, an older contemporary of Galileo who was burned at the stake in 1600. Lovelock himself points out that a similar notion had been entertained by Y. M. Korolenko, Vladimir Vernadsky, and the father of geology, James Hutton. For the first Earth Day, the microbiologist Rene Dubos wrote "the surface of the earth is truly a living organism."[28]

We might never have heard of Lovelock's theory had it not been for his neighbor, William Golding, author of *Lord of the Flies*, who suggested that such an important superorganism ought to have a fitting name, and proposed that "she" be called Gaia, after the Earth Goddess of Hesiod's *Theogony*, mother of Uranus and the Titans. So the superorganism was first anthropomorphized, then deified, then became Mother Earth, then Mother Goddess, and finally the Mother Of Us All. Even then there was no way to foresee how powerfully her image would seize the minds of so many in the growing environmental movement. Today there are hundreds of thousands, perhaps millions, who worship this Mother as the literal embodiment of our environment, our sacred Earth. For many, she is able to work miracles.

Not everyone worships the same Gaia, however. To some, she is nurturing, and they are grateful to her. To others she is weak and suffering, and they must protect her. To still others, she is fearsome and vengeful, and they must take care not to anger her. Lynn Margulis is one of these. Her picture of Gaia is that of a *survivor*, able to adapt indefinitely despite insult after insult after insult. In her article, "Gaia is a Tough Bitch," she says, "This planet's surface and its atmosphere and environment will continue to evolve long after people and prejudice are gone."[29]

The idea that some kind of quasi-transcendent entity is meaningful to all of us as an object of our profoundest commitment may turn out to be important to ecohumanism. I suspect, however, that the nature of this entity may differ from person to person. To be honest, Gaia doesn't work well for me. Perhaps it's because there is so much claimed for "Her" in the name of science, not all of which makes sense to me. I'm also frankly turned off by all the sentimentality I have found surrounding "Her" worship, focusing on imaginary characteristics that have no meaning for me. I prefer to identify something I can see as a genuinely transcendent entity, and then develop metaphors to express the feelings such an entity evokes.

I'm still working on this transcendent entity, and I'm still trying out ideas, but I must say I've been particularly impressed by the way E. O. Wilson describes his naturalistic view of the sacred. In a *Salon* interview (April 22, Earth Day, 2000) which he titled "Living in Shimmering Disequilibrium," he talked freely about his conviction that a concept of what is sacred is valuable, even necessary, to a humanist. Here are some of the things he said in that interview:

> The world is very different from the vision of traditional religion. And far more complex, far larger, far vaster, far more interesting in many ways. The human species—in achieving its independence from that universe, its ability to survive in good part by understanding how the universe works—has achieved

something truly magnificent. And what we need to offer in the way of reverence should be not to some imagined higher power, but *to each other* [italics mine]. And we need to dedicate ourselves to preserving *the one home—seemingly the only home* [italics mine]—that we're ever likely to have as a species.[30]

The Future of Ecohumanism

Looking back at this brief history of environmentalism, what are we to make of this jumble of confusing and often contradictory values and supposed facts? And what kind of program for the future can we, as card-carrying ecohumanists, or simply humanists for short, envision for the human environment? How can we decide on the best course of action in any particular environmental conflict, recruit others to our position, and design and implement a practical plan?

First, we must be content to let ecohumanism change, to grow and develop, to evolve. We are nowhere near the place where we might be able to articulate a fully detailed humanist philosophy of the human environment, and it is possible that in one sense we never will be. With respect to the human environment, human knowledge, human circumstances, and therefore human values will never be static. Consequently, in my judgment ecohumanism *must* be a changing philosophy, and *must* contain a philosophy of environmental change—how it occurs, and how we can adapt to meet it.

But we must not simply regard environmental change passively. We must actively promote the sorts of environmental change that will help us to achieve the universal humanist goal of a better, more fulfilling life for everyone. Clearly this is a never-ending process. "Better, more fulfilling" implies "better and better, more and more fulfilling" indefinitely. In the context of the preceding paragraph, we *must* work constantly to increase human knowledge of the environment, to improve human environmental circumstances, and to refine and continually re-refine human environmental values. Let me take each of these three imperatives separately.

Like every other area of humanist concern, ecohumanism *must* be based in reality, "external," inter-subjective reality—not on revelations, ideologies, wishes, or hunches. If pressed, most environmental scientists would tell us that their own knowledge of environmental science is rudimentary, and that the voting masses upon whom our democracy depends for environmental decisions know practically nothing at all. The imperative to "increase human knowledge" of our environment therefore means we *must* vigorously promote *both* (1) scientific investigations into what remains unknown about ourselves and our environment *and* (2) attempts to help not only young people but people of all ages to know and understand clearly the facts about themselves and their environment, their stake in it, and what can practically be done if it is necessary to do something to change it. To that end it will be especially important to instill new habits of critical and quantitative thinking in the global public mind, making the best possible use of all means of communication, including television and the Internet as well as newspapers, books, and magazines. Humanists *must* take a strong initiative in these endeavors. If we do not, who will?

The imperative to "improve human environmental circumstances" means that ecohumanism *must* enlist the most able among us to engage others, no matter how reluctant they may be at first, to join in a great public dialogue about the issues of the human environment that affect us all and our posterity. This dialogue will require the highest standards of well-informed, rational thinking and sympathetic understanding, since these issues are typically complex and frequently come laden with strong personal and ideological biases; since all the participants will come to realize that they have an immense personal stake in the enterprise; and since all will undoubtedly be asked to give up something in order to reach solutions in the common interest. If Humanists do not take a strong initiative in ensuring that these high standards are met, who will?

Finally, since our values depend upon our knowledge of the scientific facts and the circumstances we encounter, it is imperative that ecohumanism be ever flexible in the face of changing scientific knowledge and changing circumstances. Indeed, the continual need for refinement of human values could in the long run make the most onerous demands upon humanists. One can imagine the eventuality that the evolving human situation may one day in the—we may hope far distant—future impose a terminal lifeboat ethic upon the inhabitants of planet Earth. In that day humanists will be called upon to display not merely sophisticated judgment and the wisdom born of experience, but that most outrageous of virtues, humility, and the grace of serene submission to the inevitable. If we do not, who will?

Notes

1. Astronomy data in the first three paragraphs are from Terence Dickinson, *The Universe and Beyond* (Rochester NY: Camden House, 1992); Patrick Moore, *Rand McNally Atlas of the Universe* (Chicago: Rand McNally, 1994); and Roy A. Gallant, *National Geographic Picture Atlas of Our Universe* (1994).

2. Patrick Moore, *op. cit.*, pp. 34-5; and Jared Diamond, *The Third Chimpanzee* (San Francisco: Harper Perennial, 1992). The quoted phrase is a reference to the classic work by biochemist Lawrence J. Henderson, *Fitness of the Environment: An Inquiry into the Properties of Matter* (New York, Macmillan, 1913).

3. For this and the following paragraph, see Freeman Dyson, *Infinite in All Directions* (San Francisco: Harper and Row, 1988), ch. 6, "How Will It All End?"

4. Al Gore, *Earth in the Balance* (Boston: Houghton Mifflin, 1992).

5. Corliss Lamont, *The Philosophy of Humanism* (Amherst NY: Humanist Press, American Humanist Association, 1997), Appendix, Humanist Manifestos I and II, pp. 311-328.

6. Thomas Hobbes, *Leviathan*, Pt. I, Chapter 13.

7. Gertrude Himmelfarb, "The Ghost of Parson Malthus," *Times Literary Supplement* 4947 (January 23, 1998), pp. 4-5.

8. These estimates from UN sources, according to Microsoft *Encarta 98* CD-ROM, "Environment"; see also Sandra Postel, *Pillar of Sand* (on irrigation), Worldwatch Institute (New York: Norton, 1999), and citations in: Jim Motavalli, "Down the Drain: The Coming Water Crisis," *In These Times* 24 no. 10 (April 17, 2000), pp. 18-20

9. See 5 above.

10. Quoted in Warren Ross, "The Marginalized Majority: UU Humanism in the 1990s," *World* [*Unitarian Universalist*] 11 no. 6 (Nov./Dec. 1997), pp. 14-19.

11. For these paragraphs I used Mark Dowie, *Losing Ground* (Cambridge: MIT Press, 1996); *Webster's New Biographical Dictionary* (New York: Merriam-Webster, 1983); and Microsoft *Encarta 98* CD-ROM, "Environment."

12. Mark Dowie, *Losing Ground*.

13. Edward O. Wilson, *Biophilia* (Cambridge: Harvard University Press, 1986).

14. Rachel Carson, *Silent Spring* (Boston: Houghton Mifflin, 1994).

15. Mark Dowie, *Losing Ground*.

16. J.R. McNeill, *Something New Under the Sun* (New York: Norton, 2000).

17. Reprinted by Buccaneer Books, 1997.

18. Dennis Meadows, *Limits to Growth* (New York: Universe Books, 1972).

19. John Harte, Consider a Spherical Cow: A Course in Environmental Problem Solving (Mill Valley CA: University Science Books, 1988).

20. Mark Hertsgaard, *Earth Odyssey* (New York: Broadway Books, 1999), especially ch. 5, "Is Your Stomach Too Full?"

21. Paul R. Ehrlich, *Human Natures: Genes, Cultures, and the Human Prospect* (Washington DC: Island Press, 2000). See also review by Vaclav Smil, *Nature* 408 (Dec 7, 2000) pp. 643-4. Smil is a well-known Czech ecologist.

22. Robert D. Kaplan, *The Coming Anarchy* (New York: Random House, 2000).

23. See statement of Dr. James Hansen, Director, NASA Goddard Institute for Space Studies, Hearing before the Committee on Energy and Natural Resources, United States Senate, June 23, 1988;

24. "Clear and Present Danger," The Year in Science, *Discover* 22 no. 1 (Jan. 2001) pp. 59-60. "Hotting Up in the Hague," *The Economist* (Nov. 18-24, 2000), pp. 81-83.

25. "Mankind 'extinct in 1,000 years,'" www.timesarchive.co.uk/news/pages/ tim/2000/09/30/timnwsnws01023.html.

26. To find this quickly on the 'Net, make a search for "Hawking" & "Klimaforscher"

27. "Beyond The Hague," *Economist* (Dec. 2-8, 2000) pp. 19-20; Paul Krugman, "Sins of Emission," *New York Times* (Nov. 29, 2000), p. A35.

28. James Lovelock, *The Ages of Gaia* (New York: Bantam Books, 1990); Rene Dubos, "The Limits of Adaptability," in *The Environmental Handbook*, ed. Garrett de Bell (New York: Ballantine Books, 1970), pp. 27-30.

29. Lynn Margulis, "Gaia Is a Tough Bitch," pp. 129-146, John Brockman, ed., *The Third Culture* (New York: Simon & Schuster, 1995).

30. This was found at:
:www.salon.com/people/feature/2000/04/22/eowilson/, with five subdivisions.

THE IMPACT OF
POPULATION ON ECOLOGY

John M. Swomley

"The projected growth in population over the next half-century," wrote Lester Brown, "may more directly affect economical progress than any other single trend, exacerbating nearly all other environmental and social problems."[1]

In 1950 the world population was 2.5 billion. By 2000 it had increased by 3.6 billion to 6.1 billion, and is projected to grow in the next fifty years to 8.9 billion, an increase of 2.8 billion.[2] By 2050, Nigeria is expected to have a population of 339 million, more than all of Africa had thirty-five years ago.[3]

This growth will continue in spite of the fact that Japan, Canada, and almost all of the industrialized countries in Europe have stabilized their size of population. There are, however, reasons for the continued growth which is expected chiefly in Asia, Africa and Latin America. One reason for continued growth is the "disproportionately large number of young people moving into their reproductive years" a group estimated at more than 40 percent of the world's present population. This includes China and the United States.[4]

A second reason is the Vatican's persistent campaign for more births. This is evident in its worldwide opposition to contraceptive birth control and to abortion, but also in the direct appeals of the Pope. An article in the *Pittsburgh Tribune Review* said: "In the early 1980s, Pope John Paul II came to Nairobi and counseled Kenyans, whose population at that time was the fastest growing in Africa, probably in the world, to 'be fruitful and multiply.'"[5] The *New York Times* reported "In preparation for next month's Earth Summit in Rio de Janeiro, Vatican diplomats have begun a campaign to try to insure that the gathering's conclusions on the issue of runaway population growth are not in conflict with Roman Catholic teaching on birth control."[6]

There has been a special strong focus on the United States by the Vatican because of its world influence and its funding of contraceptives in many developing countries. *Time* magazine reported: "In response to the concerns of the Vatican, the Reagan administration agreed to alter its foreign aid program to comply with the church's teaching on birth control."[7] President Bush also blocked all U.S. funding for the United Nations Population program. The Republican Congress in response to Vatican loyalist Christopher Smith (N.J.) has for many years linked payment of the U.S. debt to the United Nations with a provision against funding family planning, overseas of any government or private agency that was involved in funding, lobbying for, or even discussing abortion.

A third reason for world population growth is that many developing countries in Asia, Africa and elsewhere do not have enough industry to provide jobs for women outside the home. While on sabbatical leave in 1969 in the Philippines I made a population study which revealed that in two cities, Manila and Cebu, with substantial industrial development and jobs for women, there were fewer children per family and there was wide use of contraceptives. It was also apparent that in many places in the Philippine Islands there was no electricity. One government official said, "In those places there is nothing to do at night except go to bed!"

Patriarchy and the devaluation of women is also a problem. The driver of the car that took our family shopping once a week in Manila was proud of the fact that he had twenty-two children, although five wives had died in the process.

Men not only stay fertile longer than women do, but are more promiscuous. "In some sub-Saharan African countries the average man wants to have more than ten children, in part because large families serve as cultural symbols of a man's virility and wealth. Consequently, under male-dominated social systems that tend not to hold fathers accountable for the well-being of their children, the women of the Third World are increasingly finding themselves doing hard work for food as well as walking several miles every day for water and fuel wood, all with babies on their backs or at their breasts."[8]

Jennifer Mitchell in *World Watch* wrote:

In the developing world, at least 120 million married women and a large undefined number of unmarried women want more control over their pregnancies, but cannot get family planning services. This unmet demand will cause about one third of the projected population growth in developing countries over the next fifty years, or an increase of about 1.2 billion people.[9]

The World Health Organization estimates that 585,000 women die each year during pregnancy and childbirth. "The death toll," according to World Watch, "underestimates the magnitude of the problem. For every maternal death as many as thirty women sustain oftentimes crippling and lifelong health problems related to pregnancy."[10] Moreover, many of these deaths and lifelong health problems could have been prevented by access to family planning services and safe, legal abortions.

It is not only the deaths of thousands of women that make this a culture of death, but the projected deaths of some 23 million Africans because of the spread of HIV and the failure of governments to control it.[11] The Vatican has also strongly opposed any funding of condoms to prevent the spread of these diseases.

The life expectancy in Zimbabwe, Kenya, Namibia, and South Africa of millions of people has been reduced from about 65 years to 38 or 39. In some hospitals 70 percent of the beds are occupied by AIDS patients. In turn the loss of so many workers unable to work means the loss of—or reduction of—food, security, and nutrition to their families.

While epidemics as well as natural catastrophes cause the deaths of thousands in some areas, the birth rate continues to climb in China, India, Latin America, the Middle East, and Africa. In these and other areas that are already overpopulated, there are many serious dangers to the ecosystems of the world.

In one sense, overpopulation is not the cause of all the world's problems, but the effect of many causes. Yet it is overpopulation which ultimately threatens every ecosystem on the planet.

One is the loss of cropland. Urbanization takes an increasing amount of land. Los Angeles County with "more than 9 million people was the most productive agricultural county in the United States at the end of World War II." It lost its orchards to industry, freeways, and houses. "Two of New York City's worth of cropland" or almost 31,000 acres "were paved over each year between 1982 and 1992."[12] Urbanization also needs transport systems and recreational areas such as golf courses.

China expects to build 600 new cities by 2010, probably even some of them with golf courses.[13]

Mountain ecosystems have also been affected by overpopulation. A 1995 book dealing with mountain ecosystems and cultures notes that "In industrial countries, mass tourism and recreation are now fast overtaking the extractive economy as the largest threat to mountain communities and environments."[14]

It is reported that 9 million people visit the Great Smoky National Park each year, more than 275,000 going annually to the Indian Himalayas, tourism in the European Alps exceeding 100 million visitor days, more than 250 golf courses in the Alps expected to grow to 500, and comparable resorts and activities in Latin America, Japan and other areas. Pollution, diversion of water, extinction of species, carbon monoxide emissions from heavy traffic, and other damage to the natural environment are evident in many mountainous areas.

Another part of our ecosystem damaged by growth of population is the world's forests. They are being destroyed by people in need of fuel, by logging for construction, by clearing of forests for road-building, and for numerous other reasons. Sandra Postel wrote:

A forest producing wood for timber is also protecting upland soils from erosion, safeguarding downstream croplands from flooding, providing habitat for countless plant and animal species, and storing carbon that would hasten global warming if released to the atmosphere. But because these are social benefits, a private investor doesn't take them into account.[15]

Forests also provide food, fish, spices, oils, resins and medicines, as well as purifying the water. For example, "At least one third of the world's 9,000 known fish species live in the Amazon river and its naturally flooded forest."[16]

Probably the most serious result of the continuing growth of population is the growing shortage of fresh water. In 1992 various articles appeared in major newspapers about the shortage of water. "People withdraw the equivalent of Lake Huron from the world's rivers, streams, lake and aquifers each year, and withdrawals have been increasing 4 to 8 percent a year in recent decades," wrote William K. Stevens in the *New York Times*.[17] He continued:

> Supplies of water are beginning to fall behind in northern China and the World Resources Institute says shortages could reach crisis proportions in the Middle East before this decade is out. Shortages have become a familiar and serious problem in the southwestern United States, particularly in California.

The shortage of water in the Mideast is illustrative. "No matter what progress irrigated agriculture makes, Jordan's natural water at this pace will be exhausted in 2010," predicted Elias Salameh, founder and former director of the University of Jordan's Water Research and Study Center.[18] "Jordan then will be totally dependent on rain water and will revert to desert. Its ruin will destabilize the entire region."

Salameh continued, "None of the regional countries—Egypt, Israel, Jordan, Syria, Saudi Arabia or the Gulf Emirates can be self-sufficient in food in the foreseeable future, if ever. All Middle East economics must be restructured away from agriculture because of a lack of water."

In southern Africa "eleven countries with a population of more than 120 million are living under a drought previously unknown to the region in its sweep and severity. . . . Lakes have dried up. . . . 17 million people are now under direct threat of starvation" wrote Anthony Lewis in the *New York Times*.[19]

By 1999 a number of French and American corporations were competing for water contracts in the United States on the assumption that many municipal water plants would be transferred to private contractors. (John Tabliabue, *New York Times* business section, August 24, 1990) According to John Bastin of the European Bank of Reconstruction and Development, "Water is the last infrastructure frontier for private investors." (Ruth Caplan, paper distributed in Seattle at World Trade Organization protest 2000).

And Tom Osborne, a member of the Newfoundland Legislature, was quoted as saying, "Water is the commodity of the next century, and those who possess it and control it could be in a position to control the world's economy."[20]

Water is not just for drinking. "Producing a ton of harvested grain consumes about 1,000 tons of water" And grain is "the source of roughly half of the calories humans consume directly."[21]

Finally, we must consider the impact of overpopulation on poverty, unemployment, migration of people, and war. The Pentagon in its 1999 Quadrennial Defense Review justified its huge military establishment with these words:

> Some governments will lose their ability to maintain public order and provide for the needs of their people, creating the conditions for civil unrest, famine, massive flows of migrants across international borders. . . . Uncontrolled flows of migrants will sporadically destabilize regions of the world and threaten American interests and citizens.

The evidence of a planetary population problem includes the cataclysmic increase in the number of economic refugees as well as those from what have been called "population wars." According to the United Nation High Commissioner of Refugees, the world had 27.4 million refugees in 1995. This was 4.4 million higher than the year before and 17 million higher than the preceding year. Another 20 million were refugees within their own countries.

Out of a global work force of about two billion eight-hundred million people, at least 120 million are unemployed and another 700 million are underemployed or without enough income to meet basic human needs. A major reason for this is that in many countries there is not enough arable land or water to provide food for the people who live there. Nor is there enough available employment for landless people. This has been a reason for both economic migration and the tension leading to population wars.

An article by Hal Kane in a 1995 *World Watch* said, "Apart from the long-established migratory pressures of war, persecution, and the pull of economic opportunity, migrants are now responding to scarcities of land, water, and food that are much more widespread than ever before. They are leaving because of overcrowding in decrepit squatter settlements that now house huge numbers of people, because of post-Cold War changes in political climate, and because of widening disparities of income. This is why *most of the world's migration has yet to happen* [emphasis added]."

We think of this as a problem in the rest of the world, but even in America there are hundreds of thousands of economic refugees. More than one-and-a-half million refugees from Mexico, El Salvador, Guatemala, and other countries below Mexico live within 25 miles of the United States, hoping to cross the border. Hundreds of thousands live in huts, makeshift tents, lean-tos, and caves without adequate sanitation or health and law enforcement assistance. Estimates are that more than a million residents of Tijuana just south of San Diego live under these conditions. They and other millions are malnourished and many have communicable diseases, including AIDS. Their future seems dim.

Some of them are also refugees from earlier wars in Central America and Mexico, fought over control of land.

The most devastating population war in recent history is the war in Rwanda which began in 1994. It began in the most densely populated country in Africa, where virtually all arable land was in use by the mid-1980s. Michael Renner of the World Watch Institute noted that in Rwanda "half of all farming took place on hillsides by the mid-80s, when overcultivation and soil erosion led to falling yields and a steep decline in total grain production."

In 1995 there were 1,800,000 refugees living outside its borders and close to one million Rwandans had been slaughtered in the struggle between Tutsi people and Hutus. The British medical journal, *The Lancet*, said Rwanda had the world's highest fertility rate and "the fact that any country could now be in intensely Catholic Rwanda's predicament is an indication of the world's and especially the Holy See's reluctance to face the issues of population control."

Renner noted that:

the Hutu leaders that planned and carried out the genocide in 1994 relied strongly on heavily armed militias who were recruited primarily from the unemployed. These were the people who had insufficient land to establish and support a family of their own and little prospect of finding jobs outside agriculture. Their lack of hope for the future and low self esteem were channeled by the extremists into an orgy of violence against those who supposedly were to blame for these misfortunes.

The conclusion to be drawn from the catastrophes that have occurred and those that are predictable is that most can be understood in the context of population growth. The implications for dealing with the problems are enormous. Work must begin with efforts to get universal recognition that the world's material resources belong not just to the developed countries able to claim them and exploit the workers of the developing world, but to those native workers and also other inhabitants of the land, forests, rivers and oceans. We must recognize that the world's natural resources do not exist for private profit but for social benefit of all its inhabitants.

Some of the decisions regarding the increase in the number of these inhabitants revolve around personal and national recognition that women worldwide are not the property of their husbands or

Ecohumanism

fathers, but moral decision-makers with respect to their health, their lives and their future. Neither are they public property for governmental decisions that require them to become pregnant or remain pregnant against their will. Unless we recognize women's rights, the dire consequences for life on the planet are enormous.

Notes

1. "Challenges of the New Century," *State of the World 2000, World Watch Institute*, p. 5.

2. Ibid., p. 5.

3. *Vital Signs 1998, World Watch Institute*, p. 102.

4. Ibid., p. 19.

5. April 4, 1998.

6. May 29, 1992.

7. February 24, 1992

8. "Men, Sex and Parenthood in an Overpopulating World," *World Watch*, (April, 1994), pp. 13-14.

9. January/February, 1998.

10. 1997 World Watch Vital Signs.

11. State of the World 2000, World Watch Institute, pp. 4-5.

12. Gary Gardner, "Shrinking Fields: Cropland Loss in a World of Eight Billion," *World Watch* (July 1996), pp. 16f.

13. Ibid., pp 18-19.

14. Derek Denniston, "High Priorities: Conserving Mountain Ecosystems and Cultures," *World Watch Paper*, (February 1995), p. 36.

15. Sandra Postel, "Toward a New Eco-nomics," *World Watch*, (September/October 1990) p. 23.

16. Jane Abramovitz, "Taking a Stand: Cultivating a New Relationship With the World's Forests," *World Watch Paper*, (April 1998), p. 12.

17. May 5, 1992.

18. *Washington Post,* May 14, 1992.

19. July 10, 1992.

20. *Washington Post,* August 23, 1999.

21. Sandra Postel, "Dividing the Waters," *World Watch Paper*, (September 1996), p. 13.

ELIMINATING POVERTY IN OLD AGE[1]

Gerald A. Larue

In his book *Rethinking Life and Death*, Peter Singer postulates a new ethic and his "Fifth New Commandment" is "Do not discriminate on the basis of species."[2] In terms of our concern for global ecology one can only agree. However, my focus will be on the human species, and in particular the elderly men and women who live in poverty.

In a troubled world, with so many places torn apart by religious, ethnic, and political strife, with Africa plagued with genocide and hundreds of thousands migrant refugees, and with disease and starvation taking their toll in lives, it would seem that a focus on the elderly could be considered far too narrow. But the elderly do not exist in isolation. Their lives and their existence are interwoven with life everywhere on planet earth. Poverty in old age reflects a general state of poverty in the world and therefore the issue has relevance for the people of the world as a whole. Not only is it important to confront the reality of poverty, but how we respond will tell us, in part, who we are and what we are as human beings.

I begin with a dictionary-style definition of poverty, which, like most dictionary statements, tends to be barren and rather cold. Poverty is defined as the scarcity, dearth, lack of a socially acceptable income or means of obtaining the fundamental necessities or comforts essential for sustaining or maintaining a decent standard of living. But, we may ask, what constitutes a decent standard of living? A decent standard of living embraces basic needs such as food, shelter, healthcare, and security. What is omitted from this definition is the fact that without these prerequisites and without human contact, individual life lacks energy, purpose, meaning, or hope, and often includes suffering and isolation leading to an early death. The issues embraced in a focus on the elderly in poverty grow out of ethical concern for the well-being and welfare of an ever-increasing older population.

Today's elderly are unique. We live in a time when science and technology have changed our view of who and what we are. We, the elderly, represent the first generation to have seen the earth from outer space. We have been made cognizant of the fact that humans are no more nor less than one of millions of life forms that, over billions of years, have evolved as habitants of a rather small piece of cosmic matter circling a rather small star in the immensity of space. We know that what Darwin proposed in 1871,[3] namely that human life originated in Africa and over the millennia migrated from that continent to develop into the multidimensional families of humankind, has now been confirmed by recent DNA studies.[4] We know, too, that through this same DNA research, it can now be established scientifically that we are all of one family, offspring of African parents. Like children in any family, we have our similarities and our unique differences and needs. These scientific findings suggest that any reasonable approach to poverty in aging must rest on a global familial ethic rather than a global village concept.

The problem with the current global village image is that it may emphasize communal differences and group-separateness rather than our familial oneness. The familial ethic requires that my personal concern for poverty in aging recognize that those who suffer poverty, wherever they might live in the world, are not just my neighbors in a global village, they are my brothers, my sisters, my children, and my parents. They are not those others who may live in my village, they are my family.

DNA/RNA studies are presently informing us that all earthly life forms originated billions of years ago as virus in the primeval seas. Human beings share with all flora and fauna a common origin. All life forms on planet earth are interrelated and our existence and well being are intimately tied to these other life forms. Deforestation, atmospheric pollution, soil and water pollution, and our growing population continue to place new strains on the plant and animal life that eons ago saved earth from a fate similar to the greenhouse effect on planet Venus.[5] We are informed that presently we are losing about one million species per year. This kind of information suggests that our efforts on behalf of today's elderly and the elderly of tomorrow must not ignore ecology.

With familial ethics as our starting point, our concern becomes universal and rises above national, religious, ethnic, and sexual boundaries each of which contributes to artificial divisions that only serve to separate the human family into conflicting, and often warring. camps. Solving the plight of elders in poverty cannot be the responsibility of any one nation or any one group. The problem is a family problem and only as we act together as members of a global family will we be able to lift burdens of poverty and pain, loneliness, hunger and despair, from the lives of the elderly throughout our one world.

What is involved in a family ethic approach?

1. A familial ethic begins with the broad recognition that all members of our human family, including the elderly, have the right to food, clothing, shelter, education, health care, and both environmental and economic security. What must be acknowledged is that as members of the one human family we

have responsibilities to guarantee that these basic survival rights are observed.

2. A family ethic, focused on the poor elderly, recognizes that among the elderly are those who have the ability to work and contribute to society and that these persons have a familial duty to engage in work that will contribute to society and that will help to provide for their own care and for the care of significant others.

3. A familial ethic calls upon family members who are business owners and managers, upon those in government and in positions of power and authority, to recognize the work potential of their elderly family members and to open doors of opportunity to enable the elderly to continue to work and earn so long as they are able. In other words, the family ethic decries the ageism that denies competent elderly the right to work and earn income. For most of us, involvement in life and work contributes more to feelings of worth and dignity than retirement from life.

4. The familial ethic calls upon all family members to protect, honor, and nurture the elderly when they become frail and are no longer able to engage in productive work, to give honorable recognition to what elders have contributed to society by providing a life–enhancing environment for their remaining years of life.

5. The degree of commitment to a family ethic can be determined by the ways in which the elderly poor are faring.

How do we begin to respond to the demands of a familial ethic? We begin with a commitment that calls upon each member of the human family to work towards building a more humane society— a society designed to enable human beings to act in their personal relationships and in the larger community to help create a better world. Our commitment is to the worth and dignity of the individual and to treating each member of the human family in ways that evoke the best and finest attributes. Our commitment is to the present and to the future.

Our initial responsibility is to discover what we can learn from one another. By sharing knowledge, programs, and ideas, we draw from experiences and successes and learn from failures, as we move toward the day when poverty will no longer be a problem. For example, one problem faced by the elderly poor is lack of proper health care. All first-world countries, with the exception of the United States and South Africa, have embraced cradle-to-grave national health programs. Consequently, men and women in countries with a national health program will enter old age in a healthier state than if they had been without health coverage throughout their lives. In the United States some *43* million people are presently without health insurance. Some of these are the men and women who will be tomorrow's elderly. They will enter into old age with medical problems that should have been addressed earlier and which, because of neglect, will have grown in complexity over the years. Among the present American elderly are those whose income is so limited that they exist on the edge of poverty often too poor to pay for medications and the costs of Medicare-provided medical treatment and yet not poor enough to come under the protection of Medicaid which is designed for those who are in dire poverty and have nothing. This shameful state of affairs suggests that we can learn little about the elimination of the elder healthcare problems related to poverty from the United States of America or from South Africa. Instead, these powerful nations are to be educated by other first world countries. Furthermore, reports on retirement homes and nursing homes for the frail elderly indicate that the some of the best information will come from Europe.[6] From European government-supported institutions, like those in Nor-

way, we will find the models and essential guidance for the protection of the frail poor elderly.

The task of eliminating poverty among the elderly worldwide
must be approached from two stances: one where a nation relies on
help from the outside; the other related to the empowerment of
elders within a country. Presently, response to crises threatening
human wellbeing in any one country is international that is to say
that help comes from the outside. Immediate needs for food and
medicine prompt shipments of food and aid from other nations.
What we learn from these humanitarian responses to crisis is the
willingness of members in our human family to reach out to those
in need even to the extent of risking the lives of those who would
be of service.[7] However, the attacks on the barracks of the International Red Cross in Chechnya and the murder of six workers in December, 1996, led the International Committee of the Red Cross to
re-evaluate some aspects of their humanitarian outreach. Similar
evaluations are being undertaken by Doctors Without Borders and
the British organization Medical Emergency Relief International.
Humanitarian aid under the protection of United Nations armed
forces raises problems in that the international troops tend not to
be recognized as "neutral" by combatants. Further, beyond risking
the lives of those who would deliver aid, is the frustration that
grows out of the looting of resources by warlords and other bandits
who utilize for themselves or sell the stolen food and medical supplies.[8] Anti-humanitarian acts committed by those in power may
serve to limit international outreach to populations in need.

What is ignored in short-term rescue programs is the reality of
long-term poverty that impacts upon the elderly whose needs are
often set aside in favor of the young who constitute the future.[9]
What also may be ignored is the danger of ageism inherent in humanitarian outreaches, particularly when groups such as the elderly
become the primary targets of rescue operations. Ageism is the

tendency to view the elderly as a group, helpless and perhaps incompetent and unable to help themselves. The notion of elder im-
potence is not accurate. Most elderly persons live independent
lives, taking care of themselves and determining their day-to-day
patterns of living. Only when crippling infirmities afflict them do
they turn to others or to social services for help. On the other
hand, when negative ageist attitudes become pervasive, the elderly
suffer as victims of a stereotyping that limits their potential for
self-expression, self control and self rescue. What is even more
troubling is that the stereotype may become a self-fulfilling prophecy should competent elderly accept the negative image and actually become helpless and incompetent.[10]

The focus on elder poverty raises a complex problem. The
meaning of poverty may vary in different contexts. Let me set the
stage. We are in an era of dramatic change. Those of us who are
older, who were born during the first quarter of the 20th century,
have lived through more changes in one lifetime than any other generation in human history and we have, for the most part, adapted
to these changes. We have survived. Among the many changes that
have taken place, the following four are important:

1. the increase in human longevity resulting in growing numbers
    of elderly people

2. generational mobility and the changing nature of the family
    which contributes to problems faced by the elderly

3. population growth, which threatens the future of the world
    with potentials for starvation and conflict and which gives
    promise of ecological problems through the ruthless exploita-
    tion of natural resources

4. the expansion of rapid communication systems

No one of these four developments stands alone they are, as we shall see, interrelated.

Modern sanitation, medicine, and pharmacy have made possible the conquest of diseases that once took the lives of children.[11] Those who, in earlier times, would have died in childhood now live into adulthood and old age. Today, modern engineering, combined with modern medicine, has produced machines that make possible the prolongation of life for the elderly—indeed keeping alive some who are in a persistent vegetative state and no longer able to function in or relate to the external world.[12] The sophisticated information and equipment produced by such life-sustaining developments are shared throughout the world by way of modern transportation of hardware and electronic communication of data. As a result, the numbers of the elderly and the numbers of frail elderly are on the rise worldwide. However, in developing nations, where the poverty levels reach as high as 46 percent, the lives of citizens are shortened proportionately. In countries like Japan and the United States, children born today can expect to live well into the late seventy years of age. In poverty stricken developing countries, the age expectancy is under fifty years of age for today's newborns. Our concern with poverty must look beyond today's poor elderly to those who will comprise the coming elder generation. As skills in life extension continue to develop, we can expect those who come from poverty areas to enter into old age with illnesses that will tax budgets for medical treatments.

Generational mobility refers to the migration of family members often in search of employment. The trend towards urbanization draws individuals and families from rural areas to the cities. Young people, who in past generations remained with or near their aging parents, now find employment in distant cities where they establish new homes and develop ways of thinking and living that do not always coincide with traditional familial patterns. The result is the dissolution of family networks. Recent longitudinal research by my colleague, Dr. Vern Bengston, has demonstrated that there is solid evidence that in the United States traditional ethnic values are still in effect.[13] The elderly are often provided with familial support whether that support derives from a sense of duty, or fear of failing to live up to expected ethnic responsibilities, or out of familial bonding and love.[14] But the patterns are changing. Because of distance, familial gatherings can become sporadic. Communication depends upon the telephone, the postal services and, perhaps, electronic equipment such as Fax or e-mail. These communications are important but they lack the benefits derived from in-person contact the energizing warmth of physical hugs, the opportunity to observe what is truly happening in the lives of the elderly and the insights that derive from extended conversations. The elderly are often left to fend for themselves until some tragedy brings the family together. In countries where the social ethic has taught youth that they are responsible for the welfare of their elders, the erosion of support patterns may be slower, but the erosion is taking place.

Lack of familial support, and lack of personal income, compel many elderly to become almost completely dependent upon the government for survival including healthcare, food, and shelter. Funding for elder care comes from taxes. With the growing numbers of frail elderly, the costs of elder care are on the rise and tax burdens for the younger generations are increased. Consequently, intergenerational tensions are developing and they find expression through the public media newspapers, magazines, radio, television, and the internet.[15]

Tensions also exist within individual families. Even as patterns of family living undergo change, support of elderly parents continues to be of concern for the younger generations; but responsibility for the care of the frail elderly often creates intergenerational problems. In families where both parents work to maintain a decent standard of living and try to pay for advanced education for their offspring, costs and responsibilities for the care of elders can become a burden. When elders sense that they are burdens, feelings of self-worth degenerate. Sometimes, due to familial stress, elders are abused. Reports of elder abuse are increasing worldwide. Neglect, abandonment, psychological and physical maltreatment are tangible expressions of the frustration, impatience and anger felt by children toward their aging parents. The shrinking boundaries of the place-world of the frail elderly, plus their growing dependency upon others for companionship, food, shelter, and healthcare, lowers self-esteem and produces depression and despondency, to the end that many look forward to death.[16]

Much of what I am reporting is based on an analysis of what has been occurring in the United States. At the present time, the majority of the elderly population in first world countries is independent and able to care for itself.[17] Much of the care for frail elderly is in-home. However, in the United States there are some 6 million elderly persons suffering physical impairment, more than 3 million have Alzheimer's disease and these handicaps place particular stresses on the family. It is not surprising to find that more than one million elderly are abused or neglected. About 12 percent of the population of the United States is composed of persons over 65 years of age and by the year 2030 that percentage will swell to 25 percent. These figures, together with the erosion of the traditional family with its patterns of familial support, suggest the potential for increasing isolation of the elderly, the growth of ageism and increase in elder abuse.

Throughout the world, schematic depictions of age patterns have undergone dramatic change. In the past, the diagram employed was that of a pyramid featuring a broad base of younger people who could easily support the narrow peak representing the relatively few elderly at the top. Today, the diagram is rectangular with the elderly equaling in number the population counts in younger generations. The slight bulge in the rectangle, which represents the baby boomers who are about to enter the category of late adulthood or old age and retirement, suggests that the diagram may soon become top-heavy with more and more individuals reaching old age and requiring more and more help in sustaining life. In 1953, in the United States, there were 16 workers to every retiree. Today, there are five and by 2030 there will be fewer than three.[18]

How do we confront these problems? What can we learn from one another? What steps must be taken to help our aging fathers and mothers today? What can we do to guarantee life free of poverty for the millions who will constitute the aged of tomorrow?

We must begin with facts. Problems associated with poverty and the dissolution of the traditional family in one country may not be those in another country. For example, Holland and Sweden are relatively small countries when compared with the United States or Russia or China. While there will be migration of children within those nations, the distances that separate families will tend to be less than in larger countries. Visitations and family gatherings can be more frequent thus encouraging intimate familial support for the aged and thereby diminishing the elders' feelings of isolation and abandonment. Where thousands of miles separate family members, regular family gatherings are limited and the plight of aging parents may be more readily ignored or dismissed. Lack of physical contact with the life situation of elderly parents, opens doors to unrecognized or ignored poverty and need. What immediate steps must be taken to alleviate poverty among the elderly? Our intentions are noble, we want to help, but too often we feel handicapped and impotent. But we are not entirely helpless and there are some things we can do to begin the process of change.

1. To begin, we need information. There is a growing field of knowledge about the changing status of the elderly in the

various countries of the world.[19] What we need to know now is what constitutes poverty among the elderly in countries throughout the world poverty defined in terms of local needs—food, shelter, healthcare, security and feelings of self-worth. We need to know how these needs are defined in different settings and what is being done locally to meet these needs. We need to know what percentage of the population of the elderly in any given country are poor? Although the basic needs will be similar, details in the definitions of poverty will vary from place to place. It seems to me that the time has come for the formation of an International Committee to determine the nature and extent of poverty among the elderly in the different countries of the world and what is needed in each case to alleviate the situation.[20]

2. We need to be able to determine how the needs of the elderly poor are best responded to in different countries. Desperate situations may call for immediate assistance from nations outside of the local situation, but long term protection for future elders must also be developed locally.

3. Where there is elder abuse, places of refuge must be established immediately.[21]

4. Where health needs are not being met, a national health care program must be established with provisions for nursing homes and long-term care facilities. The nature of health care programs may differ from locale to locale, but successful patterns presently in existence can provide working models.

5. Where poverty results in lack of proper nutrition, food surpluses must be directed to meet the needs of the hungry whether they are young or old. It has been estimated that 800 million people are presently undernourished. The bulk of the underfed population, those receiving less than 2,100 calories

per day is concentrated in sub-Saharan Africa, Haiti, Afghanistan and parts of Central and South America.[22]

6. These responses, which combine short term and long term programs, need always to be entered into with an eye to the future and, in particular, the future for those who will become old during the 21st century. It is time to take a serious look at the burgeoning world population.

7. During the past 26 years over one billion people have been added to the world population. At the present rate of growth, it is estimated that by the year 2150, the world population could reach 694 billion.[23] We have been told that the earth's maximum "carrying potential" lies between 12 and 13 billion which, at the present rate of growth, could be reached by 2050. Ninety-five percent of that growth will take place in poor countries. One can visualize the spread of areas of poverty and disease that will dwarf the already overcrowded, festering slums of Calcutta, Mexico City, Sao Paulo and Bombay, to name a few. By 2020 the population of the United States is expected to increase by 29 percent, that of Guatemala by at least 60 percent and that of Mexico by *135* percent. In Kenya, fully half of the population is under age 15—or in the process of becoming sexually mature. No one will deny that discussions of population deal with fundamental and very personal, private, and often religious issues, pertaining to sex, birth, marriage, and death. Nevertheless it has now become clear that the irresponsible breeding of children, without plans or means for their support and education, is both immoral and unethical and contributes to the spread of hunger and malnutrition, particularly among women and children and the aged. Two hundred million children go to bed hungry every night. There is no estimate of how many elderly go to bed hungry each night.

Efforts at population control have been made in China home of one quarter of the world's population. Unfortunately, Chinese cultural mores have created serious ethical issues. Male offspring are preferred and there are reports of the abandonment and exposure of female infants. Ancient and outmoded notions, that lie behind the preferability of male offspring,[24] underscore the need for social education concerning the equality of the sexes.[25] Without education and without the widespread use of artificial birth control, world population will continue to expand and the number of impoverished elderly will grow proportionately. We cannot talk about the elimination of poverty among the elderly without discussing the need for, and means of, population control. This means that, for the protection of the future elderly, we must call on national governments to provide access to family planning services for their citizens, to assist men and women in making decisions about the number of children they desire and are willing and able to support. Artificial birth control equipment and education must be made available worldwide. Indeed, we may be reaching a point where some national governments may be compelled to assume parental roles by determining just how many mouths can be fed, what standard of living they will be able to maintain, and how the citizens of tomorrow are to be educated and provided with potentials for meaning-filled lives. We dare not be indifferent to the implications of uncontrolled human breeding.

Poverty robs an individual of self-esteem. Without self-esteem, the elderly lose faith in their importance as human beings and their relevance in society. The result is depression that affects energy, health, and social well being. Empowerment of the elderly can contribute to self-esteem.

Empowerment requires recognition of the human right to be informed, the freedom to make choices and the freedom to act on those choices. In democratic countries, empowerment can develop through organized groups of the elderly through which they make their needs known and through which they influence the vote. By joining an association that shares common interests, the elderly will experience a sense of belonging, solidarity, and power that can give a special meaning to their existence. Few politicians ignore the power of an idea or of a group that can influence the outcome of an election. Elderpower is a reality in the free world and elders need to be organized everywhere so that they can express that power.[26] Here is where the experience of elder empowerment in developed nations can be transmitted to developing nations. Moreover, each effort toward elder empowerment within a given nation can be augmented by help from the outside. For example, there can be little question that each nation wishes to present itself in favorable terms to the world community. Reports on the conditions of the elderly within a nation and of the efforts of the elderly to change their situation, when published internationally, can affect the ways in which a nation will respond to steps toward elder empowerment. When the public media in any given nation expose the fact that elderly members of our one human family are neglected and robbed of human dignity, there will be pressure within that country to remedy that situation.

Elder empowerment is also important for end-of-life decisions. Modern medical technology is able to keep alive suffering or comatose elderly patients who in earlier times would have died. Medical practitioners, trained to preserve life, tend to employ heroic means to sustain life at any cost. The right of the elderly to make personal decisions regarding the employment or non-employment of heroic treatment for end-of-life ailments is fundamental to maintaining human dignity and personal empowerment right up to the time of death.[27] Worldwide use and legalization of documents like the Living Will and Durable Power of Attorney for Health Care can help to empower the elderly by placing under their control their wishes for end-of-life decisions. In Holland, Switzerland, and Colombia, end-of-life decisions include the right to request doctor-assisted suicide or euthanasia. As life-sustaining techniques continue to be used by the medical profession, even in cases where the patient does not wish to continue to live, there is considerable evidence that some form of end-of-life patterns similar to those available in Holland may be legislated and become legal options in other countries. For example, in the State of Oregon, doctor-assisted-suicide has been over-whelmingly endorsed by the citizens, despite opposition by the Roman Catholic Church and some evangelical Christian groups.[28]

8. Retirement programs terminate the earning power of the elderly. Where an individual is able to continue to work and earn income, he or she should be encouraged to remain employed. The argument that such a policy will produce conflict between the young, who resent the elderly working at jobs they desire, and the elderly who wish to continue working, can be answered by the fact that the expanded population of older men and women that lies just ahead is going to require a larger work force to produce the necessities of life. Therefore, without the need to increase the number of new births to sustain the elderly, the elderly can contribute to the productivity of society and to their own well-being by continuing to work beyond the generally accepted standard retirement age.

9. Finally, because our concern must be for the future, it is imperative that we begin to educate our youth and those of middle age to prepare them for the time when they will become

the elderly segment of population. This education must include information about the following:

- genetic factors

- the relationships between physical health, exercise, food and mental health

- the development of skills and interests that will carry over into retirement and provide activities that will contribute to personal satisfaction and perhaps income

- the fact that learning is a life-time experience and the ability to learn and develop does not cease at any given age

- awareness that the life-experiences of the elderly may contain wisdom that comes only with age and is worth listening to and recording

In other words, youth must be taught to prepare for their own old age and at the same time be made aware of what can be learned about life and aging from today's elders. Studies have shown that ageism extends from kindergarten into maturity.[29] Only through an appreciation of what it means to age and of what aging entails, and through knowledge of how to contribute to a meaning-filled, secure, and—we would hope—happy old age, can the future for the elderly be made secure. In other words, empowerment for the elderly of tomorrow must come through education today.

Education in aging should begin in primary school and continue into old age. Programs should move beyond the presentation of dry statistics. Education in aging must truly live up to the concept involved in the term "education" which means "to lead out." "Leading out" involves the breaking down of walls of isolation and ignorance to present new horizons and new challenges. For the young, actual in-class contact with the elderly is important. The elderly can come prepared to answer questions and talk about their life. For college age and middle-age, it will focus on understanding the aging process, the financial problems that can impact on the aged, the need to understand national policy as it relates to age, and education in the use of organizations to influence policy. The illnesses and disabilities that handicap some elderly can challenge youth to engage in research and community outreach to find ways to protect those who are presently old and themselves as they join the ranks of the old. For the elderly it will encompass ways to continue to contribute to the growth and life of the community and the world as well as the continuing development of skill and interests that enhance life.

For me, as an educator, the continuing teaching experience is both exciting and enriching in the hope that in some small way, what I do, how I interact, what I share, will contribute to a better world tomorrow. I believe this kind of involvement and response should be open to every elder.

Notes

1.   This paper was delivered in a different format in December, 1996, at the International Conference on "Eliminating Poverty in Old Age: A Developing Country Perspective" held in Malta by the International Institute on Ageing (INIA). The conference was one part of the INIA's activities in observance of the 1996 United Nations International Year for the "Eradication of Poverty" and the 1999 International Year of the Older Person – "Towards a society For all Ages." The paper was published in James Calleja (edit). 1997. *Eliminating Poverty in Old Age*. Malta: United Nations International Institute on Ageing.

2.   Peter Singer, *Rethinking Life and Death* (New York: St. Martin's Press, 1994), pp. 202f.

3.   Charles Darwin, *Descent of Man* [1871].

4.   Brian Fagen, "All About Eve," *Archaeology* (November/December, 1992), pp. 18-24; Robert Lee Hotz, "Genetic Study Says All Men Have a

Common Ancestor," *Los Angeles Times,* (April 26, 1995), pp. Al, A43; S. Paabo, "The Y Chromosome and the Origin of All of Us (Men)," *Science* 268 (1995), pp. 1141-1142; R. I. Droit, H. Akashi, W. Grant, "Absence of Polymorphism at the ZYF Locus on the Human Y Chromosome" *Science* 268 (1005), pp. 1183-1185.

5. "Rediscovering Planet Earth," *U.S. News and World Report* (October 31, 1988), pp. 56-68.

6. Victor Regnier, *Assisted Living Housing for the Elderly: Design Innovations From the United States and Europe* (New York: Van Nostrand Reinhold, 1996).

7. When Goma, Zaire, fell to rebels, United Nations Relief Workers, together with representatives from religious and national humanitarian and donor agencies, were forced to flee for their lives, abandoning millions of dollars worth of food and equipment donated to aid the needy. Also left behind were the hundreds of native Zairians employees and staff members. Most threatened by the developing situation were the elderly, the disabled, the children and pregnant women. More recently, as reported by The Associated Press, 1/20/ 97, in Ruhengeri, Rwanda, three medical volunteers with the Spanish branch of Doctors of the World were executed by Hutu militants. As a consequence of these brutal murders, Doctors of the World suspended operations in northwestern Rwanda, the British branch of Save the Children, CARL and at least eight other agencies left Ruhengeri. The murder of the medical volunteers came after attacks on aid agencies including a hospital, a UN human rights team and a UN vehicle. (Reported in The *Los Angeles Times,* Jan. 20, 1997), p. A4.

8. William D. Montalbano, "Is Giving Aid Worth the Risk." *Los Angeles Times* (Jan. 25. 1997), pp Al, 14.

9. In the United States, media appeals by various religious groups for funds to aid families in impoverished nations focuses on the plight of children—the needs of the elderly are not mentioned.

10. Extensive studies have demonstrated the negative health and attitudinal potential in "learned pessimism" and the powerful and beneficial potential of "learned optimism." For a discussion of both the negative and positive, see Martin E. P. Seligman, *Learned Optimism* (New York: Alfred A. Knopf, 1991).

11. For example, diseases like measles, whooping cough, scarlet fever, diphtheria, poliomyelitis, etc. can be controlled and virtually eliminated.

12. It is important to note that most major religions have sanctioned the abandonment of heroic medical efforts to keep alive persons whose lives would end naturally without the medical intervention and for whom artificially sustained life constitutes an indignity. One of the most widely discussed cases was that of Nancy Cruzan who was kept alive in a persistent vegetative state for

seven years before her family could receive court permission to remove the life-sustaining feeding tube.

13. Vem Bengston, *Adulthood and Aging: Research on Continuities and Discontinuities* (New York: Springer, 1996).

14. P. M. Hines, N. Garcia-Preto, M. McGoldrick, R. Almeida, S. Weltman, "Intergenerational Relationships Across Cultures," *The Journal of Contemporary Human Services* (Jn. 1992), pp. 323–338.

15. Marjorie A. Pett, Michael S. Caserta, Ann P. Hutton and Dale A. Lund, "Intergenerational Conflict: Middle-Aged Women Caring for Demented Older Relatives, *American Journal of Orthopsychiatry* (Jul.1988), pp. *405* 417; Sue Shellenbarger and Carol Hymowitz, "Over the Hill? As Population Ages, Older Workers Clash With Younger Bosses." *Wall Street Journal* (Jun. 13, 1994), p. 1; Robert L. Jackson, "Seniors' Benefits Unfair to Young, Tax Group Says," *Los Angeles Times* (Nov. 31, 1994), p. A4.

16. Gerald A. Larue, *Geroethics* (Buffalo: Prometheus Books, 1992), ch. 7.

17. Monique Vézina, "Are We Ready to Meet the Challenge?" *Long Term Care in An Aging Society* ed. Gerald A. Larue and Rich Bayly. Buffalo: Prometheus Books, 1992), pp. 13 17.

18. Rob Nelson, "Fix it Now or Risk a Generational War," *Los Angeles Times* (Jun. 12, 1995), p. B9.

19. See the data provided by Ken Tout, "Empowerment: An Aging Perspective," *Population Aging: International Perspectives* (San Diego: University Center on Aging, San Diego State University, 1993), pp. 221-274.

20. The need for cross-regional data was emphasized by Gary R. Andrews and Monique M. Hennink. "Cross-National Research: Asia and the Pacific Experience." *Population Aging: International Perspectives.* San Diego: University Center on Aging, San Diego State University, 1993) pp. 644-683.

21. In the United States, during the 1960s awareness of child abuse prompted the development of laws and the establishment of care facilities for abused children. During the 1970s accounts of spouse abuse resulted in the passing of laws and the development of houses of refuge for abused souses. The awareness of elder abuse that began to develop in the 1980s has not produced comparable legislation nor places of refuge for the abused elderly. In fact, there is solid evidence that fear of separation from an abusive family often keeps abused elderly in fearful, dangerous, and unethical relationships with family members.

22. Ron Tempest, "Ending Hunger Takes on New Complexity," *Los Angeles Times* (Nov.18, 1996), pp. A6, A8.

23. Lee Dye, "Overpopulation *Should* Be Popular Topic," *Los Angeles Times* (Jan. 17, 1996), pp. D4, D13.

24. The same pattern prevails in India where unwanted female infants are often murdered by their parents, and where ultra-sound pregnancy tests can determine the sex of the fetus resulting in the aborting of female fetuses. See Gerald A. Larue, *Freethought Across the Ages* (Amherst, NY: Humanist Press, 1996), pp. 316-318.

25. The sale of female children to be used for prostitution in Indonesia; the employment of female children in factories in India, all speak to the need for education concerning the equal worth of females and males.

26. The problems and dangers associated with the formation and development of elder groups has been clearly set forth by Pratt, Henry J. "Senior Organizations and Seniors' Empowerment: an International Perspective." *Population Aging: international Perspectives* (San Diego: University Center on Aging, San Diego State University, 1993), pp. 321-360.

27. Gerald A. Larue, *Playing God: 50 Religion's Views on Your Right To Die* (Wakefield RI: Moyer/Bell, 1996).

28. In 1996, in Australia's Northern territory and in the State of Oregon in the USA, doctor-assisted-suicide was legalized. However, in Australia, the High Court refused to recognize the *Rights of the Terminally Ill Act.* Meanwhile, there is solid evidence that doctor-assisted-death is taking place virtually worldwide under the protection of the double-effect principle by which increased doses of morphine administered to "control pain" have the "side-effect" of killing the patient.

29. Richard O. Ulin, "Aging Education in the Public Schools: A Global Perspective." *Educational Gerontology* 8 (1982), pp. 537-544; Pamela E. Rich, Robert D. Myrick, Chris Campbell, "Changing Children's Perceptions of Aging: A Multidimensional Approach to Differences by Age, Sex, and Race." *The Gerontologist* 25 (1983), pp. 182-187; Daniel Krause, Rachel Chapin, "An Examination of Attitudes About Old Age in a Sample of Elementary School Children," *Gerontology and Geriatric Education* 7 (1987), pp. 81-91; Sandra McGuire, "Promoting Positive Attitudes Through Aging Education," *Gerontology and Geriatrics Education* 13 (1993), pp. 3-12.

ECOHUMANISM
AND EVOLUTIONARY PSYCHOLOGY

Michael Werner

The modern environmental movement has a short history, but one where the tension between various strategies, goals, and tactics has delayed coherency and coordinated action. As in any new arena of thought, the movement has sought to develop concrete actions and results while still trying to understand itself. Realistically we are only in the first stages of defining the problems, collecting our data, developing an integrated understanding, developing goals, inducing change and uncovering the unanticipated results of those changes.

I think that humanism can provide some insights into some of these conflicts and possibly some resolutions. There are several lessons that I will pose here as useful tools not only for a humanistic approach to environmentalism, but applicable to the general service of environmentalism. These tools can help in the resolution of what are many times poorly understood conflicts.

Humanism maintains that all our values including environmental ones come from human needs and concerns and this warns us that we are always biased towards self-interest. Also, it is used by some to say that humanism is "speciesist" and builds a new "God" of humanity. The argument goes that this leads to the inescapable exploitation of the environment as all other species and the biosphere at large are relegated to a position secondary to human

needs. This is due to this humanist statement being viewed as a hierarchy of values rather than an ontological statement of origins. In
actuality, it is a humbling statement rather than one of arrogance in
that it says that our own subjective biases and prejudices always
mediate human values. It says that there are no external sources
inviolate of human understanding on which to ground our values.
We have no "book," "authority," or other non-human perspective
to ultimately guide us.It warns us that we are always biased toward
self-interest including any thoughts we may have concerning environmentalism.

We have multiple high values. For most religions, the highest
value is usually God. As the 20th century closes, humanism has
moved further and further away from identifying a hierarchy of
values. There is a whole pantheon of high humanist values. There
has been a strong reluctance to identify even with any single secular
idolatry moving away from any logocentric foundational base.
Most humanists would say that out of their high secular values,
human worth and need seems to be the highest value. But, when
practiced as a kind of idolatry, it can be a single-minded force
warping our other values. In his book *The Arrogance of Humanism*, David Ehrenfeld stresses that setting people as the ultimate
value can result in placing other species and, indeed, the entire biosphere subservient to human need. What he describes is a narrow-
minded humanism, one that is mostly a caricature of humanism.
Still, the seventy-year rationalistic communist experiment was al-
legedly based on placing human interest first—and we see how un-
humanistic were the actions, methods, and results when other high
humanist values such as freedom, tolerance, effectiveness, non-
coercion were not considered. We now know we must consider the
whole constellation of values without any clear way to ultimately
determine their relative importance when conflicts occur, as they
always will. This is what is really at the heart of the "speciesist"
argument concerning humanism. Human welfare and concern does

take precedence over other species, but ironically that means that specific individual human welfare must take a back seat at times to other species. It means that gorilla habitats threatened because of human encroachment from farms must be curtailed and other options found because the food needs of a few farmers are not as important as the greater human need to protect such an important species.

Some environmentalists in the humanity versus earth debate argue that human beings are likened unto weeds with their ability to adapt to almost any environment, the lack of external population control mechanisms, and the ability to dominate their ecosystem with the subsequent marginalization of other species. Some extremists have gone so far as to argue that humans are an unnatural curse on the planet that should be eliminated. Extremists on the other side argue that human need must always take precedence over any others. These debates, like most arguments, set up demonized, hyperbolic characterizations of the opponents. What is lost in the arguments is that we all have multiple high values with varying orders of importance, many times in deep conflict with each other. Whenever there are multiple values, we can expect them to be in conflict with each other at times. Our desire for perfectly rational methods to guide us in deciding which values should be regarded most highly has eluded us. We cannot evade the unavoidable conflict of values. What we can do, though, is to resist falling prey to secular or religious idolatry. We can see in the dynamic battle of values, a source of strength rather than a problem. Many times we will find a coherence of values such as when environmental destruction harms human health and existential meaning. Still, it is naive to assume that there will not be conflicts of environmental interests and human interests as well as interests for economic justice, social freedom, property rights, and the like.

How can we justify human welfare as being superior to other species? We can't, ultimately. What we can say is that all we can know is human needs. Still, the differences between species seem to grow less clear with greater understanding. Animals emote, communicate, and have a primitive consciousness. What does make us different, it appears, is language, the degree of consciousness, and the massive inner life that goes along with both. A self-reflective, reasoning consciousness does not ultimately justify placing human welfare over other animal species, but it does make it understandable and consistent with the Darwinian demand of self-preservation.

Environmentalism is best seen in both scientific and experiential ways. Our environmental understanding is a combination of our scientific interpretation of the world and its existential meanings. Humanist environmental authors such E. O. Wilson and Carl Sagan gained an appreciation of our environmental wealth through science. Along the way they became deeply passionate and aware of our environmental richness, its beauty, and its dangerous destruction. Other humanists out of the Romantic tradition such as Henry David Thoreau and Walt Whitman bathed in direct experience with nature and were transformed as well. Some have said that scientific reasoning is reductive and coldly analytical. Those statements come generally from those of the experientialist pole who have not enjoyed the elegance and experiential awe a scientist feels when unlocking the mysteries of nature. While many times a reductive lens must be used in science, science only makes sense when integrated, holistic theories evolve out of the grander range of views.

Science is our best, but not only tool for understanding and solving our environmental problems. Several other traditions have sought to lay claim as the only way to deal with the environmental crises. For example, those within a Rousseauian Romantic framework have argued that science is the cause of environmental destruction. It is argued that indigenous people, because of their closeness with the earth, are more responsive to their environment, and are better guardians of earth's survival.

Ecofeminists see male orientation towards dominance, control, rational bureaucracies, and isolated individualism harming the environment. This is in contrast to feminine attitudes toward nurturing, communitarian orientation, and more intuitional methods.

These perspectives of environmentalism, among others, have the advantage of providing deep insights with relatively narrow lenses of attention. I believe an ecohumanism has the advantage of a broader integration of various perspectives.

Environmental problems are characterized many times by both unintended consequences of human action and the balancing of known tradeoffs. We have seen asbestos being used as a marvelous nonflammable heat insulator that reduces energy consumption, only to discover years later that it cost tens of thousands of lives as well. Dams used to prevent flooding wreak havoc on native aquatic species. Coal-burning power plants ease our physical burden, but result in strip-mine wastelands and global warming. Science and technology have not lived up to their promise in many cases because of unintended side effects and because the competing costs to the environment have not been known. Scientific arrogance results in thinking we have more knowledge than we really have, and that an enlarging science can solve any and all problems. Science and technology, like any recourse, have limits. To be sure, we have no idea what astounding new developments may arise to get us over one crisis or another as evident by surprising success of the "green revolution." Still, we can no longer blind ourselves with a utopian vision of the capabilities of science and technology.

Despite its inherent limitations, science is our most powerful tool for understanding our environmental crisis. Science is our most powerful tool for predicting future problems. Science is our most powerful tool for predicting the effects of the changes we might make. Science, however, cannot tell us how to balance our many values for a given situation. It can only help predict potential outcomes from alternative strategies. Science by itself cannot effect social and political change, although it can tell us what methods might be most effective.

Science seldom changes people's hearts and value structures, but it can tell us effective ways to get those changes to occur. Technology, a source of much of the environmental degradation, can just as easily be turned towards healing those wounds if we have the resolve to do so. An effective environmental psychology makes us aware and responsive to an earth too small, and with a biosphere that is too thin, to spread toxins indiscriminately. It is a psychology that nurtures our environment and all the life forms as a response to humanity's important needs of survival, joy, and connectedness.

We can't return to prescientific and pretechnological times. We can't abandon science and technology because we need them in the service of environmental enhancement. At the same time we know that unintended consequences increase with the complexity of a system. There is currently no life sustaining system available to us larger than our planet. Consequently, our environmental science, technology and politics must remain cautious, humble and reflectively self-critical.

Using Evolutionary Psychology

Science can't effect environmental change—only people can. To my mind, there is no greater immediate need than to uncover how to motivate ourselves, our neighbors, our country, and all the world's people to the urgency of our environmental crisis. Some environmental utopianists envision a retreat to a prescientific society, some look to "earthbased" religions. Some see changes occurring by purely political means and some by purely technical means. As in most stubborn problems, a multipronged approach is probably going to be most useful.

One area that I believe can help us is that of evolutionary psychology. This burgeoning field tells us that there is a human nature that is predisposed to help our genes survive. Traits of survival, tribalism, reproduction, social status, danger avoidance and dominance are "hardwired" into us. These powerful urges can at times override the most powerful social inducements.

Evolutionary Psychology offers both an understanding of the origins of our environmental crisis and some of the solutions. Elaborate, abstract reasons are sometimes given for overpopulation, ignoring the reality of sexual gratification. We ask why even educated environmentally aware people fall prey to over consumption, when those that observe human motivation can easily see we gather goods as symbols of social status. We bemoan how indigent Brazilian farmers clear out rain forests only to have the soil turn infertile after two to three years. The simple answer is survival. Many times we think we can work to eliminate these drives by education and consciousness raising. While we can and should work to minimize the destructive elements of human nature, they can never be fully overcome and our instincts, like a Phoenix, will rise out of the ashes of naive social engineering. The Soviets thought they could eliminate self-interest; the Catholics thought they could eliminate sexual drive in their clergy; more primitive, egalitarian societies are quickly converted to societies based on status symbols and conspicuous consumption and not the other way around. History tells us clearly that trying to fool Mother Nature doesn't work very well.

Rather than trying to change or ignore human nature, a better approach is to ask how we can turn our instinctual drives to our benefit in environmental issues in concert—with our cultural methods. Some environmental programs are designed to change people's minds or hearts by consciousness raising. The premise is, if the more rational of us knew the facts and the more emotionally oriented were emotionally transformed, we would act differently. This is of course true, but only to a point.

The question that is still in its infancy is how can we get our basic instinctual urges to work for environmental benefit rather than against it. A plan for development might include asking these questions:

1. How can we confer high status to those who live lives without wastefulness and unbridled consumerism?

2. How can we use sex/survival/social status etc. to reduce overpopulation?

3. How can we link our personal drive for survival with biosphere survival?

4. How can we promote public awareness that our technological addiction may be a barrier to human and environmental values?

While these are just some jumping off questions, progress has already been made on some of these motivational reformulations.

For example, in the Cairo population conference of 1993 sponsored by the United Nations, it was unanimously agreed to promote four solutions to reduce population. The interesting thing is that it was based on scientific evidence that in some cases was counterintuitive or seemingly not connected. The four points are:

1. Raise the literacy rates of women.

2. Provide employment opportunities for women along with access to banking, credit, education, and civil liberties.

3. Lower the infant mortality.

4. Provide access to birth control and family training education.

These are empirically proven methods, when one thinks about them, that represent how using our instinctual drives may benefit us. For example, point two makes sense if one sees economic independence (read as survival) as a way to reduce dependence on their children. Point three makes sense only if we understand that increased infant survival rates improve parent's confidence in the survival of their genes. They become less anxious concerning their own future as they age and are more willing to have fewer, more survivable children. Another example of using Evolutionary Psychology is the experience of the state of Texas in developing an effective antilitter campaign. Earlier programs appealing to beauty, civic duty, cleanliness, and courtesy failed miserably. They then settled on a slogan campaign that radically transformed the behavior patterns of Texans and led to a dramatic cleanup of roadside litter. It simply said, "Don't mess with Texas." By appealing to more chauvinistic tribalism, it became unfashionable to litter and is still their most successful program.

Garrett Hardin, a prominent environmentalist, has long been an advocate of using our evolutionary drives towards environmental policy. He has been a consistent critic of programs that are not in people's self interest, saying they are doomed to failure. His programs always ask how we can get a people's self interest working towards the environment. He has not been afraid to point out that freedom must be tempered by responsibility, and that governmental control limiting freedom in some cases cannot be avoided.

E. O. Wilson, the father of evolutionary psychology, has called our natural affiliation with nature "biophilia" and hopes that we can use this urge towards environmental interests. Critics have pointed out that we also seem to have biological urges to over-populate and use up an environment. Still, if we can awaken our primal love and exploration of nature, it can be an important source of motivation in environmental service. Zoo programs, for example, have been important promoters of awakening biophilic urges.

Some years ago I was involved in the startup of two chapters of Sierra Club. I thought it was interesting that most of the early members were humanists who seemed to find an outlet for their human needs for awe, connectedness, and a certain type of tran-scendental emotional fulfillment in the glories of nature. Following in the footsteps of the early great naturalists, we were heady with the assurance that only youth can have regarding what the problems were and how to solve them. The environmental movement has adapted and changed and the competing tradeoffs for our multiple values appear more apparent with time. Any ecohumanism for the 21st century will see the tragedy of having to choose and have some aspects of our highest values compromised. We might not have the luxury of having a sustainable ecology without some government interventions that are distasteful to freedom lovers. We will constantly have to make choices between human welfare and the welfare of other animals. We will be forced to confront dwindling resources and bite the bullet of our excesses. We will have to give up our ideas of equating progress with growth. We will see that technology cannot always be the savior. We will have to enlarge our minds and hearts while at the same time acknowledging that self-interest is our major driving force. We will have to find ways to extend our altruistic drives that are generally reserved for our families and close tribe members, to humanity at large and our biosphere. We will be forced to confront the reality that building a sustainable future inherently means giving up something of value to us. These are not easy tasks which is why we must garner all our best tools of mind and heart with a wisdom that sees our lives imbedded in a nature that is all and enough.

THE HUMAN IN THE CONTEXT OF NATURE

Harvey B. Sarles

Removal of the Human from Nature

In attempting to develop the concept of ecohumanism, the definition of the human—human nature, the human condition—seems
central to our quest. Although the notion of the human seems apparent, even obvious at times, it is caught up in the history and
politics of ideas which range from metaphysics and religion to notions of economy, psychology, and anthropology.

This is so because the very idea of the human has included an
implicit set of presumptions about nature, thence the place of the
human within or removed from the natural world. These presumptions include actual and apparent differences between what is human and what is not. While the idea of the human might seem to
stand on its own, it has rather been a depiction of the human as
having a certain place or standing among other species. Much of
this thinking is embedded within particular philosophico-religious
traditions whose critique demands that the very idea of what is
human needs to be rethought and recast within an ecohumanism.

Rethinking and reexamining the human is important because our
tendencies deriving from various traditional ways of thinking have
driven ideas of the human as being variously unique, thus separate

211

or independent from other aspects of nature: different in kind from the flora of the world, removed and usually placed above other animal species. In the traditions of thinking about the human, our removal of place from and responsibility to the rest of terrestrial nature has been one of continuous and expanding privilege and arrogance.

In the context of what I will call the *human uniqueness* arguments, much ground of what human means has been developed. However, since the arguments have been particular and often exclusionary, they have focused fairly narrowly on certain characteristics attributed to the human, and have literally neglected or omitted from our view and critique, a great deal of the being and experience of the human condition.

This is to say that our notion of the human has been less than complete and accurate, as we continue to think of the human within often narrow constraints and by-pass much of what, Dewey, for example, calls *human agency*.

No one would deny that we ourselves enter as an agency into whatever is attempted and done by us. That is a truism. But the hardest thing to attend to is that which is closest to ourselves, that which is most constant and familiar. And this closest 'something' is, precisely, ourselves, our own habits and ways of doing things as agencies in conditioning what is tried or done by us...the one factor which is the primary tool in the use of all these other tools, namely ourselves, in other words, our own psycho-physical disposition, as the basic condition of our employment of all agencies and energies, has not even been studied as the central instrumentality.[1]

In addition to the neglect of such basic properties of the human as human agency, much of the depiction of the human has been cast within the attempt to celebrate our uniqueness. There has been a sense that what is human is not only different from, but *better than* any common ancestors or related species. Thus the unique human has been deserving of whatever we can figure out to do with the world in behalf of justifying, celebrating, and advancing what has seemed particularly human. The very idea of a deity who is claimed to have created the human, exemplifies this idea of human removal and privilege.

Historical claims as to the uniqueness of humans are philosophical, but they have also been political. "Man is made in the image of God, and has dominion over all the other species (Gen. 1.26)." In this context, the celebration of human uniqueness is clearly linked with politics, interpreted either as responsibility to preserve, or to utilize the earth. To note this is to remind us that there is a usually implicit politics contained in the definition of the human: particularly (in my experience) within the contexts of those who have actively attempted to remove the human from our evolutionary forbearers. As part of this sense of the human, we are described as being able to do as we wish with all other species.

But human uniqueness arguments have also been utilized in the context of our relations to (the rest of) nature: the justification of using the world's resources in order to benefit and increase the human domain, encouraging us to turn a blind eye to the current moment of impending ecological crises. It also seems to encourage us to devise newly engineered species to serve human ends more than, or rather than to preserve the histories of life on earth in the existences of naturally evolved species.[2]

An implicit politics is also found in what poses and passes as philosophy—but also in science—where the uniqueness of the human usually due to language, rationality, or consciousness is proclaimed, usually prior to much examination of what is particularly human. As an extension of this thinking, many observers are busily listening to signals from outer space searching for extraterrestrial intelligence and the insight into the human which it might offer, rather than actively observing the human within our natural terrestrial contexts to discern how and what we are. Or they are at-tempting to figure how our genes evolved as humans, even as they resist or avoid tuning in to their own bodily experience. Perhaps more astoundingly, from my perspective, we continue to resist the idea-observation promulgated by the philosophical pragmatist G. H. Mead, that we are a social species by our nature. And that we are related to other species, who are also social. Rather, we promote the idea that human consciousness due to our brain is *the* defining attribute of the human.

Indeed, much of the history of thinking about humans essen-tially separate from the rest of nature, is implicit in the Western tradition of so-called idealist thinkers from Plato to Descartes to the present in both science and the humanities. In separating mind from body—a pervasive dualism shapes our thinking about ecohu-manism. In the case of the idealist tradition, existing particularly within the humanities using texts as the guide to truth, the sense of the human especially as the mental leads to the notion that human is particularly the representation of the human in texts and in asso-ciated arts. On the oppositional material side which exalts the body as the human, the current idea that our knowing the brain will somehow explain the human essentially denies much, perhaps most, of human experience.

Within dualism of either axis of body or mind, an incomplete portrayal of the human attempts to determine and explain the hu-man exhaustively. In either case, we end up with an incomplete or false portrayal of the human condition and human nature, omitting most of human agency, for example.

From the idealist tradition, the belief or acceptance of any objec-tive truth, leads many to think that the discussion of the human is either empty or fully political. From the materialist-mechanist tra-dition the human discussion is seen as apolitical. Both of these ap-proaches tell a partial story, leaving us with a human who is peculiarly outside of nature; but both carry a strong set of implications. And their particularities and politics remain pervasive—difficult to note and comprehend—but crucial to extending an ecohumanism.

The re-currency of American Pragmatism attempts, especially, to examine the nature of human agency and experience in our being. Following Dewey, Peirce, and Mead, especially, it is seeking to set out paths of examination of ecohumanism which are more accurate to our nature, and include human agency and experience in defining and understanding the human.

The Human in Nature

One of the principal constructs of humanism is the idea that humans exist within nature. Humans are not removed or remote, not specially created by some grand designer, or coming to the earth from some place different from our prehuman predecessors. We are parts of this earth, having developed or evolved as aspects of nature; engaging in the natural processes shared by all of life; participating particularly in the lines of development and evolution which have led to vertebrates, mammals, and primates—of which we are one line of development.[3]

This is not to say that humans aren't different or unique in many ways—the recognition of the human species indicates that we share some features in common which are different from those of other species. The very definition of species implies human commonalities and some differences from other species. It is to claim that we have evolved naturally, and that we are related to all of terrestrial life, and continue to be aspects of nature, rather than removed or remote from other species.

In attempting to avoid falling into similar presumptions about the human which Western thinking persuades us to follow, it is important to consider critically what it means to think compara-tively. Lest we continue to fall into our historical presumptive thinking, comparative thought needs to proceed, for example, by looking first for commonalities among species. Differences will ap-pear fairly quickly in this fashion. But if we proceed as usual, by presuming to elaborate what we presume to be different about the human, we may well spend eons in elaborating what we have pre-sumed to be unique. And, *pace* Dewey, we will likely neglect and overlook much of what is truly human.[4]

Prior to considering the idea of human within its proper place-ment as an aspect of nature, however, it seems important to recog-nize and critique this considerable history alluded to above. Com-plicating this is the fact that most of us as Western thinkers have been educated to think within dualistic traditions of body and mind. Here the temptation of humanism has been to side with the materialistic-mechanical side of the dualist argument, without pay-ing much attention to the actualities of human experience.

We have been very concerned with how we got here, a sense of what Philip Regal refers to as an *ultimate* biology (how we got here, as distinct from a *proximate* biology which explores what we are doing here).[5] Impressed—reasonably—with the idea that we are related to other species and have co-evolved with them, we tend to call attention to explanations of how genetics *got* us here. We pay much less attention to how humans actually are, having tried to prove that we are aspects of nature, and doing this quite success-fully; at least from the point of view of naturalism.

And while all of the work on evolution helps to undergird the idea that human is an aspect of nature, our examination of the hu-man in and of nature, remains incomplete—as Dewey notes. We are left with a humanism which remains at various odds: with re-ligious ideas of the human as specially created by a deific power; but also at deep odds with much of the humanities, the thinkers and disciplines who favor the idea of the human as represented in and by the texts of all of time. This includes, of course, the Western biblical texts, which create a fairly detailed description of the human removed from nature.

Call it Postmodernism: an attempt to undercut the ideas of nature as aspects of nature; an attempt to shift the idea of external reality from nature to talk or narrative. It stems ultimately (in the West) from the splintering and splitting of the human into the two aspects of being body or mind, and sides with the idea of reality as being located somehow in the mental attributes of the human.

Although the critique of the Postmodernists is cast within the mentalistic side of the mind-body dualism, and neglects or refutes the idea of the human within nature and any ecohumanism, its concerns about the materialistic approach to the human does contain some valid criticisms. Namely, that there is an implicit politics within a so-called scientific approach to the world which neglects to study the history and politics of thought. The recent moves of sociobiology and evolutionary psychology to proclaim that genetic evolution will somehow explain the nature of the human, exhaustively, falls into the 19th century thinking and politics of Social Darwinism. The nature of the human is fully determined, in this thinking, without including the emergent experience and being of the human condition; e.g., human agency as described above by Dewey, or the transformative sociality of our being per Mead.

Ecohumanism within a Recurrent Pragmatism

The future of ecohumanism will be placed with the context of a recurring Pragmatism. Pragmatism attempts to get the study of the human beyond the politics—particularly of Social Darwinism—which have led our thinking to focus primarily on those human attributes which are held to distinguish humans from other species. We have much in common with the rest of nature, and the commonalities need to be further explored and pursued before we seek out what may be particularly unique to humans.

Following Peirce and Dewey, we can begin to rethink the human condition by focusing on the active aspects of our being—in our thinking as well as in our doing. In Peirce's notions of *abduction*, for example, the human is active in perceiving a simple geometric figure. The nature of this activity yet remains, as Dewey tells us, mostly unexplored. There is a great deal of being human which remains implicit, out-of-awareness as linguists are wont to say. All of what Dewey calls human agency is background and presumption to our proceedings, and calls out to be examined thoughtfully, purposively, and soon.[6]

As Pragmatists have claimed since their beginnings in Boston in the metaphysical group led by Chauncey Wright, much of the problematic of the human has been created within the Platonic-Cartesian idealist tradition of the false separation of body and mind. That is, most of our theories and counter-theories of the human have been embedded within thinking processes who have taken one side or the other of these ancient dualisms.

We need to find new paths to understand what is human, and Pragmatism will help locate such paths outside of celebrating one or the other side of the dualism, or attempting to find some interface between them. Once we accept and explore the body-mind notions of Dewey, for example, the idea that the human has been dominantly depicted as male, can no longer be sustained.[7] We are of two kinds—male and female—and this is a deep fact of our continuing and active existence.

When we think of the human within ecohumanism, it is necessary to be inclusive of all peoples and cultures, in this time, and in the past. We carry a great deal of pseudo-history to this study. As our thinking about the human has stemmed from a presumption of human uniqueness, the stories which have been used to characterize us have also echoed this thinking. Humans are presumed to have moved from animal to man via language, and in parallel ways, from savage or primitive to civilized.

We now know that the languages of all humans are of a single sort, the thinking of humans is not very difficult to translate from one culture or tradition to all others. Our earlier (and some residual) thinking about humans had been based on stories about non-humans, and we had spent much time trying to explain ourselves without much observation.

Boas, an anthropologist and close colleague of Dewey at Columbia, sent his students around the world to examine languages and cultures. This work literally got us to understand the unity of the human condition, and led directly to the United Nations Declaration on Human Rights, drafted by two of Boas' students, M. F. Ashley Montague and Juan Comas. This is to say that any speculative history of humans now alive on the earth, does not tell us much about how we got here.

An emergent Pragmatism will examine—instead of speculative history—the actuality of humans and other species, the questions that Peirce and Dewey raise concerning agency, and not a priori underrate other species on presumptive grounds.

In this context, it is important to include the work and thinking of Darwin, especially of his later work, *The Expression of Emotions in Man and Animals.* Darwin set out an arena of study, which remains little pursued. He points toward study of: 1) all humans; 2) animals; 3) children 4) old age; 5) the insane; and, 6) art. An eco-humanism within Pragmatism will take up and extend the suggestions of Darwin.[8]

Darwin's late work also returns us to the Pragmatism of G. H. Mead, whose ideas that we are social by our very nature set out a very different study for a productive ecohumanism. In the context of *expression*, it first becomes clear that we are social: an-other is observing and interacting with us. The very idea that we are individuals by our nature—the idea that has prevailed in Western thought—is shown to be incorrect, if not false. Since F. F. Darling's work beginning in the 1930s, it has been well known, if not taken to the study of the human very often, that related species to humans, are also social.[9]

This observation of the intrinsic sociality of the self problematizes the question of our individuality, and redirects both ecohumanism and Pragmatism. It will ask us to study the nature of the human, of the self, as *emergent* from sociality, rather than attempting to explain questions of our sociality, morality, and so on, as emerging from an individuality taken as a given in the human condition.

Since the effective disappearance of Pragmatism with the passing of Dewey and some colleagues in the early 1950s, there has been some very interesting and productive work done in the context of the implicit. Deriving much from parallel work across languages, in which *phonemic* methods were developed to gain insight to the cognitive structures of other languages—thence one's own—the implicit or out-of-awareness aspects of our language and thought has been described by Ray L. Birdwhistell, Erving Goffman, Harold Garfinkel, and Edward T. Hall.[10]

Hall introduced the idea of *The Silent Language*, that much of interaction occurs via the body, and that much of this can be studied. His work on *Proxemics*, for example, was groundbreaking in pointing out precisely the distances between interactants when talking with one another.

Birdwhistell's work in *Kinesics* began to explore the actual use of gestures in communication, and much of the implicit in interaction. His friend and student, Erving Goffman, explored much of the presumed in his *Presentation of Self in Everyday Life*. Garfinkel laid out some methods for proceeding to explore the implicit in his *Ethnomethodology*, in which he places the observer in the context of returning *home* wearing new observational lenses in developing what I like to dub an Anthropology of the Ordinary.

Reviewing these works and ideas brings us to the present moment, one of the re-currency of the progressive Pragmatism which inspired most of the works mentioned in this essay. The more recent work has indeed explored issues of human agency which Dewey dubbed the *central instrumentality* of our being.

A pragmatist ecohumanism will attempt to avoid the ancient battles of mind and body which have effectively separated us from nature, and from many aspects of our own being. In order to pursue such an ecohumanism, we need to take up Dewey's quest to uncover more and more aspects of our own agency.

Beyond a reconsideration of the histories of thought which have led us to think of humans as being effectively outside of nature, and to concentrate almost all our efforts on analyzing what has been taken to be the humanly unique, a Pragmatism will ask us to engage ourselves increasingly in our studies. What are the active aspects of our own viewing of ourselves, of what we bring to the reading and inspection of ideas?

I suggest that it is important for us to re-view our own being, to begin to review the nature of our observational and intellectual habits in the Deweyan sense. As Dewey studied his body with F. M. Alexander during the last 30-plus years of his life, it will also be useful for us to engage in some similar study of our habitual being. Toward this end I propose the study of an Archeology of the Body.[11]

Finally, in the context of a Pragmatism which focuses on the nature of our experience, and the taking of our social critiques into the shaping of the future, the field of ecohumanism requires our active participation.

Notes

1. John Dewey, "Introduction" in Frederick Matthias Alexander, *Constructing Conscious Control of the Individual* (New York: E.P. Dutton, 1923), p. xxxii.

2. An associated argument is also found in our frequent interest in cosmology. A recent book by Peter D. Ward and Donald Brownlee, *Rare Earth: Why Complex Life is Uncommon in the Universe* (New York: Copernicus, 2000) underscores the search for intelligent life outside of earth, in claiming that there is not likely to be any life except on earth. We have been tempted, at least since Pythagoras, and driven by the thinking and work of Carl Sagan, to search for the meaning of the human extra-terrestrially. Sagan's work on CETI has encouraged the search for extra-terrestrial intelligence, and is implicated in the lack of interest in our earthly relatives and descendants. Carl Sagan, ed., *Communication with extraterrestrial intelligence (CETI)* (Cambridge: MIT Press. 1973).

3. In the context of seeking for paths around the mind-body dualisms of Western thought, we should remain open to the idea that species which are not in the direct line of development of the human form, may have much more in common with us than a directly formal development model would presume and suggest.

4. See Harvey B. Sarles, "On Comparative Thought" (1975ms).

5. Philip Regal. Personal communication. Ongoing, 2000.

6. The question of religion, a presumed deity or creator, will also become rethought in a recurrent Pragmatism. As we more fully understand the human condition with respect to those aspects of our being which Dewey alludes to as human agency, the question of a creator will, I suggest, fade, and we will further appreciate the complexities of being human.

7. John Dewey, *"Nature, Life, and Body-mind," Experience and Nature* (Carbondale and Edwardsville: Southern Illinois University Press, 1988), ch. 7.

8.   Charles Darwin, *The Expression of the Emotions in Man and Animals* (London: J. Murray, 1872). In Darwin's second last book, *The Descent of Man,* it is useful to note that he claimed that the difference between man and animals with respect to language is quantitative, not qualitative: a most important idea within the history of ideas, and justifying a broad comparative and open approach to the study of human and other animal nature.

9.   F.   F.   Darling, "Social Behavior and Survival," *Auk* 69 (1952), pp. 183–191.

10. Much of this work was inspired as well by Birdwhistell, Smith and Trager, who were variously associated with Hall and Goffman. They worked within the Chicago School of Symbolic Interactionism, deriving from Mead. Works include: Ray L. Birdwhistell, "Kinesics," *International Encyclopedia of the Social Sciences* (New York: Crowell, Collier, and Macmillan, 1968) vol. 3, 379-85; Erving Goffman, *The Presentation of Self in Everyday Life* (Garden City, New York: Doubleday Anchor Books, 1959); Edward T. Hall, *The Silent Language* (Greenwich: Fawcett, 1959); Harold Garfinkel, *Studies in Ethnomethodology* (Englewood Cliffs, N.J.: Prentice-Hall, 1967).

11. Harvey B. Sarles, "Archeology of the Body" (2000ms).

ECOHUMANISM:
A HUMANISTIC PERSPECTIVE

Vern L. Bullough

At the beginning of the twentieth century, what we would now call an ecological crisis seemed eminent. The world's population was rapidly increasing, almost double what it had been hundred years before. People were also migrating across boundaries more than ever before in history. Millions took ships from Europe to the U.S. with the height being reached in 1907 when 1.3 million arrived in the United States. Millions of others migrated to Argentina, Chile, Uruguay, Brazil and other areas in South America. Smaller numbers migrated to Australia, New Zealand, South Africa and elsewhere. Everywhere there was a vast migration of rural people into the city as more and more people abandoned agriculture as a means of support. Migration was not limited to the new world or to recently explored areas of the Pacific. Hundreds of thousands of Ashkenazi Jews from Poland and Russia entered Germany in the nineteenth century and additional numbers moved to other European countries as well. What had been small isolated Jewish communities became major groupings of peoples. Traditional ways of life seemed under attack and inevitably there was a reaction against such rapid changes, some rather passive but others quite virulent such as anti-Semitism. It was in such a setting that the first tentative awaken-ings of what eventually became the ecology movement appeared in Western Europe and America. Its emphasis, however, was more on population control, although there was some concern with preserving the beauties of some wilderness areas.

Perhaps this failure to deal with other issues was that these same Europeans and Americans were the ones who most threatened the long homeostatic relationships between humans and their environment. European explorers and adventurers had opened up Africa, taken over India, undermined China, colonized Australia and New Zealand, conquered the Philippines, and sent Christian missionaries everywhere. Following in their footsteps, loggers were clear-cutting forests of southern Brazil, India, and elsewhere and forests that were ancient when humans first began to cultivate crops had all but disappeared in many parts of the world. In the United States forests of white pines that had extended in their millions from the Atlantic to the Great Lakes were gone.

The growing cities added to the crisis as they grew larger and more complex. Chicago, which had acted as a portage center for canoes in 1800, had a population of over 2 million by 1900. San Francisco, nearing a million, had only emerged as a city after 1848. Boston, Philadelphia, Baltimore, and similarly-sized cities also had their teaming millions, as of course did New York, London, Paris, Berlin, Mexico City, Buenos Aires, and others, all of which except Paris had been fairly small cities in 1800. The growing public health movement was campaigning to bring public recognition to many of the problems but they were not yet seen as ecological ones. The public health campaign to keep animal wastes off the streets taxed the resources of the cities while the problems of outhouses and urban flats created major sanitary and disease problems. Simply bringing water to the cities required major changes in streams and rivers and lakes. Rapid industrialization was creating other problems. The steam locomotives polluted the air wherever they went and the growing steel mills and smelters made it difficult to see the sun in some of the major industrial cities. Food and water supplies were often contaminated and disease and epidemics were endemic. Vast slums appeared in the rapidly growing cities and disease, crime, and corruption seemed to be inevitable.

Living creatures were being wiped out. The vast herds of buffalo which had dominated the Great Plains were deliberately destroyed by Americans in an effort to break the back of Indian resistance, changing an independent people to a reservation-confined one dependent mostly on the federal government for support. In Africa, Rinderpest, a virus disease of cattle characterized by high fever, diarrhea, and lesions of the skin and mucus membranes, previously unknown in Africa south of Sahara, appeared in 1896, probably brought in by Italians who imported cattle from Asia to feed their troops fighting in Somalia. The disease swept south, traveling as fast as twenty-five miles in a day, killing millions of cattle and wild ungulates, reducing large numbers of Africans to hunger and even starvation and death, disrupting African societies and opening the way for European imperialistic advances. Whole species, such as the quagga (a species of zebra), died out and vast herds of wild animals disappeared from most of Africa. In the United States the passenger pigeon which once numbered in the billions became extinct in 1914, largely because of intense hunting. In fact it is estimated that 25 to 40 percent of all bird life in America died off in the last half of the nineteenth century due to environmental changes, disease, and other factors associated with expanding settlements of people. Most of these changes were seen as the price of human progress and only a few expressed concern but their actions were very localized. Several groups organized under various titles in an effort to prevent cruelty to animals and one of the lasting contributions of the British in many parts of the world was the appearance of such groups. When I lived in Egypt, I felt there was such a society still in existence and I felt it compared to Don Quixote attacking the windmills since the basic problems underlying the ill treatment were ignored.

Though the 1890s had seen the discovery of a variety of bacteria which caused different diseases, we were not yet able to use the knowledge to advantage, although vaccination for small pox was a sign of the future. Syphilis was epidemic as was tuberculosis and malaria. Gonorrhea was widespread. Diphtheria, small pox, polio, and other diseases which we learned to control and prevent during the twentieth century were not yet under control. Even as late as 1918 the Spanish flu killed half a million people in the U.S. and 20 million in the world, a more efficient killer than World War I, and the greatest single demographic catastrophe in terms of absolute numbers to be suffered by humanity. The list of crises and ecological disasters could go on for many more pages.[1]

It was the age of exploitation with vast fortunes being made by a rising industrial, commercial, and banking classes all over the western world. In the United States we can still remember them, if not always for the industries and business they created and exploited, for the charitable trusts which were eventually established in their names: Rockefeller, Ford, Carnegie, Guggenheim, Woolworth, Stanford, Huntington, Eastman, Chandler, Duke, Vanderbilt, and literally hundreds of others. The rich grew ever more wealthy while the number of poor seemed to increase almost geometrically. Labor unrest was generic and the new prophets Marx and Engels were winning converts.

Many people were appalled at the momentum of change. Henry Adams warned that humanity was emptying the organic treasury of the planet, exhausting reservoirs of petroleum and natural gas, digging up the peat bogs, razing whole forests, systematically decimating large animals, and replacing them and many wild plants with feeble domesticated organisms.[2] Other joined with him. It was not that people were unaware of what was happening to the environment that was the problem, but rather what to do without threatening the growing industrial complex. In the United States, for example, we began to establish a national park system and set aside forest preserves. Jane Addams in Chicago, Lilllian Wald in New York, and their counterparts in cities throughout the United States established settlement houses, well-baby clinics, and helped develop new types of caring professions such as nursing and social work. Public health efforts expanded, food inspection was established, sewers were built, toilets moved indoors, automobiles began to replace the horses, better public transportation developed, child labor laws were enacted. The government gradually entered into areas of public welfare although not on any large scale until the 1930s. Gradually workers became better organized, education was extended beyond the elementary school, minimum wage standards were set, public housing developed, and a whole list of changes and improvements were made. Still, in terms of the overall ecological picture, conditions can only be said to have worsened because often the various changes caused greater ecological distress. Automobiles, for example, solved the problem of streets strewn with manure, but the internal combustion engine itself in the long run posed a greater environmental threat. Moreover, the ecological movement itself was not very well organized and those parties who were most active did not agree on goals. Although many of the groups such as the Sierra Club, the Audubon Society, the Wilderness society, and others appeared, their original scope was very narrow, and it took much of the twentieth century for them to recognize major ecological problems. They did encourage national parks and forests, but predators, such as wolves which threatened domestic herds were gradually exterminated. It took nearly a century really to educate Americans (and for that matter other peoples of the world) about the dangers threatening the environment. There was, however, one simplistic solution which early on served to motivate many wanting to see a change in the factors which to them seemed to threaten the survival of civilization as they knew it, namely effective control of population growth. The answer was not the pollution of industry nor the exploitation and exhaustion of some national resources nor the unthinking acceptance that humans were set aside by some deity to be masters of the world, but rather to define what kind of humans best deserved to survive and reproduce and enjoy the benefits of the world that they were remaking.

Though science was their guide, as it should be ours, it was selective and simplistic assumptions put forth in the name of science which most, if not all, of the "ecologists" accepted as their guide for their relationships with their environment. For much of the first part of the twentieth century, the major ecological problem was a very human one of overpopulation. It was not simply overpopulation however, but the rapid growth of the poor, the feebleminded, the physically handicapped, foreigners, troublesome minorities, sexual "deviates," who were threatening the hegemony of the best and the brightest, and even the survival of the world. It was Charles Darwin and his great scientific findings, they said, which had explained it all through his theory of evolution and the survival of the fittest. But evolution was extended by others into Social Darwinism which could help direct evolution to desirable social ends if only humans were willing to act. The answer was Eugenics, a term coined in 1885 by Francis Galton who defined it as an applied biological science concerned with increasing from one generation to another the proportion of persons with better than average eugenics, that is, better prepared by their intellectual endowment to meet the increasing demands of an ever more complicated and evolving world. Galton, a cousin of Charles Darwin, and a major figure in nineteenth-century science, was a great believer in heredity as a means of improving the "race" and thus in the importance of sexual selection as the key to the survival of humans. Those who rose to the top in any society were there because of the survival of the fittest. But eugenicists were not just willing to make such statements based on their personal beliefs, they wanted to do "scientific" re-

search to demonstrate, and to this end Galton endowed first a fellowship and later a chair at University College (University of London). The first holder of both was Karl Pearson, a brilliant mathe-
matician and also, I must add, a free thinker. Pearson was convinced that environment had little to do with the development of
mental or emotional qualities and that both were the result of heredity. From this assumption he concluded that the high birth rate
of the poor was a threat to civilization and that the "higher races"
must supplant the "lower." Control of population was the first
step in any ecological planning since we had to remove the human
threat of deterioration before other factors could be considered.
Though the English Eugenic Society, founded by Galton, eventually opposed Pearson's racist and ethnic views, large segments of
the Eugenics movement had racist overtones, and the American
Eugenics movement, founded in 1905, adopted Pearson's view
wholeheartedly. So, should I add, did the Germans. In simple terms
it emphasized the survival of the fittest—those who were the poor,
the dispossessed, the alien, the racial and religious minorities, were
simply, in harsh terms, the dregs of history, and it was the rapid
increase of such people which threatened the environment. The
major crises such as poverty and overpopulation were not necessarily due to the rapid changes taking place and other complex issues, but simply because those of inferior ability were too plentiful
and potentially would have too much control. Scapegoats were
needed, and those who did not quite fit in were to blame. Anti-
Semitism, as an instance, was justified in order to put down inferior
beings; discrimination was accepted as a fact of life and necessary
for self protection. The teeming hordes of Africa, Asia, and the rest
of the world had brought on their own problems by their continual
need to procreate. In simplistic terms it was this growing mass of
people which led to the cutting of virgin forests, the death of various species of animals, and other ecological disasters. Some "true
believers" even went so far as to hold that helping out such peoples

only made the problems worse because subsistence living still allowed them to reproduce.

This eugenicist scenario explained everything. Labor unrest and the riots were led by rabble rousers who were trying to disestablish the rule of the best people, and the main sources of discontent were the new immigrants who were recruited and led by "subversives" who themselves were not really Americans but foreigners. The fear of immigrants led to the passage in America of limits and quotas, attempting to cut down people from "undesirable areas of the world" such as Italy, Poland, Spain, India, all of Black Africa, and by the so-called oriental exclusion act, almost all oriental peoples, except for the Filipinos who, while discriminated against, had special privileges because they came from an American dependency, as did Puerto Ricans. Even though the African Americans had been emancipated following the Civil War, rigid segregation was established in the south and elsewhere, and where there was not legal segregation there was unofficial segregation by banks, lending institutions, hotels, transportation system, and everything else, against not only African Americans but identifiable Jews, Mexicans, Indians, and others. Mentally compromised and mentally ill were institutionalized, often hidden away, and even denied by their families.

As a group, the American eugenicists believed that the white race was superior to other races and that within the "white race" the Nordic "white was superior to other whites." It also assumed that upper-class people had superior hereditary qualities justifying their being the ruling class. To document this assumption they gathered any evidence supporting their interpretation. Intelligence tests, introduced in the early 1900s by Alfred Binet, for example, in spite of opposition by Binet himself, were held to be measures of innate genetic intelligence. On the basis of such tests, the eugenicists classified all people whose IQs gave them a mental age of 12 as feebleminded or morons, without regard to the educational background or deprived environment that might have led to such tragic results. Criminality was considered a concomitant of feebleminded-ness. Insane, idiotic, imbecilic, feebleminded, and epileptic persons were often sterilized, either voluntarily or involuntarily—as in some areas were habitual criminals, "moral perverts," and other deemed socially undesirable. Studies by some of the America eugenicists, such as R. L. Dugdale and Lothrop Stoddard on the pseudonymous Jukes and Kallikaks, were taken to prove that thousands of persons were feebleminded or criminal types because of the inheritance they had received from a single ancestor five or six generations previously.[3] Later, much of the data was found to have been fabricated. Many states passed law for sterilization of such misfits in society so that future generations would not be compromised. What the eugenicists offered was a simple solution to the world's problems, namely to curtail the birth of the poor and poverty stricken as much as possible, and to eliminate reproduction of specified categories through sterilization. Many of the activists in the birth control movement adhered to some of the principles of eugenics, although it was never the dominant theme. Carried to its extreme, this doctrine could be interpreted to mean that the poor and helpless were there because of their own deficiencies and while charity could be given to them they could not be allowed to grow in numbers or political influence. Ultimately, it was the extremes to which the Nazis took such pseudoscience that broke the back of the eugenics movement in America and much of the world. But it did not eliminate it.

Fortunately the intellectual underpinnings of the late twentieth century ecology movement discarded such simplistic answers and based on the research of Rachel Carson and others began to look more deeply at what humans themselves were doing to cause a degradation of the environment. It was not enough to simply control population growth but it was essential to take more positive steps to protect the environment. Legislation to stop some of the pollutants was enacted in United States and throughout most of the world, but in spite of this the twenty first century starts with many of the problems that faced those in the twentieth remaining unsolved although the causes of the problems might be somewhat different.

In fact the ecological crisis faced some 100 years ago seems in retrospect to be relatively mild in comparison. The world's population, even though there has been a decline in birth rate, is still doubling in a shorter time period than before, in part because people are living longer. People continue to migrate across boundaries in great numbers, and vast numbers of people still come to the United States including millions from Asia and Africa who previously had not voluntarily come in any significant numbers. In Los Angeles there is not only Chinatown, common in many major cities in the United States in the immediate past, but Japanese town (mainly for tourists, however, since most Japanese are now widely dispersed and emigration from Japan to U.S. has declined), Korea town, Thai town, Vietnam villages, Cambodian enclaves, Muslim mosques for various varieties of Muslims, Buddhist and Hindu temples, Sikh worship centers, and a wide variety of Christian churches from Syrian Orthodox, to Armenian to Coptic to Ethiopian to Korean Baptist, and new varieties appear every year. The migration of rural people into the cities continued until we have megalopolises such as Mexico City and Cairo, two or three times the size of New York. While European colonizers have more or less disappeared from Africa and other parts of the world, exploitation continues, often by the indigenous peoples themselves. In many areas of the world it is no longer the loggers and miners who are destroying the indigenous environment but the growth of suburbs and encroachment of hordes of recreationists who threaten the natural environment. Demands for water have led to the building of ever more dams while the fear of flooding has led to other ways of impeding the natural flow of rivers. In Los Angeles, the river about which the city was built is now mainly a cement ditch running for nearly 100 miles. Free-running rivers are almost an anachronism. Hardwood forests are disappearing, and there is now a determined stand in California to preserve one of the last great tracts of Redwoods, which outside of a few national parks are almost nonexistent. The pollution of the environment by man-made machinery and equipment continues. Automobiles and their exhausts have almost made some areas of the country unlivable and even such "beauty spots" as Salt Lake City and Denver suffer from serious bouts of smog. Though cities like Pittsburgh, Cleveland, Youngstown, Lackawanna, have eliminated much of their industrial smog, it was not necessarily voluntary. Quite simply the industrial complexes which created so much of it simply have disappeared from U.S. only to reincarnate in many parts of the developing world, bringing them the pollution problems we once had. Left behind are rusting mills and decaying towns and migrating citizens. A major result of the loss of major industries has been a radical drop in wages for many of the nation's poorer citizens. To complicate matters even further, in spite of modern medicine, one of the world's worst epidemics, that of AIDS, is raging uncontrolled, and large sections of Africa are seeing their peoples dying off.

But what has this to do with ecology, the relationship of organisms to each other. Quite simply, some have argued that to be effective in ecological planning, humans will have to accept the importance of other forms of life, and not put humans at the center of their planning. This paper argues that no planning can be effective in the long run unless they take into account the human factor. But this human factor has to involve all peoples and must be humanistic. Large segments of the world are now beginning to recognize ecological problems and are more willing to take steps to seek solutions than earlier. Many positive steps have been taken, and ecology groups hold worldwide conferences to try to find solutions, solutions which a good segment of the world's countries are willing to adopt, if they could afford to do so. Proposing solutions and taking steps to enact them are different things, and the welfare of all humans must be considered. One of the interesting and troubling things I noticed in my travels, however, is what again might be called the neglect of the human element. I noticed this particularly in South Africa where a significant number of the wealthy and powerful residents of European background have taken to establishing large scale wild animal parks, dedicated to preserving the flora and fauna of Africa. Endangered species such as cheetahs, leopards, hippos, rhinoceros, are gathered on vast estates and encouraged to breed and reproduce. This struck me as a wonderful idea, but I was troubled by the fact that this basically is a withdrawal from the real world of South Africa and this very withdrawal could doom all their efforts. It allows them to ignore the problems of integration, of the melding of conflicting cultures, the vast disparity in incomes, high crime rates and unemployment. In their vast isolated conclaves, many surrounding Kruger National Park, these devoted ecologists with their private airports, vetted tourist groups, and dedicated employees, are removed from the real life of South Africa. That this is a dangerous solution is indicated by what is happening in other parts of Africa, where the recent civil wars and mass exterminations in Ruanda and elsewhere, have driven hundreds of thousands of refugees onto previous sacrosanct game preserves where they cut the trees, kill the animals, and destroy the undergrowth that had remained stable for centuries. Many other countries in Africa are threatened with bankruptcy, and their concern is no longer on ecological issues but simply survival.

This only emphasizes the point of ecohumanism, the need to take into account the humans. We can draw up all kinds of world statements, do excellent planning, make people aware, but unless we deal with the human miseries no ecological program will be successful in the long run. It is not just a problem of developing countries—the anxieties and fears are present everywhere. Austria is a good example. Though unemployment in Austria is among the lowest in Europe, and immigration is modest and strictly regulated, the Austrians. apparently worried about what they felt was the economic crisis of possible unemployment; and the dangers of almost non existent emigrants threatening their culture, have been flirting with "racist" and neo-Nazi solutions.

If Austria has problems, imagine those in most of the rest of the countries of the world since the majority of the world's population is at the poverty level. Even in a country such as the United States, it is difficult for the poor struggling to survive to be concerned with ecological issues. In United States, studies done in January 2000 indicated that the average income of the top fifth of the country was above $137,000, more than ten times the bottom fifth ($13,000) Moreover, in eighteen states incomes of the lowest fifth have actually declined over previous samplings.[4]

The issue is complicated by newer versions of the old Social Darwinism or eugenics which have emerged with increasing force. Repetitively, the attempt to come to terms with our serious problems at the end of the twentieth century, ecological and others, seem to follow some of the same concepts found at the end of the nineteenth and the simplistic answers are in many ways similar. Fueling the glowing embers are such books as *The Bell Curve*,[5] a book widely accepted and believed in spite of the challenges to the efficacy of the standardized I.Q. tests.[6] It argues in a sense that large numbers of people fail because they do not have the innate ability to succeed. Intellectual biology is destiny, something with which I disagree. My own research on intellectual and creative achievement, for example, emphasizes the necessity of opportunities for education, an intellectual and cultural milieu that encourages achievement, a modicum of economic well being, as essential. It is almost impossible for a person born in poverty and with little opportunities for education to break through the barriers to make important contributions in intellectual and creative areas, regardless of their innate intelligence. If this is true in countries like United States, the issue is further complicated in the underdeveloped and third world countries where hundreds of millions of people are still condemned to devoting all of their energy to getting enough to eat and put shelter over themselves. Even if a relative handful break the barriers and do manage to go to school, significant achievement cannot usually be done in one generation but rather necessitates a three-generational process.[7]

The United States itself is suffering from a backlash against the vast number of new immigrants. Affirmative action has been challenged and in many areas discarded. If we cannot deal with our own people problems, think of the difficulties in other areas of the world, and the implications for ecology. New discrete forms of discrimination have appeared. Police, for example, tend to stop black and brown drivers more than white. There is mass unemployment of African American youth and our prisons have an ever-increasing population of the dispossessed and minorities. In fact, until this year, the prison budget in California threatened to be larger than the one for education.

In short, my worry about ecohumanism in the twenty-first century is that it will, if not fail, be severely compromised because we will not be able to deal with the human problems. I know this makes ecology a more human centered problem than many would prefer but it takes humans to solve the issues even though they created most of the problems. Ecology issues cannot be dealt with in isolation, and they cannot be solved by withdrawing from real life (as some of the South Africans seem to be doing) nor ignoring the real human cost that is involved. The rich minority (of either peoples or countries) ultimately cannot dictate to the rest of the world what to do. This is simply because ecological solutions have human consequences. Even in rigid authoritarian countries, it is difficult to predict the consequences of attempted solutions designed to ease perceived threats to the world's ecological balance. A good example is China which with its ideal of one child family is attempting successfully to cut down the birth rate although the population will not top off until well into this present century. Anyone who visits China, however, sees some of the consequences of this policy. Since the ideal of one child, and enforcement of the ideal is very strong in some areas, the sex of the child becomes all important, and males are desired if only because they traditionally have been the ones to support the father and mother in their old age. The result has been a disproportional birth of male babies—so much so that there will be a real shortage of adult women of child bearing age. This will perhaps curtail the population growth more radically in the future but at what cost to the millions of males who will go without mates? How will the spoiled single child adapt to the real world when it reaches adulthood? Who will take care of the older persons? There are undoubtedly solutions to these problems, and China is beginning to experiment. In Shanghai, for example, volunteers tending to the elderly exchange, under the supervision of community government groups, hours of service now for care of themselves later. "This old couple's today is my tomorrow," is one of the motivating slogans.[8] China might well be able to adopt and more less effectively enforce a one-child family, but can a democratic country do so? One of the problems with modern Japan is the aging of the population with the median age rapidly rising because of the declining birth rate over the span of the past thirty or forty years. While individuals often deplore the youth culture so omnipresent in our society as of now, a youth culture is more experimental, both more daring and more troublesome, than a culture that is aging. It is the younger generations in our society which have created the computer, the internet, and the digital revolution, changed our music styles, set the fashion trends, and are more demanding of change than the older generation which I represent. Will an aging population cut down on innovation and change? Some experts blame the economic decline of Japan on its aging culture which finds it more and more difficult to change, needs less goods and demands more services.

In sum, I think, an ecological disaster can be avoided only if we incorporate a much stronger element of humanism than it now has. But it has to be a humanism which is concerned about the welfare of all, the rich and the poor, the handicapped, the ill, the young and the old, the alcoholic and drug addict, the student and the prisoner, men and women and children. Ecohumanism can work but in my interpretation the emphasis on humanism must come first for it to succeed. The ecology experts can point out the problems, but it is the rational humanist thinkers who have to attempt to solve them, and we always have to remember that any solution will have human consequences. This makes the problems particularly difficult to solve and there are no easy solutions.

Probably the easiest solution is to take incremental improvements. Planting trees to stop encroaching of desert in Africa, cleaning up car emissions by changing to alternative fuels or alternate forms of transportation, continuing to encourage family planning, encouraging education, working on lessening the effects of poverty, discrimination, and segregation, returning refugees to their home lands, and similar measures. These are not world-shaking solutions but their ultimate effect might be.

Notes

1. See, for example, Alfred W. Crosby, "The Past and Present of Environmental History," *American Historical Review* 100 (October 1995), pp. 1177–1189.

2. Henry W. Adams, *The Education of Henry Adams* (Boston: Houghton Mifflin, 1927), pp, 492, 497; Henry W. Adams, *A Letter to Teachers of History* (Washington DC: J. H. Furst, 1910), pp. 79, 131, 188.

3. For some of these works, see Lothrop Stoddard. *The Rising Tide of Color* (New York: Scribner's, 1922) and *The Revolt Against Civilization* (New York: Scribner's, 1923); Alfred P. Shulz, *Race or Mongrel* (Boston: L.C. Page & Co., 1908).

4. *The Nation* 270 (February 7, 2000), p. 7.

5. Richard J. Herrnstein and Charles Murray, *The Bell Curve* (New York: Free Press, 1994).

6. Stephen Jay Gould, *The Mismeasure of Man* (New York: W. W. Norton, 1981).

7. See, for example, Vern L. Bullough, "History and Creativity," *Journal of Creative Behavior* 15 (1981), pp. 102-16; Gerhard Falk and Vern L. Bullough. "Achievement Among German Born Jews," *Mankind Quarterly* 37 (Spring, 1987), pp. 337-65; "Dissenting Thoughts on Intellectual Achievement," *The Humanist* 40 (January-February, 1980), pp. 43-47, 53.

8. Ching-Ching Ni, "New Twist of Saving for Old Age," *Los Angeles Times* (February 7, 2000), col. 1, p. 1.

HUMANISM'S MISSING LINK

Carol Wintermute

How many times have you heard a humanist say, "We'd fill this place to the rafters if we just did a better job of getting our message out to the public." The point being that if only they could just know what we stand for they'd be beating the doors down. How many of you think that is true? I once believed that to be true. The fact is that the humanist movement is at a standstill. I do not hear any of our groups talking about their achievements in growth. I've come to the conclusion that it is not that our potential public has no idea of what we think—but it is because there really is a gap between our message and our behavior.

So, what is this gap? I will call it a detachment from our emotional selves, which involves our inability to see that actually we act more often from emotions than reason. We, of course, proudly deny this fact. We insist that we are creatures of logic, making decisions based on reason and science. In fact we embrace just about as many unfounded ideas and beliefs as anybody else. While they may willingly swallow incredible myths and stories with great swoons of zeal, we persuade ourselves that we operate from beyond the hysteria of emotions dealing only in facts that can be proven by the scientific method.

No, I think not. Science and reason are tools that we use in both good and sometimes misguided ways. Where we go astray is that

243

we take something we think or believe and use science or reason to back us up, thereby arriving at our conclusions in a seemingly objective way. What we do not own up to, is the subjective motive for why we wanted to find that conclusion. Let me illustrate.

Harriet Humanist writes a letter to the editor of her city newspaper protesting the report that the Catholic Church continues to refuse women entry into the priesthood. She has all the facts about women being just as capable as men to do this work and the fact that many did so in the beginning days of Christianity. She tells herself that she wrote this letter in the hopes of showing those of that faith that they are on the wrong track and should correct this mistake or even better, leave the church and join the humanists. What Harriet is denying is that she is still furious at being a member of that Church as a child and discovering that she felt like a second-class citizen in that fold. She does not even see that her so-called reasonable rhetoric is filled with invectives and sarcastic slams at the church.

Now I am not after Harriet to show that she was dishonest in her intentions. I think Harriet is cheating herself from a real understanding of what is guiding her behavior. She is angry and rageful at what she feels she suffered in that particular faith. By denying that and thinking she is acting because reason demands that the truth be told, she is keeping a very significant truth from herself. That truth is that she has a life-long hurt that is going unattended and is being disguised as truth seeking.

Those of us who believe as Harriet does, read her article and say, "Boy, did she nail them." Those whom Harriett hope to convince, see a woman denied and suffering who is mad as hell at her experience in the Catholic faith. Do they see the truth of her position? Probably not, because the rage she is displaying is more pungent than the logic of her arguments. Her behavior is more truthful than her thinking. Thus there is a gap between her behavior and reason.

Which brings me to a book that helped to generate my thoughts for this talk. It is a book about words and images. It is a book about how our brains handle words and images, and how our adoration of the written word and it's related linear thinking has created an imbalance in how we use our brains.

Leonard Shlain as chief of laparoscopic surgery at California-Pacific Medical Center in San Francisco has performed many brain surgeries. He is author of *Art and Physics: Parallel Visions in Space, Time, and Light*.[1] His current book, from which I am drawing, is *The Alphabet Versus the Goddess: The Conflict Between Word and Image*.[2]

I heard Shlain speak at a conference on madness and creativity this summer in Santa Fe. I was intrigued with his presentation, which consisted of words, of course, and of artistic images drawn from the dawn of humankind until today. Dr. Shlain's thesis is that the development of literacy is indeed one of the most significant and important aspects of human culture. But it is one of those precious gifts that has a dark side that we have ignored in our awe and gratitude for the light literacy has brought.

He points out that when we speak and listen we use both sides of our brain. The left processes the words literally and the right evaluates the non-verbal parts of the message, such as body language and voice tonality. Literacy or reading depends primarily on the left side of the brain, which is involved in linear, sequential, reductionist, and abstract thinking. The right brain is involved in holistic, simultaneous, synthetic and concrete views of the world. The left brain fosters what we have come to call a masculine outlook and the right brain, a feminine one.

Thus the pernicious effect of literacy, which has gone unnoticed, is that masculine values and a patriarchal perspective have diminished feminine values. Now this is a very simplistic summary of Shlain's thesis. He makes an elaborate case, as an amateur anthropologist, that history is replete with examples of how the creation of an alphabet and the written word has both benefited societies and at the same time caused a splitting off and devaluing of an equally important human mode of perception, creating an imbalance in the way we use our brains. Non-literate societies are greatly dependent on oral learning, which requires both, left and right spheres of the brain to work together to form a perception. These perceptions are based on exchanging images. These societies, for the majority, are more egalitarian in relationships between men and women.

In literate societies, in which the left brain is dominant, hierarchies have formed and men subjugate women. Thus Shlain says, "Misogyny and patriarchy rise and fall with the fortunes of the alphabetic word." Further, he says:

> Among the two most important influences on a child are the emotional constellation of his or her immediate family and the configuration of his or her culture. Trailing a close third is the principal medium with which the child learns to perceive and integrate his or her culture's information. This medium will play a role in determining which neuronal pathways of the child's developing brain will be reinforced.

Images are primarily mental reproductions of the sensual world of vision. These reproductions in our heads are concrete and taken in as a whole, all at once. Words involve a different process. The eye scans individual letters in a sequence. The letters are abstract symbols that are combined, one at a time, in rapid-fire fashion until meaning emerges.

To perceive through images, the brain uses wholeness, simultaneity, and synthesis. To get to the meaning of alphabetic writing, the brain uses sequence, analysis, and abstraction. Images are associated with the feminine aspects of ourselves and writing, with the masculine side.

Thus non-literate cultures are image based and tend toward the feminine values—the goddess cultures. She was dethroned by writing and the masculine values. Shlain says, "Whenever a culture elevates the written word at the expense of the image, patriarchy dominates. When the importance of the image supersedes the written work, feminine values and egalitarianism flourish."

At this point you are probably wondering what this has to do with Harriet Humanist. Bear with me and I will come to that, soon.

I would love to regale you with Shlain's analysis of Judaism, Christianity and Islam, all of which are literate religions and all exemplars of patriarchy. Each feature an imageless Father deity whose authority is based on *his* revealed *word* sanctified in written form. This imageless entity paves the way for the kind of abstract thinking that inevitably leads to law codes, dualistic philosophy, and objective science.

Okay you say, what's so wrong with those results. Well, the law codes became instruments to reduce women to being property and conquered peoples to slaves. Dualistic philosophy helped to split our world into one that is natural and another, which is beyond this reality and is supernatural. Objective science has—wait, I better stop, I think I'm getting into trouble.

What could possibly be wrong with science? It's the whole basis of humanism, isn't it?

Here is my point. Science is indeed our greatest tool for finding verifiable truths about our natural world. But is science the only way to know something about reality? There are truths from which we operate as human beings in this world that do not come from science or reason. These truths reside in the human experience. When the written word and science eradicated the image as a vehicle to understanding the world, it lopped off a most important method for gaining truth. The humanist movement—devoted to physics and metaphysics—has been so blinded by these dazzling subjects that it has yet to reunify one of its essential philosophical parts to its whole. Aesthetics is at the heart of the criticism that humanism is coldly intellectual and emotionally crippled. Yes, we humanists love the arts and support them as enhancing life adornments, but don't see that with them lie truths that cannot be expressed in words or scientific symbols.

Our building[3] contains no permanent images associated with our life stance. In this room and the upper auditorium we see only abstract symbols and abstract artworks with the exception of the Ben Shahn's civil rights portraits on the back of the upper auditorium wall. We rely completely on the word to deliver our cognitive message. If it were not for the art and music committees and the minister's poignant poetic images and an occasional dramatic presentation, we would be left to only the reasoned word.[4]

Aesthetics addresses both the cognitive and the affective aspects of our nature. It is impossible to exist at only one end of the continuum between thinking and feeling. But humanism appears to be a masculine, value-written word movement trying to operate from the head, desperately trying to hold the heart in check or at least keep it from displaying itself in public. Poor Harriet thought her words would be the influencing aspect of her letter. She was disconnected from her emotions, and was tripped up when they emerged between the lines to present a very different image of what she was about and that left her with a most unconvincing logical argument.

I am afraid we humanists are often like Harriet. We protest loudly that we are seeking truth and exposing what Professor Emeritus of Communications and Education, and Humanist Institute graduate Bob Wolsch calls, "double-speak, pseudoscience, false syllogisms, half-truths, red herrings . . . and other forms of verbal trickery and abuse." While we are busy exposing the false and presenting our version of the true, he notes that:

> Visitors to our groups are commonly ignored, while leaders neglect their host functions. We gossip. We back-bite. We could support a laundry with the dirty linen we display or share by mail. Perhaps we can become as nice to each other (and I add, to non-humanists) as we try to be to the recipients of our social services.

Here again, like Harriet, instead of overwhelming others with our brilliant position and impeccable logic, we are actually leaking all over with repressed and unresolved emotions like anger, rage, and hurt. Perhaps we need to face our feelings and not run from them into that safe haven of objective reasoning. Truth will never be found until we find out why we want to think as we do. Words won't tell us; only our images, which lead to our feelings, can expose these inner truths that really guide us.

There is a natural relationship between aesthetics (image) and science and philosophy (writing) that recognizes the equal contributions of each in seeking truth without putting them in competition with each other for being the final authority. Science gives us verifiable knowledge. Philosophy presents us with systems of meaning for comprehending the universe, and aesthetics leads us to understanding human experience. We humanists can restore the balance of the so-called feminine and masculine values, which the written word has destroyed, by attending to what the image has to say as well.

The hero who can come to the rescue of restoring the balance between image and word is humanism's philosophical champion. John Dewey was America's most famous philosopher when he died in 1952. Revered by liberal educators, he was considered the country's intellectual voice. That was only 48 years ago and I'll hazard a safe guess that very few people know his name today. We humanists should. I would never have read him on my own. I discovered him at the Humanist Institute and I will be eternally grateful. When I want common sense and deep wisdom he is a fabulous guide, more current today than ever.

Dewey helps resolve the unnecessary duality and impasse between word and image, reason and emotion, science and art. For Dewey experience is the center of his philosophy and aesthetics is the heart of it. Experience is the personal interaction of self and environment and the subsequent changes in both. Art (or the arts) is the unification in experience of things that lead to a fulfillment. It is characterized by a dynamic flow of intellectual and emotional responses between artist and audience. The aesthetic experience is appreciating, perceiving and enjoying that which was lovingly rendered and which speaks to the human spirit. It clarifies and concentrates meanings contained in scattered and weakened ways in the material of other experiences. All I have ever thought or felt about death is captured by Samuel Barber's "Adagio for Strings". All I need to know of loneliness and longing is encapsulated in the film version of "Death in Venice" with Mahler's haunting *Adagietto* from his Fifth Symphony.

In art we have a triadic relationship: the speaker, what the speaker says and the one spoken to. The artwork is the connection. While the artist is working, she or he must step back and vicariously become audience to see or hear if the connection is coming through. What the artist is conveying is the substance and how it is said is the form. The artist draws on material that is the stuff of common experience. The artist assimilates this material in a distinct way, reissues the material in a public form that now becomes a new object. In time perceivers may recognize that new object as one relating to older objects that refer to common experience. The new object or artwork then becomes acknowledged as a universal expression. The material is public; the way of saying it is private. Picasso's "Guernica" stands in a building of it's own in Madrid, for good reason. The subject is the familiar one of the horror of war, but how Picasso says it is so very unique—it has never been said this way before and no words will suffice to capture what it portrays.

The perceiver can look at art intellectually or emotionally to satisfy a certain need, but looking at art aesthetically, she or he will create an experience that is new. The raw material of the artwork is of the same old stuff of the world, but bringing one's individual experience to it creates an interaction with that old material and produces something in meaning that had not been experienced previously. Both artist and audience continue to find new and different meanings in the aesthetic interchange, every single time they connect with the artwork. I hear something new every time I listen to the Beethoven's late piano works and with each piano artist who interprets him.

The universality is not to be found in a single correct interpretation of the work, but in the recognition that one's own experience is called into relation to a common aspect of human experience by the artwork.

The quality of the experience is what binds all the constituent elements and makes it a whole. It is an immediate awareness, not one of reflection. Aesthetic perception is an instant elicitation of a sense of wholeness and belonging to the universe in reaction to a work of art. It produces what Dewey calls "a feeling of exquisite intelligibility and clarity." One look at Michelangelo's statues of the slaves or prisoners says more about oppression that a thirty-page essay and it says it with a poignancy and immediacy that is overwhelming.

Dewey points to a kind of spirituality based on aesthetics. The term spirituality is repugnant to some humanists who find it too closely tied with religion. For Dewey a religious feeling has nothing to do with established religions. It is an adjective that describes "experiences having the force of bringing about a better, deeper and enduring adjustments in life." He says that the immediate sense of connection with the whole universe of human experience "explains:...the religious feeling that accompanies intense aesthetic perception. We are, as it were, introduced into a world beyond this work, which is nevertheless the deeper reality of the world in which we live in our ordinary experiences. We are carried beyond ourselves to find ourselves." We've all read fiction about characters from other times and places, but whose experiences and inner lives mirror something of our own. They tell us new things about ourselves we didn't know before. Jane Austen, Milan Kundera, and a host of others have opened my inner eyes at various stages of my own development.

Thus we can see why Dewey calls art the highest human achievement. This experience is imaginative. It is imagination that makes the conscious adjustment between prior experience and the artist's vision as expressed in the artwork. During the interaction process of artwork speaking to receiver, thoughts and emotions are floating around. Imagination connects these floating thoughts and feelings of the here and now to the vast past. Dewey says:

> Imaginative vision is the power that unifies all the constituents of the matter of a work of art, making a whole out of them in all their variety. Yet all the elements of our being that are dis-

played in special emphases and partial realizations in other experiences are merged in aesthetic experience.

Imagination is what holds all the elements of aesthetic experience together in a conclusion. Aesthetic experience is not just emotion, reason, sense or activity. It is all of these and more. It is the beauty found in the ordering of particular elements and unifying them into a whole, which bears meaning and truth, which is grasped by all of our faculties. Dewey believes that art is preoccupied with imaginative experience, which is our only vehicle for visioning a more ethical and moral world. He says, "The first intimation of wide and large redirections of desire and purpose are of necessity imaginative. Art is a mode of prediction not found in charts and statistics, and it insinuates possibilities of human relations not to be found in rule and precept, admonition and administration." Many of Dickens's fictional works served to bring attention to, and gain sympathy for the needed social reforms of his day that were eventually enacted.

So if Dewey finds that art speaks truth, then it must be in competition with science. He says, "science states meanings; art expresses them". The scientific statement is useful as direction toward an experience. If it disclosed something about the inner nature of things, then it would be competing with art. But it doesn't. Science operates in the dimension of correct descriptive statement. It points to experience. Art constitutes one.

Thus Dewey has elevated aesthetics to its former status as a major domain of knowledge and human achievement, which is a counterbalance to science and reason, ethics and other branches of philosophy—but not a challenge to their areas of authority. Aesthetics is lodged in the house of experience—not in the house of verifiable knowledge or science. Aesthetics is a process that results in finding meaning, but not a logical system of meaning like philosophy. Aesthetics makes connections to vast areas of human experience that result in deeper understanding, but it does not solve problems or is used to make decisions as does reason. Aesthetics is a catalyst for taking the links made from past and present actions to forming new possibilities of human satisfaction, but it is not a system of moral behavior, which is ethics. This branch of knowledge is different but equal to all these others.

Dewey has eliminated dualism by rooting the aesthetic branch of philosophy in the world where humans live and breathe, not in some ideal world or heaven beyond. His aesthetics has dignity and importance in the areas of knowledge and understanding. It deals with the expressive aspect of our nature and gives life its vitality, depth, significance, and hope.

Aesthetics is the key to our missing link. It is nonverbal. It is image. It requires both left and right brain. It provides a balance to science, reason, and philosophy with its truth about experience. That experience is stored both in our conscious memory and in our unconscious warehouse of emotions. To be whole persons, to be a whole movement, humanists must open those doors and begin talking about how feelings and emotions are a valid part of our human nature. Let's own these rages, passions, compassions, hurts, sufferings, and the whole gamut of feelings we try to stuff. Letting them out in the light will do much to defuse their power and allow us to move on.

We do such a wonderful job with our memorial services. The honored person comes fleetingly to life again as each grieving friend and family member adds memory after memory of moments in which they were deeply touched by the deceased. The full scope of emotions embraces the participants—laughter, tears, joy, and sorrow. The person suddenly has new facets, some admirable, some quite human in the form of foibles. We know them as a completely new and whole personality. How sad, now that they are gone from us. We must find ways to know each other in full while we live.

Just think what kind of effective letter Harriet could have written if she were to have told her story, and been upfront with her feelings, thus acknowledging her human experience, and then made her arguments with a clear head and heart uncontaminated with pent-up rage and suffering. She would have presented the image of a whole person with human experiences that can be understood. She would have made her arguments in a context that would have given them honesty and power. Images with words can really be enlightening. Reason informed by one's emotional investments can be most powerful. Science and aesthetics as partners can shed great beams of light on our world and the human condition.

Humanists could again be in the vanguard if we would publicly acknowledge, accept, and nurture the emotional side of our beings. Images, feelings, happenings in our lives—all those things of the aesthetic experience, of the right brain, have too long been subjugated by the left brain values of the written word, reason and science. Put them all together and we have a whole movement speaking to whole persons.

Notes

1. Leonard Shlain, *Art and Physics: Parallel Visions in Space, Time, and Light* (New York: Morrow, 1991).

2. Leonard Shlain, *The Alphabet Versus the Goddess: The Conflict Between Word and Image* (New York: Viking, 1998).

3. This paper was initially a Forum Lecture in a series sponsored by the Humanist Institute at the First Unitarian Society of Minneapolis, Minnesota.

4. The minister is Rev. Dr. Kendyl Gibbons.

NURTURING NATURE

A PERSONAL VIEW OF THE NEED TO NURTURE NATURE AND TO LET IT NURTURE US

Gwen Whitehead Brewer

The pun in the title of my paper is intentional. Because nurturing has a double meaning, nurturing nature means both that nature nurtures us and that we nurture nature. I will explore both meanings.

Daniel Farber has looked at the environment from a pragmatic, public point of view, exploring costs, public attitudes, official policies. He finds that "our society [has] a strong commitment to environmental values, but it also recognizes the legitimacy of economic goals."[1] His rational, pragmatic approach is essential for creating and maintaining public policy. But it is important not to limit ourselves to the rational and pragmatic, as I think we humanists sometimes tend to do. For a personal view, we need to add the emotions. My personal, individual approach supports Farber's, but I want to involve the emotions of people, stirring them to activate their "commitment to environmental values."

When I first chose this approach, I decided I should look at some feminist theory. I did, but I didn't feel comfortable with most of it. With deep roots in Judeo-Christian and Greek and Roman civilizations, out Western society has been a very patriarchal one. Men have largely been the shapers and movers. Feminist books I read blamed Western civilization for spawning the science, technology, and competitive economy that have dirtied the air and the water, that have turned fertile land into deserts, that are destroying the oxygen-producing rain forests, that are warming the earth. Distinct species of plants or animals that previously evolved over millennia are now becoming extinct in a matter of years.

In condemning men for all these ills, however, feminists are throwing the baby out with the bath water. Men, with the support of women, have produced great civilizations, powerful religions and philosophies, impressive art and architecture, systems of ethics and conduct. A good part of all this is admirable. I have always enjoyed my intellectual life in the male world. And as a woman, I am most grateful to be able to have a long healthy life, to be an active professional, to have a solid relationship with a man in my life without worrying about getting pregnant every other year, to cook delicious, nutritious meals without spending all day in the kitchen–all things that I attribute largely to Western science and technology. As Rosemary Radford Ruether says, we need to "harness rather than reject technology."[2]

I do strongly identify with the nurturing part of feminist thought. Feminists have been concerned about women world wide, supporting, for example, programs that educate third-world women about economic independence and birth control. Though skeptical of the irrational mysticism evident among some feminist writing, I feel it is important to read them because of their feelings about the environment. I like very much their recognition of the importance of the emotions in humans. Our spirits need to be nurtured, and we need to care for the animate and inanimate parts of the only world we know. No longer can we thoughtlessly use the earth for our own immediate, selfish purposes. We need to change our ways in order to protect the health of the only planet we know to be life sustaining. We must consider ourselves in our whole environment.

That is, we must be ecologically conscious and must actively participate in contributing to the health of the earth. The feminist theologian Rosemary Radford Ruether has put it very well: Our goal should be "an ecologically sustainable earth community."[3] As members of the earth community, we must nurture nature and let it nurture us.

Since I have been an English professor all my professional life, it is perhaps inevitable that I will use literature, especially poetry, to illustrate my points. A theory rampant among English teachers is that not until we articulate an idea do we know what we really think. Verbalizing an idea, especially through writing, helps us focus and develop and link and limit. Poets are able to do this well, and their words can help us see the importance of sustaining the good health of our earth. Great poems, writes one critic are an "inexhaustible source of stored energy" which continues to "sustain life and the human community."[4]

The world's great civilizations, as reflected in their religions and philosophy, have been strongly anthropocentric, and we ourselves, naturally enough, are strongly anthropocentric. When we do consider nature, we look at how we can use it, how it can benefit us. Most important, we have nurtured nature for basic survival: it shelters us and feeds us. Keats in his "Ode to Autumn" richly describes the plenitude of autumn and the "maturing sun" which "conspire" "to bend with apples the moss'd cottage-trees,/ . . . To swell the gourd, and plump the hazel shells/ With a sweet kernel. . . ." The farmer has cultivated apples and hazel nuts to sell, controlling nature for the benefit of humans. I vaguely remember a poem written about Dr. Samuel Johnson, the great eighteenth-century man of letters: It began something like "Sam Johnson, Sir, you are most like/ a tractor and a plow" and went on to say how Dr. Johnson with his great intellect tried to create order out of his world, forcefully making the earth yield its potatoes and cabbages. But we all need to do that.

The question is how much of earth's plenitude do we need to reap for our own perceived needs and how much is extraneous? Most writers and poets who examine the plight of our earth think we have gone too far. D. H. Lawrence, writing in the early part of the last century, gives a homely example in his poem "The Snake." When on a hot summer day he went to the water-trough to get a pitcher of water, he had to wait because a poisonous golden snake was already drinking there. His Western upbringing tells him, "If you were a man/ you would take a stick and break him now, and finish/ him off," but Lawrence "confesses how I liked him,/ How glad I was he had come like a guest in quiet, to drink at my water-trough/ And depart peaceful, pacified, and thankless,/ Into the burning bowels of this earth."[5] Lawrence's conflict was between his human-centered phobia about the poisonous snake and his respect for an awesome noble creature from the earth.

We view nature anthropocentrically in other ways. It affects our moods. It can fill us with foreboding or with joy or with peace. Just from breathing in summer air, Emily Dickinson becomes a "tippler":

> I taste a liquor never brewed
> From tankards scooped in pearl;
> Not all the vats upon the Rhine
> Yield such an alcohol!
> Inebriate of air am I,
> And debauchee of dew,
> Reeling, through endless summer days,
> From inns of molten blue.[6]
>   [from "I Taste a Liquor Never Brewed"]

Wordsworth was similarly transported. He "wandered lonely as a cloud" until he saw "a host of golden daffodils/ . . . tossing their heads in sprightly dance." In "such a jocund company" he "could not but be gay." But he goes farther. Because human memory makes reliving the experience possible, years later "in vacant or in pensive mood," the daffodils flash again into his mind and his "heart with pleasure fills,/ And dances with the daffodils."[7]

Anne Finch, living in early 18th-century England, finds peace in her garden, feeling the breeze and the restful river banks; observing the glowworm, the shadows, the clouds; smelling fresh night scents; hearing the nightingale, falling water, the "nibbling Sheep," the cows "rechew[ing] the Cud," and the "loos'd horse" tearing "up Forage in his Teeth"—all "whilst Tyrant-Man do's sleep."[8] These personal responses to our uses of nature are pleasurable, but not enough to involve us in creating a healthy earth.

Humanists, especially, an intelligent, pragmatic group of people, need to know and feel our dependence on the ecology of the earth. We tend to be rational activists who can make a difference. We also tend to be very focused on humans and their treatment of each other. Humans were the focus while most of us were growing up and establishing our basic values. Serious consideration of animals, plants, and rocks seemed interesting, but peripheral. Now we need to shift a bit. Now it is time to incorporate animals, plants, and rocks—and their interrelationships and their relationship with us—into the most fundamental part of our value system.

A good way to begin is to observe or hear or feel or touch some aspect of nature that has no useful impact on our lives. Tennyson watched an eagle and then captured his remote height and his abrupt plunge to earth so that you and I can visualize him:

He clasps the crag with crooked hands;
Close to the sun in lonely lands,

Ring'd with the azure world, he stands.
The wrinkled sea beneath him crawls;
He watches from his mountain walls,
And like a thunderbolt he falls.[9]

Keats, noting that "the poetry of earth is never dead" listens to the music of the grasshopper in summer and the cricket from a warm corner of the house in winter. [On the Grasshopper and the Cricket]. Emily Dickinson goes farther. She is a part of a garden community in which all kinds of creatures dwell: "Several of Nature's People/ I know, and they know me—/ I feel for them a transport/ of cordiality—" but she never meets the snake, a "narrow fellow in the grass," "Without a tighter breathing/ And Zero at the Bone—."[10]

Robinson Jeffers is reclusive like Emily Dickinson. Also like her, he is carefully observant and responsive to nature. His nature, however, is wild and often violent. He writes, for example, of a steelhead "sculling uneasily/ In three inches of water: instantly a gaunt herring-gull hovered and dropped, to gouge the exposed/ Eye with her beak; the great fish writhing, flopping over in his anguish, another gull's beak/ Took the other eye. Their prey was then at their mercy, writhing blind, soon stranded, and the screaming mob/ Covered him."[11] Jeffers sees clearly the cruelty and suffering in Nature and in humans, and his poetry makes his readers starkly aware of them.

But perhaps the most thoughtful, sustained response to Nature is that of Henry David Thoreau, a bright, well-educated New Englander, who wrote three significant books communicating his increasingly careful and minute observations about Nature, probing his own—and human—relationship to plants, to animals, to the earth: *A Week on the Concord and Merrimac Rivers*, *Walden*, and *Journals*. Nature was a magnet to Thoreau: he was pulled to observe it and seemed almost compelled to write about it. Nature nurtured him and matured him. He became a committed scholar of Nature itself. Many have been pulled to nature in this way, but few write about it in such a way as to make other humans understand that we are part of it. My most vivid memory from my first reading of *Walden* is the great battle between the small red and the great black ants. One day Thoreau discovered that his whole woodpile was covered with tenacious combatants in a battle that went on for hours. He focused on a specific pair locked in "deadly combat," the red "fastened like a vice to his adversary's front" though he had already lost several legs. After a time, a fresh red ant came to the aid of his brother, springing "upon the black warrior and commenc[ing] his operations near the root of his right fore-leg." Observing the three combatants through a microscope, Thoreau saw that the breast of the first red ant "was all torn away, exposing what vitals he had there." When he looked a half hour later, the black ant "without feelers and with only the remnant of a leg" was struggling "to divest himself of" the severed heads of the two red ants that were still hanging from his sides. Facetiously parodying other historians who have recorded ant battles, Thoreau compares his ant battle to the Battle of Bunker Hill, but he has carefully and seriously observed the ant battle for its own sake.[12] Like Emily Dickinson, he lives contentedly but alertly among the inhabitants of his earth community. His absorbed study of the nature around him made him want to walk lightly on the earth. He went to Walden Pond for two years to see how simply he could live and still have a satisfying, contented life. He condemned an "unclean and stupid farmer" who "had ruthlessly laid bare" the shores of his large pond because he "loved better the reflecting surface of a dollar. . . , regard[ing] even the wild ducks, which settled on it as trespassers."[13] This farmer was not living lightly on the earth. He was not a steward. He was an opportunist using the earth for his own selfish purposes.

The American Indians are peoples who in general lived lightly on the earth, nourishing it and asking it to nourish them. They often accommodated and respected the spirits of the many other earth-dwellers and frequently addressed those spirits. Before cutting cedar bark, for example, a Kwakiutl woman speaks to the cedar tree:

> Look at me, friend!
> I come to ask for your dress,
> For you have come to take pity on us;
> For there is nothing for which you cannot be
> used, . . .
> For you are really willing to give us your
> dress,
> Long-Life maker,
> For I am going to make a basket for lily roots
> out of you.
> I pray you, friend, not to feel angry
> On account of what I am going to do to you;
> And I beg you, friend, to tell our friends about
> what I ask of you.
> Take care, friend!
> Keep sickness away from me,
> So that I may not be killed by sickness or in
> war, O friend![14]

Living inside cities, surrounded in our homes by manufactured goods far removed from their natural sources, we do not have objects in our kitchen or garages that we call "friends." But maybe we should call these objects "friends," or at least recognize them as relatives.

But what does this mean for the twenty-first century? We know that science and technology have in many ways made us look at the world differently than the Kwakiutl Indian woman did. The phenomena of television, air travel, and the internet have made the culture, the arts, the economies, the ethics, the religion of people around the world accessible to us. We know that the indigenous peoples of the Amazon are having a hard time surviving in the disappearing rain forests. The tribal people of New Guinea are no longer cannibals, but the seemingly unavoidable transition to an acquisitive money economy is painful and questionable. And not only people are changing because of Western science and technology. The plight of elephants is similar to that of the Amazon natives. Whales become beached and die, some probably because of human sonar experiments in the ocean. Examples of serious human impact on the natural world abound.

Our world has become smaller also because science has increased our understanding (and shown us our ignorance) of the universe and of matter. I used to think that the earth's place in the universe and the human place on the earth was solid, and I considered people in old stories who were frightened of comets or sunspots or eclipses superstitious. No longer. What we now know—and don't know—about the expanding universe, its forces, and the kinds of bodies in it makes me realize that our earth is very fragile. Thinking of the minute world around us has the same effect as thinking of the universe. Molecular biology is much in the news. Which molecules are permanently part of our body? There are evidently "extra-chromosomal elements" that can move from one cell to another, from one body to another, and perhaps even from one species to another.[15] We are part of this earth which is our home, and we must be conscious of the interdependence of all things on it. Like the Kwakiutl woman, we need to realize that the cedar tree—or the mountain lion, or even the vacuum cleaner—are our relations. We are on this earth together. How can we preserve it? How can we make it more healthy?

We can nurture it—not just to get its wheat and apples and meat, not just for the peaceful or buoyant effect it has on us, not just for scientific inquiry, but for the health and the well-being of everything existing on it. We can do it in two steps. First, feel; second, act. Become friends with animals, plants, rocks—with the inhabitants of earth beyond immediate need. Do it your own way, perhaps through monitoring insects in your back yard, perhaps through watching nature shows on television, perhaps through climbing a mountain. Denise Levertov observed a mountain in Mexico:

> Golden the high ridge of thy back, bull-
> mountain,
> And coffee-black thy full sides.
> The sky decks thy horns with violet,
> With cascades of cloud. The brown hills
> are thy cows. Shadows
> of zopilotes* cross and slowly
> cross again
> thy flanks, lord of herds.[16]
>   *buzzards

My theory is that this kind of involvement with nature will motivate us to act. What we do will be very individual. All of us can recycle and can conserve gas. We can all reduce consumption. Some of us can get involved in larger things. I live in Ventura County, California, which contains the Oxnard Plain, a rich agricultural area that yields citrus fruits and up to four crops a year (strawberries, lettuce, carrots, broccoli). It is situated between the Pacific Ocean and Los Angeles, one of the most heavily populated and fastest growing places in the world. Ventura County has become a popular place to live. In order to keep agriculture and open space (we have mountains), citizens of the County passed an initiative that prohibits any building on open land unless citizens vote approval.

How do we make it work? For a starter, we established the AG Futures Alliance in which all kinds of concerned citizens representing all points of views—developers, business people, farmers, city council members, members of non-profit organizations—meet to try to understand each other's point of view, to learn to talk to each other. Not until they have met together for ten months will they start to make decisions implementing this attempt for sustainability in our county. Will it work? We are trying.

We all need to nurture nature so that it will continue to nurture us.

Notes

1. Daniel Farber, *Eco-pragmatism: Making Sensible Environmental Decisions in an Uncertain World* (Chicago: University of Chicago Press, 1999), p. 200.

2. Mary Mellor, *Feminism and Ecology* (New York: New York University Press, 1997), p. 51.

3. Rosemary Radford Reuther, "Introduction," *Ethics for a Small Planet: New Horizons on Population, Consumption, and Ecology* (Albany: SUNY, 1998), p. xiv.

4. William Rueckert, "Literature and Ecology: An Experiment in Ecocriticism," *The Ecocriticism Reader* (Athens: University of Georgia Press, 1996), p. 108.

5. D. H. Lawrence, "Snake," *Seven Centuries of Verse, English and American* 3rd ed., (New York: Scribner's, 1967), p. 624.

6. Emily Dickinson, "I Taste a Liquor Never Brewed," *The Complete Poems of Emily Dickinson*, ed. Thomas H. Johnson (Boston: Little, Brown, 1960), p. 214.

7. William Wordsworth, "The Daffodils," *Seven Centuries of Verse*, p. 301.

8. Anne Finch, Countess of Winchelsea, "A Nocturnal Reverie," *Eighteenth Century English Literature, ed. Geoffrey Tillotson*, et al. (New York: Harcourt Brace Jovanovich, 1969), pp. 795-96.

9. Alfred, Lord Tennyson, "The Eagle," *Seven Centuries of Verse*, p. 433.

10. Emily Dickinson, "A Narrow Fellow in the Grass," *Complete Poems*, p. 986.

11. Robinson Jeffers, "Steelhead," *The Selected Poetry of Robinson Jeffers* (New York: Random House, 1959), p. 578.

12. Henry David Thoreau, "Brute Neighbors," *The Variorum Walden and the Variorum Civil Disobedience* (New York: Washington Square, 1968), pp. 174-76.

13. Thoreau, "Ponds." *Walden*, pp. 148-9.

14. "Prayer to a Young Cedar," *American Indian Prose and Poetry: An Anthology*, ed. Margot Astrov, (New York: Capricorn, 1962), p. 280.

15. Neil Everndon, "Beyond Ecology: Self, Place, and the Pathetic Fallacy," *Ecocriticism Reader*, p. 95.

16. Denise Levertov, "Sierra," *The Jacob's Ladder* (New York: New Directions, 1958) p. 28.

ARE WE STRIPPING THE EARTH OF ITS MYSTERY?

WHEN SPIRITUALITY AND ETHICS COLLIDE

Richard Gilbert

Mark Twain's anecdote "Slide Mountain" is the most famous legal dispute in Nevada's history that never happened. About ten miles north of Carson City in the Washoe Valley we find Slide Mountain, an uncertain terrain if ever there was one. One day back in the nineteenth century a group of practical jokers set out to dupe a U.S. attorney by the name of Buncombe.

> Dick Hyde, who was in on the joke, came busting into Buncombe's office. A landslide, he cried, had caused his neighbor Tom Morgan's ranch to slip down on top of his property, burying it to a depth of 38 feet. Worse yet, Morgan now claimed possession of both layers of real estate. Weeping, Hyde pleaded with Buncombe to represent his interests in the buried land. Buncombe agreed.

> Justice was speedily attended to later that afternoon. The judge, who was also in on the gag, listened to testimony and then pretended to make up his mind: "Gentlemen, it ill becomes us, worms as we are, to meddle with the decrees of Heaven." "If Heaven," he continued, "chose to move the Morgan ranch to the benefit of its owner, then what right did mere mortals have to question the act's legality? No—Heaven created the ranches and it is Heaven's prerogative to rearrange them."

"An act of God had deprived Hyde of his property," he ruled, "and there was no appealing God's decision." Buncombe, incensed by the stupidity of the ruling, begged his honor to reconsider. After appearing to mull over the matter again, the judge told Buncombe that Hyde still had title to his land, a perfectly good right, that is, to dig his buried ranch out from under all 38 feet of Morgan's property. Enraged by this gross miscarriage of justice, the U.S. attorney marched off in a huff. Buncombe, to put it mildly, "had been had."[1]

Twain points out, in his inimitable way the inherent contradictions in human nature. What arrogant creatures we are to think that we "own" a piece of earth. It is a mark of our greed. However, it should be noted that while Twain critiqued this acquisitive human nature, he was himself a zealous, though failed, capitalist.

Who owns the earth? It is a religious, not an economic question. It is commonly assumed in our culture that property rights are inviolable. But what does it mean to "own" a piece of the earth?

A personal example. Over 20 years ago, throwing caution to the wind, my wife Joyce and I bought a cottage on Seneca Lake. It was a combination investment, retreat, and summer residence. Becoming a property owner for the first time (and in debt for the first time), I had cause for reflection.

Rummaging through what the previous owners had left, I had a fresh realization of the passage of time. I became very nostalgic fumbling through the overcrowded tool shed, remembering what a labor of love the place had been to the man who built it. Now I must put my clumsy mechanical skills to work to make it mine as he made it his.

For a time there was a feeling of elation—at last I owned a piece of the rock (albeit the bank thought it did too, for many years). Then, horror of horrors, I remembered one of my ecology sermons!

We do not "own" the land, we are merely its trustees. The land "belongs" to the earth; our task is to care for the land as earth's trustees.

Henry David Thoreau once asked Ralph Waldo Emerson if he might build a cabin on a piece of Emerson's property on Walden Pond. Emerson offered to give it to him, but Thoreau intimated that it really belonged to the raccoon and the beaver and it wouldn't do to change ownership.[2]

The question of ownership of the earth goes back a long time. I recall a seminal essay by scientist Lynn White in 1967. In it, he blamed the Bible for western civilization's environmental sins.

He quoted from the Revised Standard Version of the Bible, Genesis 1:28, one of the Creation stories. God has just created the earth and humanity: "And God blessed them, and God said to them, 'Be fruitful and multiply, and fill the earth and subdue it; and have dominion over the fish of the sea and over the birds of the air and every living thing that moves upon the earth.'"[3]

These words, according to White and others, gave humanity license to treat the earth as a mine, to exploit it for purely human purposes. This selfish spirit, they contend, set the stage for the western philosophy of exploitation of the earth. However, poet Wendell Berry points out that there is another translation of that section. In the earlier King James Bible we read, "Be fruitful, and multiply, and replenish the earth, and subdue it." There is still sanction for the population explosion, still we are admonished to subdue the earth, but there is that divine caveat—we are to replenish the earth—to treat it as good stewards. The earth is not so much a mine which will one day run out, but a garden which continually replenishes itself—with a little help from the gardener.

Berry resurrects the concept of "Usufruct," the right of temporary possession, use, or enjoyment of the advantages of property
belonging to another without causing damage or harm.[4] In this case
the property really belongs to Nature, the earth, or God. Berry
concludes that "It is our present principled and elaborately ration-
alized rape and plunder of the natural world that is a new thing under the sun."[5] He calls for a new sense of a biblical ecology.

I don't really know why there is this crucial difference in the
translation; nor do I know if or how much that biblical account has
influenced the propensity of western civilization to risk emptying
the earthly mine and polluting the earthly garden. I do know, however, that spiritually this is an important distinction. How we view
the earth is not only a spiritual matter, but also an ethical issue.
Earth is a mystery to be celebrated, and a problem to be solved.

Berry uses his poetry as a weapon in this struggle for the earth:

> Let us pledge ourselves to the flag
> And to the national sacrifice areas
> For which it stands, garbage dumps
> And empty holes, hold out for a higher
> Spire on the rich church, the safety
> Of voyagers in golf carts, the better mood
> Of the stock market. Let us feast
> Today, though tomorrow we starve. Let us
> Gorge upon the body of the Lord, consuming
> The earth for our greater joy in Heaven,
> That fair Vacationland. Let us wander forever
> In the labyrinths of our self-esteem.
> Let us evolve forever toward the higher
> Consciousness of the machine.

> The spool of our engine-driven fate
> Unwinds, our history now outspeeding
> Thought, and the heart is a beatable tool. [6]

Our American ethos is to grow, grow, grow, go faster, faster, faster, make and consume more, more, more. Not long ago there was a serious proposal from a Los Angeles engineer who wanted to siphon water from Western Canada to the arid Southwest, necessitating the reversing of the flow of some of North America's largest rivers, transforming land on which thousands of Canadians live into reservoirs and eliminating the city of Prince George, British Columbia. A similar proposal has been resurrected recently as some contemplate exporting water from the Great Lakes around the world—much as the Gulf nations export oil.

I was in the Southwest recently and heard about their looming water crisis. Arizonans are making a concerted effort to create green those sections that nature intended brown. They want this area to support more people than it naturally can. Here we find a terrible tension between human ingenuity to make nature do our bidding, and an incredible arrogance that we know more than nature.

Locally, we have a developer who wishes to build expensive homes on one of the few remaining woodlots in the city. On the one hand, this would mean more taxable property for an economically pressed city, and as a city taxpayer I would welcome a larger tax base. On the other, this is vital green space for physical and spiritual renewal. The "owner" of this piece of land said not long ago on a radio talk show that he was going to build there and no one could stop him.

Does he "own" that land? Legally, I suppose he does. But ethically, if the public is deprived of a woodland in the urban area, is he free to do whatever he wants? And, spiritually, does he really "own" that land?

It is this arrogance that leads to suburban sprawl in Monroe County; to a village I saw in the Philippines being washed away after clear cutting of a mountain forest; to the ugly brown coal strip-mining in the former East Germany which I visited in 1992; to the struggle for water rights in the Middle East I saw last summer; to mining and lumber companies complaining about increased rents on public lands as taxpayers subsidize their profits; to a *Wall Street Journal* article pointing out that we can save as much as 75 percent of our electricity but may never do so because business requires paybacks of less than three years.

We have not yet learned to live within our limits, to befriend the land, to savor earth's mystery. We are still hell-bent on subduing it—on owning it for our own narrow purposes. We continue to exploit the earth with little sense of replenishing what we take from it or cleaning our own nest. All this reveals is a preoccupation with controlling nature and making it work for us. We try to transform nature into mere property which we can own.

It reminds me of Antoine de Saint-Exupery's story of the little prince who discovered a businessman, who, as he counted stars and marked them in his accounting book, was asked by the innocent Little Prince, "And what do you do with these stars?" "What do I do with them?" "Yes." "Nothing. I own them."[7]

The late John Wood, friend and Unitarian Universalist minister, put it well:
>Who can own a sunset or the view from the
>top of a hill?
>Where is the deed to the wind,
>or the copyright on the song of a bird?
>Ownership? It was all here -- the sun, the
>song, the hills, the wind.
>We came.

And the marks of our coming are upon the
land—giver, taker, intruder, helper, destroyer,
appreciator, lover, pretender.
The wind chuckles among the hills at the pre
tense of our ownerships.[8]

The issue is powerfully dramatized for me by Barbara Meyn's
reflection "At the Planning Commission."

That it should come to this—that we—movers of earth, cutters
of trees, polluters of springs and streams should sit in a heated
public room deciding where fences shall be run over the unre-
sisting land, decreeing where power lines should go—and houses
of the rich be planted! In the beam of the overhead projector a
French-curve map stains the wall, lots laid out like steaks and
chops on a butcher's cutting chart.

I've seen this mountain in another light, toothed with the quiet
symmetry of firs, after a night when deer and fox and owl fed
and went to sleep, coyote's song brought the dark alive and
skunk left a subtle warning on the wind.

Restlessly I cross my legs, uncross them. I have had my say.
Now it is up to the five behind microphones at the front of the
room, visibly tired, thinking of dinner, craving a cigarette, a
coffee break.

I forgot to tell them about the salamanders, dark as chocolate,
torpid with cold that move up the mountain about this time
every year, how easy it is to drive right over them if you are
unaware. I forgot to tell them about the golden eagle that clings
to the top of the transmission tower, feathers in blue air, talons
clutching metal, half in his world, half in one we made.

I cannot resolve these contentious issues—the tension between
spirituality and ethics; between our religious sense of the earth as
sacred and our ethical weighing of its uses for human purposes. I
can only suggest earth is a mystery that we try to reduce to ownership at our peril. In making the earth merely a mine for our exploitation, we not only ravage and pollute our global home, but we lose

that sense of reverence toward creation which separates us from the beasts of the field and the birds of the air; which enriches our brief sojourn on this earth so it means more than just daily getting and spending.

I close with a story that suggests how difficult it is to be a trustee of creation, to live responsibly on planet earth. It is about a man whose uncle considered himself the family environmentalist. The uncle's main concern was preserving the giant redwoods of California. He would tell all his relatives about the importance of these old-growth trees that were so beautiful and needed to be saved.

But one summer the uncle found that he needed to replace the pier at his lakefront home. He was advised that the best material for a new pier was redwood, which he proceeded to use.

The uncle still considered himself the family environmentalist, the story continued, but he no longer talked about saving the redwoods. Instead he became an enthusiastic defender of whales.[9]

All of us have a long way to go to get beyond our sense of owning the earth, to learn to live with the mystery of creation, to truly respect that interdependent web of all existence of which we are a part.

Notes

1. Theodore Steinberg, *Slide Mountain or the Folly of Owning Nature*, (Berkeley, Los Angeles, London: University of California Press, 1995), pp. 3-4.

2. Richard S. Gilbert, "On Owning a Piece of the Rock," Rochester *Unitarian* (June 1, 1975).

3. Genesis 1:28.

4. Wendell Berry, "Let Us Pledge," *The Amicus Journal*, National Resources Defense Council, New York, 1990, reprinted in *Harper's Magazine* (November 1990).

5. Ibid.

6. Ibid.

7. Antoine de St. Exupery, *The Little Prince* (New York: Harcourt, Brace and Company, 1943), p. 45.

8. John Wood, "On Owning the Earth or Parts Thereof." Mimeographed].

9. Beth Baker, "Green Worship," *Common Boundary* (September/October 1996), p. 40.

UNIVERSALISM AS PARTICULARISM

Timothy J. Madigan

When some one reproached him with his exile, his reply was, "Nay, it was through that, you miserable fellow, that I came to be a philosopher." Again, when some one reminded him that the people of Sinope had sentenced him to exile, "And I them," said he, "to home-staying."

Diogenes Laertius, "Diogenes"[1]

The topic of "universalism" is one I have been interested in for as long as I can remember. I grew up in an Irish-American household on the West Side of Buffalo, New York. We were somewhat out of place, since most of the families in the immediate vicinity were of Polish or Italian backgrounds. There were definite culture clashes, although not as heated as ones which had occurred when my parents were young—they had been virtually forbidden to interact with other ethnic groups.

What united all these immigrants and their descendants was the common feature of belonging to the Roman Catholic Church. I can well remember the feeling of deep-fellowship I would experience every Sunday at mass, when I would contemplate the fact that communicants not only in Buffalo but literally all over the world were celebrating the exact same mass. Regardless of our ethnicity, language or other uncommon attributes, we were one family united by a common faith. This feeling was captured for me by reading the book *Borstal Boy* (1959) by the Irish writer Brendan Behan. It describes his experiences as a member of the Irish Republican Army, imprisoned at the age of sixteen in an English jail for his terrorist activities. Lonely and frightened, he nonetheless takes consolation in his membership in the Roman Catholic faith:

> But I did not want any prayer book to follow the Mass. That was the same the whole world over, from one end of it to another . . . I had never given up the Faith (for what would I give it up for?) and now I was glad that even in this well-washed smelly English hell-hole of old Victorian cruelty, I had the Faith to fall back on. Every Sunday and holiday, I would be at one with hundreds of millions of Catholics, at the sacrifice of the Mass, to worship the God of our ancestors, and pray to Our Lady, the delight of the Gael, the consolation of mankind, the mother of God and of man, the pride of poets and artists, Dante, Villon, Eoghan Ruadh O Sullivan, in warmer, more humorous parts of the world than this nineteenth-century English lavatory, in Florence, in France, in Kerry, where the arbutus grows and the fuchsia glows on the dusty hedges in the soft light of the summer evening.[2]

Like Brendan Behan, I was well aware that "catholic" meant "universal," and I was happy to belong to an organization that united so many people. But I was still nagged by the fact that not *all* Christians worshipped in the same way that I did, and I hoped for the reconciliation of followers of Jesus. My favorite hymn was called "They'll Know We Are Christians By Our Love," and I especially liked the verse that went: "We are one in the spirit/We are one in the Lord/And we pray that our unity/May one day be restored." It was only when I went to college that I became really aware of the many religious traditions *other* than Christianity. I came to feel that organized religions of any stripe were too divisive, too obsessed with defending dogmas which ultimately were matters of pure speculation or authoritarian dictums. Still motivated by a concern for what might unite human beings rather than drive them apart, I found myself intrigued by the motto of the Ancient Stoics, which I learned in an Introduction to Philosophy course: "faiths divide, reason unites." This concern for a rational way of life led me to the humanist movement. Here, surely, was a group that advo-

cated *true* universalism, a concern for the core needs of human beings, and a desire to better life here on earth.

While I still consider myself a "humanist", it did not take me
long to see a paradox in this point-of-view. While seemingly universal in its advocacy of transcending doctrinal differences among
humans, humanism itself is a minority point-of-view, appealing to
a small group of people with specific interests. It is very much a
particularistic approach to life. This was demonstrated very
graphically in 1988, when I helped to organize a World Humanist
Congress, which met in Buffalo, New York. This gathering of self-
proclaimed humanists from throughout the world attracted almost
800 participants, which I thought was a goodly amount, until I
learned that the evangelist Billy Graham, in town at the same time,
had averaged over *100,000* attendees each night at his "Crusade".
And unlike the Graham Crusade, the Humanist Congress was a
homogenous gathering, overwhelmingly composed of white, well-
to-do elderly men. It didn't seem to quite capture the real world's
perspective.

It is unlikely that the human race will ever be united under one
banner. Yet the dream for human cooperation is not a new one, nor
has it died out completely. The philosopher Martha Nussbaum has
recently examined this desire for unification and the manner in
which the Stoics promulgated reason as the key to cooperation.
Her book *The Therapy of Desire* (1994) gives an extensive treatment of the significance of the Stoics, as well as the Epicureans and
Skeptics. Since my own favorite Hellenistic philosophers were the
Cynics, I was sorry to see that this group was not addressed in her
work. Nussbaum states in the introduction to the book that:

> A more problematic omission is that of the Cynics, practitio-
> ners of a quasi-philosophical form of life that challenged public
> conventions of propriety as well as intellectual conventions of
> appropriate argument. The Cynics are certainly important is
> some way in the history of the idea of philosophical therapy;

and the reader of Diogenes Laertius' life of Diogenes the Cynic will find them fascinating figures. On the other hand, there is, I believe, far too little known about them and their influence, and even about whether they offered arguments at all, for a focus on them to be anything but a scholarly quagmire in a book of this type. With some regret, then, I leave them at the periphery.[3]

I am happy to report that Nussbaum has since then given full attention to this movement, and its relevance to present-day concerns. For instance, she wrote the following blurb for the 1996 book *The Cynics: The Cynic Movement in Antiquity and Its Legacy*: "The Cynics' strange combination of shamelessness and integrity, of shocking behavior and cosmopolitan humanism, has proven perpetually fascinating to philosophers and politicians in the Western tradition."[4]

Nussbaum herself has been influenced by Cynical cosmopolitanism. In late 1994, she wrote an article for *The Boston Review,* entitled "Patriotism and Cosmopolitanism," which initiated a broad debate on the need for educational reform. Over thirty leading intellectuals (including Hilary Putnam, Benjamin R. Barber, Amy Guttmann, Arthur Schlesinger, Jr., Charles Taylor and Michael Walzer) responded to her plea for a greater focus on internationalism in contemporary educational systems.

Nussbaum begins her essay with a quote from Diogenes Laertius' life of Diogenes the Cynic: "When anyone asked him where he came from, he said, 'I am a citizen of the world.'" Such a motto, she argues, is even more appropriate to the present day, and one can learn from the practices of these ancient vagabonds, who had a continuous awareness of the common struggles of humanity. She traces this to the influence of Diogenes the Cynic, whose statement about being a world-citizen typifies his refusal to be defined merely by his local origins. Nussbaum writes:

... he insisted on defining himself in terms of more universal aspirations and concerns. The Stoics who followed his lead developed his image of the *kosmou polites* or world citizen more fully, arguing that each of us dwells, in effect, in two communities—the local community of our birth, and the community of human argument and aspiration ... it is this community that is, most fundamentally, the source of our moral obligations.[5]

The Stoics expressed this view by looking upon humans as consisting of a series of concentric circles: self, immediate family, extended family, neighbors and local group, city-dwellers, fellow countrymen, humanity as a whole. Our identity should be expanded to embrace the whole. This is universalism. The task is to "draw the circle closer to the center," considering all human beings to be fellow city dwellers. She continues:

We need not give up our special affections and identifications, whether ethnic or gender-based or religious. We need not think of them as superficial, and we may think of our identity as in part constituted by them. We may and should devote special attention to them in education. But we should work to make all human beings part of our community of dialogue and concern, base our political deliberations on that interlocking commonality, and give the circle that defines our humanity a special attention and regard.[6]

The Stoics gave three arguments for defending cosmopolitanism. The first was egoistic—the study of humanity is valuable for self-knowledge. We can understand ourselves more clearly by examining others. To know thyself is to know how one is similar to or different than others. The second argument is practical: we are better able to solve our problems if we can get beyond factionalism and local allegiances. And the third is intrinsic: cosmopolitanism is valuable in-and-of-itself. It recognizes the common aspirations and fundamental decency of all human beings.

Such a universalist position tries to override passionate commitments to local policies and practices. Nussbaum recognizes that, for many people, this cosmopolitan view is less rich and exciting than adhering to local identifications. It is harder to lose one's self in a crowd or mass movement.

> Becoming a citizen of the world is often a lonely business. It is, in effect, as Diogenes said, a kind of exile—from the comfort of local truths, from the warm nestling feeling of patriotism, from the absorbing drama of pride in oneself and one's own. . . . If one begins life as a child who loves and trusts its parents, it is tempting to want to reconstruct citizenship along the same lines, finding in an idealized image of a nation a surrogate parent who will do one's thinking for one. Cosmopolitanism offers no such refuge; it offers only reason and the love of humanity, which may seem at times less colorful than other sources of belonging.[7]

But cosmopolitanism has its own ideals: a view of humanity, struggling together, putting aside metaphysical differences, using reason to solve problems and arriving at a common code of behavior. Still, this is a very particularist view. And it is not one that is likely to motivate the masses.

The problem, then, with this view—a problem pointed out by most of Nussbaum's critics—is that it tends to be thin and unmotivating. To whom does this vision appeal? In her 1991 book *Strangers to Ourselves,* the philosopher Julia Kristeva states:

> . . . such a cosmopolitan universalism was to remain utopic, even as, along with Stoicism, big Hellenistic monarchies took over from the former city-states. One of the reasons it was impossible to carry out the Stoic doctrine was that, under the cover of its egalitarian aspect, an elitism of the reasonable wise man was unfurled; that wise man was separated from the rest of mankind, which, no matter what didactic efforts were considered, could not have access to virtue. The pride of the wise Stoic actually produced, under the guise of a reason apparently acknowledged in all, a new class of foreigners: those who did not attain virtue, did not live according to the law, or talked nonsense.[8]

Universalism is thus criticized for not only being too vague, too ungrounded, and too uninspiring, but also for being elitist in its aspirations: those not ruled by reason are relegated to second-class citizenship.

But is this cosmopolitan desire really so uninspiring? Certainly in the hands of talented artists (such as Rabindranath Tagore, the Nobel Laureate whom Nussbaum mentions throughout her article) this stress on the commonality of humanity can be quite moving. The Stoic idea of "concentric circles" reminds me of a passage in the book that did more than anything else to propel me away from Catholicism toward a more human-centered approach to life: James Joyce's autobiographical work, *A Portrait of the Artist as a Young Man*. Young Stephen Dedalus, Joyce's alter ego, doodles the following in his geography book:

Stephen Dedalus

Class of Elements

Clongowes Wood College

Sallins

County Kildare

Ireland

Europe

The World

The Universe

This foreshadows Stephen's own later break with his family, his country, and the Catholic Church; and his decision to become an artist, dedicating his life to art rather than religious devotion.

Stephen describes his decision later in the book in the following famous words:

> Look here, Cranly, he said. You have asked me what I would do and what I would not do. I will tell you what I will do and what I will not do. I will not serve that in which I no longer believe whether it call itself my home, my fatherland or my church: and I will try to express myself in some mode of life or art as freely as I can and as wholly as I can, using for my defense the only arms I allow myself to use—silence, exile, and cunning.[9]

One sees in the story of Stephen Dedalus a relentless self-education, which is further enhanced in Joyce's following book, *Ulysses,* through Stephen's interactions with the Jewish Leopold Bloom, a member of a community which Stephen's own family and friends refuse to associate with.

The key element in the Cynics's movement is continuous education, which includes an openness to traditions and peoples alien to one's self. Two other statements of Diogenes the Cynic express this quite eloquently: "Education, according to him, is a controlling grace to the young, consolation to the old, wealth to the poor, and ornament to the rich . . . Being asked what was the most beautiful thing in the world, he replied, 'Freedom of speech.'"[10]

It is interesting to note that Nussbaum frames her article as the beginning of an ongoing discussion. In answer to her critics, Nussbaum writes:

> When we think as world citizens but also as citizens of nations, what will we decide about our obligations? . . . My focus in the piece was on the formation of citizens who could be intelligent participants in debates about those questions; I did not want to prejudge how the debate should come out, though I do have views about that. Let's now begin that debate.[11]

Kristeva is pessimistic about the effectiveness of universalism as a political force. She writes:

In today's circumstances of unprecedented intermixing of foreigners on earth, two extreme solutions are taking place. Either we are headed toward global united states of all former nation-states: a process that could be contemplated in the long run and that the economic, scientific, and media-based development allows one to assume. Or else, the humanistic cosmopolitism shows itself to be utopic, and particularistic aspirations force one to believe that small political sets are the optimal structures to insure the survival of humanity.[12]

But why present this as an either/or proposition? For those who are inspired by a vision of human beings interacting with mutual aid and respect, it makes perfect sense to encourage the particularism of universalism—recognizing that it is unlikely to sweep the world or convince everyone, yet seeing it for what it is: a powerful and time-honored position which has continually transcended the boundaries of ethnic, religious, and other distinctions that keep humans from interacting with each other.

Notes

1.   Diogenes Laertius, *Lives of Eminent Philosophers,* vol. II, translated by R. D. Hicks (Cambridge: Harvard University Press, 1970), p. 51.

2.   Brendan Behan, *Borstal Boy* (New York: Alfred A. Knopf, 1959), pp. 53-54.

3.   Martha C. Nussbaum, *The Therapy of Desire: Theory and Practice in Hellenistic Ethics* (Princeton: Princeton University Press, 1994), p. 8.

4.   R. Bracht Branham and Marie-Odile Goulet-Caze, editors, *The Cynics: The Cynic Movement in Antiquity and Its Legacy* (Berkeley: University of California Press, 1996).

5.   Martha C. Nussbaum, "Patriotism and Cosmopolitanism," *The Boston Review* XIX, no. 5 (October/November 1994), p. 4.

6.   Ibid.

7.   Ibid., p. 6.

8.   Julia Kristeva, *Strangers to Ourselves,* translated by Leon S. Roudiez (New York: Columbia University Press, 1991), p. 58.

9. James Joyce, *A Portrait of the Artist as a Young Man,* in *The Portable James Joyce* (New York: The Viking Press, 1975), p. 519.

10. Diogenes Laertius, p. 71.

11. Martha C. Nussbaum, "Asking the Right Questions: Martha Nussbaum Responds," *The Boston Review* XIX, no. 5 (October/November 1994), p. 34.

12. Kristeva, *op. cit.,* p. 98.

ECOHUMANISM: SO WHAT'S NEW?

GOD, HUMANITY, AND NATURE—
CARING FOR CREATION

Sarah Oelberg

For a long time, Humanism has been bearing the brunt of blame for our growing environmental problems and ecological crisis. I have never understood this, for it has always seemed to me that the notion that humans have dominion over all other forms of life on earth comes more directly and reasonably from Genesis, and God's message to man and woman to "Multiply and fill the earth and subdue it; you are masters of the fish and birds and all the animals. "Environmentalists have long blamed this Biblical tradition for providing cultural sanction for the Industrial Revolution and its plundering of the earth.

Father Thomas Berry, a solitary monk in earth shoes, suggests that the problem is not that the Bible says the wrong things about human's relation to nature, but that it, along with the other major religions of the west, Islam and Judaism, gives too little theological significance to the world of nature at all. As people of the book, he says, Jews, Christians and Muslims too, turn primarily to sacred texts for God's revelation. What matters most in these texts is human redemption, not divine creation. If religious leaders want to know what God thinks about nature, Berry says, books like the Bible and the Koran are the wrong places to look. The universe it-

289

self is God's "primary revelation," and the story it tells of its own evolution from cosmic dust to human consciousness provides the sacred text and context for understanding our place in God's creation. "The natural world is the larger sacred community to which we all belong," Berry writes. "We bear the universe in our being even as the universe bears us in its being."

Berry criticizes Christianity for its preoccupation with "redemption out of this world through a personal savior relationship that eclipses all concerns with cosmic order and process." Judaism and Islam too, err in his eyes by overemphasizing human's relation to a transcendent God, and thus ignoring humankind's primordial genetic attachment to the natural world. "The same atoms that formed the galaxies," Berry likes to remind his audiences, "are in me."

Alan Watts, in his book *Nature, Man and Woman*, offers another critique of Christianity. He finds a deep incompatibility between the atmosphere of Christianity and the atmosphere of the natural world. He writes:

> It has seemed well-nigh impossible to relate God the Father, Jesus Christ, the angels, and the saints to the universe in which I actually live. Looking at trees and rocks, at the sky with its clouds or stars, at the sea, or at a naked human body, I find myself in a world where this religion simply does not fit. Indeed, Christianity itself confirms this impression, since 'my kingdom is not of this world.' Yet if God made this world, how is it possible to feel so powerful a difference of style between the God of church and altar, for all his splendor, and the world of the open sky? . . . I have found it a basic impossibility to associate the author of the Christian religion with the author of the physical universe. This is not a judgment as to the relative merits of the two styles; it is only to say that they are not by the same hand, and that they do not mix well together.[1]

Watts goes on to try to discern why Christianity differs so in style from the natural universe. One reason is because Christianity is a construction of ideas or concepts "playing together on their own," without adequate relation to that world of nature which ideas represent. In Christianity, the stress is upon belief rather than experience. Immense importance is attached to an acceptance of a correct formulation of a dogma, doctrine, or rite. Early in it history, Watts reminds us, Christianity rejected *gnosis*, or direct experience of God, in favor of *pistis*, or the trust of the will in certain revealed propositions about God. "In the beginning was the word," and Christianity has ever since been obsessed with the realm of words and thought symbols—separate from experience and nature.

Another reason, according to Watts, is that Christianity sees a universe that has been *made*. Outside the church, we are in a universe that has *grown*. Thus, the God that made the universe stands outside it as the carpenter stands outside his creations, but the source that grows the world is within it. Christian doctrine admits, in theory, that God is immanent—in the world—but in practice it is his transcendence, his otherness, which is always stressed. And, seeing humans and the universe as made, Christianity tries to interpret them mechanically, and understands the workings of the universe in terms of logical laws—the mechanical order of things viewed in a linear series of causes and effects. Thus, it never really sees nature. It sees only a pattern of geometrical forms which it has managed to project upon nature. But nature is not like that. It is a jumble of all sorts of shapes and forms, intertwined and interconnected in many ways, constantly changing and evolving, ebbing and flowing, waxing and waning.

Finally, Watts suggests, however poorly Christianity fits with nature, it fits very well with human nature. God is reflected in nature nowhere as clearly as in humans—indeed, they are "made in his image." Therefore, the appeal of Christianity is to very human and very powerful feelings—the love of humans for their own kind, the bedrock of nostalgia for home and one's own people, coupled with the fascination of the heroic, the challenge to believe in the possibility of an ultimate victory over evil and pain. And the result, according to Watts, is that deep in our heart of hearts, we do feel alien from nature, and we do desire to control and decrease it. He claims that the Western experiment in changing the face of nature by science and technology has its roots in the political cosmology of Christianity.

If this be true, then why is it that humanism has become the primary target when it comes to the environment? Some suggest that it is because humanism is now thought to be the dominant force behind civil society—our "civil religion"—which determines public policies in the world today. Sometimes the downside of "winning" is that you then get the blame for whatever happens. Others blame a different kind of "success"—that in finally severing human/human interaction from interaction with supernatural deities, humanism *also* seems to have separated humans from nature, since nature, creation, and God are inseparable to many people. Or, perhaps it is, as Watts suggests, simply "human nature" to want to protect the human species above all else!

It is not difficult to see where and how humanism is open to criticism for being anthropocentric, however. Many of our writings put humans at the center, if not the top, of everything. This is, as David Ehrenfeld has pointed out, a bit "arrogant." He blames our faith in the superiority and abilities of humans and our triumphs in science and technology for a catalogue of disasters into which our attitudes toward nature have led us. He may be right when he claims our technologically enhanced anthropocentrism has become ugly and dangerous. Like the Christians, we may be guilty as charged, much as we might like to think otherwise. After all, the *Humanist* magazine still carries on its masthead the statement: "Humanism . . . derives the goals of life from human needs and interest." Period. As long as we continue to so publicly declare our anthropocentrism, it is not unreasonable for others to get the impression that we do not care about nature.

Recently, a strong critique of both Christianity and Humanism has come from the ecofeminists, who contend that a large part of the problem with humanity's relation to nature is that we call it *mother* nature, and that anything which is perceived as female is fair game for desecration and being "used" for the benefit of men. They point out that Christianity and Humanism are hierarchical, patriarchal, and anthropocentric, putting MAN at the center of the universe. In contrast, they claim, earth consciousness and woman consciousness often go together. Furthermore, ecofeminism discloses a profound understanding not only of the earth's suffering, but also of the social and socio-psychological causes of this suffering. Eco-feminists find meaning in liberation theology merged with a view of the earth as sacred in and of itself—in fact, the most sacred thing. Theirs, too, is a critique we need to take seriously. We need to define and defend a similar approach to nature which comes naturally from our humanist stance—ecohumanism.

While acknowledging the validity of these and other critiques of humanism as it relates to nature, I am not willing to accept them without rebuttal. The humanism that is so often criticized is a kind of parody of the humanism I grew up with and love. Yes, I have encountered the arrogance Ehrenfeld describes, mostly among "secular" humanists, but underneath it I also find a deep caring for the earth and its inhabitants—all of them. And even Ehrenfeld was willing to concede that the protection of human interest is a useful rationale for conservation—as a starting point. My humanism has always embraced the idea of our "oneness" with nature; that as human beings we are part and parcel of the physical and natural universe. It is Nature and not the supernatural that provides me with my sense of meaning, wonder, and awe; the discovery of my place in the context of the cosmos. I find my religious meaning in the context of the natural. My humanism is concerned with "earthly" cares and concerns, individually, socially and literally.

I have written elsewhere about being raised on the wide, open plains of the Midwest, and how the liberal religion that emerged and grew in the West differed from that of the more restricted and convention-loving East. I have even suggested that humanism fits best with the experiences and attitudes that come from living in a more open environment.[2] The humanism I grew up with was very connected with nature, perhaps because, living on the prairie, I witnessed the interdependence and power of nature, and realized its intrinsic value. I also sensed, from childhood, that the more I understood and cooperated with nature, the less frightening it became, and the more both humanity and nature would flourish.

And I found verification for my experience in various humanist sources, starting with Manifesto I: ". . . religious culture and civilization. . . are the product of a gradual development due to interaction with the natural environment and social heritage," and that we are "part of nature . . . emerged as a result of a continuous process." I liked Curtis Reese's humanism which, "while abandoning the supernatural. . . expands the natural."[3] I agreed with the Morains who saw the interrelationship of humans with each other and with nature as inseparable and think "the good moral life is justified in terms of having proper relations with nature and each other."[4] And I would have applauded John Dietrich when he attacked critics whom he felt misunderstood the humanist view in relation to nature:

> The mistake that all these critics make is in separating man [sic] from nature, and looking upon nature as antagonistic to man's purposes and ideals. They do not seem to realize that we are an inseparable part of the universe. We are not alien children in a strange and foreign land. We are a product, the natural development of its forces and condition. Every human function—physical and mental and moral—has developed as a result

of constant and successful adaptation to natural conditions. And therefore, as I hope to show you, what we call human values, while they may not exist outside of human consciousness, are an essential part of the universe because they are a part of man. Here is the crux of the whole problem. We are a part of the universe, and cannot be separated from it. We were with it when our universe was star-dust swinging out in the open spaces.[5]

Certainly, part of the genius of humanism is a preparedness to deal with human beings as we are. That means embracing evolution and thereby locating humans in nature, not apart from it.

But perhaps humanism has changed—has become a "victim of its excesses"—and I am out of touch. Last summer, David Burwasser posted three propositions on the Friends of Religious Humanism chat line, and asked which of these positions on the relationship between humans and their environment would be acceptable in contemporary humanist thought. They were:

1. We need to attend to the environment inasmuch as it is necessary for human existence or helpful to the human enterprise. So, if we need the oxygen provided by phytoplankton, let's not pollute the phytoplankton; if there's a cancer cure in some vine in the rainforest, let's not slash and burn the rainforest.

2. We are embedded in the natural environment in too many ways for us to sort out based on current knowledge. We know we depend on it as a species but are confident that the extent of our dependence is deeper than we have discovered. We therefore should prevent, where possible, any endangered species from going extinct, because we will never know until it is too late just when we have shredded the interdependent web beyond its ability to support us.

3. The interdependent web has value in and of itself. We should, for example, resist the cutting of old-growth forest, even if the pulp and paper company that owns it will replace it with new trees of the same species, because a 500-year-old stand of trees is inherently more valuable than a fresh stand of seedlings, even of the same species.

Burwasser then goes on to "rate" the propositions. He assumes #1 gives no problem to contemporary humanists, and that #3 is not a contemporary humanist statement; that a humanist of today might accept and act on it, but would in that event be doing so out of other values or attachments than humanism. Then he asks where contemporary humanism comes down on #2. I left for Europe right after this post, and therefore did not get to see any of the responses. My own, however, is that I have the most trouble with #1, precisely because it *is* arrogantly anthropocentric, selfish, and foolish. If that is what contemporary humanism is all about, we deserve all the criticism leveled at us.

I also have no problem with #s 2 and 3, although even #2 reeks of anthropocentrism. What I find most disturbing, however, is his suggestion that any humanist who accepts #3 would be doing so only out of other values than humanism. Is he suggesting that we can so compartmentalize our life and thought that some things derived from our human experience are "legitimate" because they fit some narrow definition of humanism, and all else is suspect? Excuse me, but I thought one of the things that differentiated humanism from, say, Christianity, was our reliance on experience as the method—Dewey says "the only method—for getting at nature, penetrating its secrets, and wherein nature empirically disclosed . . . deepens, enriches and directs the further development of experience."[6] Furthermore, this experience, says Dewey, is the same for the scientist and the man on the street—stars, rocks, trees and creeping things are the same material of experience for both. So why would not human experiences which lead one to embrace the philosophy in #3 not be consistent with humanism? I am sorry, but I cannot accept that values I adopt as a result of my human experience are not valid because they did not come from precise empirical scientific evidence. Human experience is not only *of* nature, but also *in* nature.

I would like to suggest that there are four "models" which are all legitimately humanist, but vary in their basic assumptions. The first is what I would call the Pure Naturalistic Humanism. This is the kind of attitude espoused by Burwasser in his first proposition, where nature is perceived as having value only as it is experienced and interpreted as directly benefiting humans. This approach is so elitist it borders on speciesism—attaching an exaggerated importance to our own species, *Homo sapiens*. This model, insofar as it still exists, is so antiquated and problematic that it only deserves to die.

The second model I will call, at the risk of contributing even more to a trend toward hyphenated humanism, Ethical Naturalistic Humanism. This is an approach toward nature which comes from the strong humanist dedication to ethical and moral behavior; that "moral values derive their source from human experience" and that "ethics is autonomous and situational" (Manifesto II). It is based on the premise that humanism in rooted in ethical behavior, and, as Joseph Wood Krutch suggested, an ethical attitude toward nature is "better in the longest run for humans, too." He said that the modification of nature by humans could be appropriate and beneficial "only up to the point where it did not interfere too drastically with the ecosystem as a whole. "He also said we should have "sympathy with other living creatures."[7] In a 1954 essay entitled "Conservation is not enough," Krutch claimed that the old-style utilitarian and anthropocentric resource management was insufficient to save nature (and, ultimately, humankind) from human selfishness.

Roderick Nash, in his useful history of environmental ethics, claims that ethical standing cannot begin and end with human beings; morality ought to include the relationship of humans to nature, and vice versa. He says: "Ethics should expand from a preoccupation with humans (or Gods) to concern for animals, plants, rocks and the environment or nature in general."[8] Perhaps the most ardent advocate for an environmental ethic is Aldo Leopold, who argued in the 1940s for a holistic, biocentric morality he termed "the land ethic." His land ethic affirms "the right to continued existence" of not only animals and plants but waters and soils as well. The life-forms that share the planet with people should be allowed to live "as a matter of biotic right, regardless of the presence or absence of advantage to us." This means "there are obligations to land over and above those dictated by self-interest," obligations grounded in the recognition that humans and the other components of nature are ecological equals.[9] This does not mean humans should have *no* impact on nature, but that only human action "to prevent the deterioration of the environment" should be undertaken. Leopold's is an ethical system that "includes the whole of nature, and nature as a whole."[10] He pushes us to think of ethics as more than what is "right" for humans, but to include the concept that nature has "rights" also.

This is also the position Ehrenfeld takes when he declares that "long-standing existence in Nature" carries with it "the unimpeachable right to continued existence." He wants "recognition of the rights of 'non-resources,' including species that have no significance to people or even to the healthy functioning of the ecosystem." He thinks the only firm base for ethical respect was "existence value," a kind of ecological because-it-is-there attitude.[11] The Ethical Naturalistic Humanist, then, recognizes the intrinsic rights of all species to exist and assumes a moral duty to protect and preserve them.

The third approach I call Ecological Naturalistic Humanism. This model sees that the human response to nature has to go beyond human need and interest, for the needs and interests of humans and nature are intrinsically intertwined to such an extent that they cannot be separated. This stance comes directly from scientific research and observation, especially biologist Henry Cowles, whose study of the Illinois prairies led him to document the complex environmental factors that went into determining the distribution of plant communities in the 1890s; and Frederic Clements investigation of the succession of plants and the process that leads to "climax" vegetation, which he described as a "complex organism." What he meant was that many living things functioning together resemble a single being. They were mutually dependent; plants interrelated with climate, soil and each other to form a predictable vegetative association such as a grassland.[12]

In 1914 the Scottish biologist J. Arthur Thompson first described this quality with the phrase "web of life." That phrase anticipates the more current ecosystem. There is a very dynamic, interactive, and cooperative community going on—many species are dependent upon and contribute to other species—geology, botany, soil chemistry, wind, fire, and water must all be in some sort of balance. This finding is the basis for the Seventh Principle in the Unitarian Universalist Principles and Purposes, "the interdependent web of all existence." It has broadened the concept of community and the consequent notions of rights and ethical behavior still further.

Arguably, the most comprehensive philosophy of interdependence was that of Alfred North Whitehead, who contended that the identity and purpose of every object in the universe arose from its relationship to everything else—every organism, indeed every atom, had intrinsic value if only for the contribution it made to the ongoing reality of the universe, which he called "process." Whitehead ultimately hoped that science would embrace what he called "organicism," abandon objectivity, and lead humankind to a recognition of the intrinsic worth of every component of the environment. The Ecological Naturalistic Humanist, then, honors and protects each and every bit of matter, because it is so interwoven with everything else that no one species or atom can be isolated; thus, the continued existence not only of humankind, but of all life, depends on preserving everything.

My final model I call Reverential Ecological Humanism. It comes primarily from Albert Schweitzer who was cruising down a river in Africa, pondering the question what was the most valid basis for ethics, when it flashed upon his mind the word *Ehrfurcht*, which means, roughly, "reverence for life."[13] From this, Schweitzer built a theory of value and ethics based on the "will-to-live" that he understood every living being to possess. Right conduct for humans, then, meant granting to "every will-to-live the same reverence for life that he gives to his own." The preservation, promotion, and enhancement of life in general became the basis of Schweitzer's ethics—"a man is ethical only when life, as such, is sacred to him, that of plants and animals as well as that of his fellow men."[14] Perhaps it is more realistic to think of "reverence for the cycle of life and death, intertwined and each as a precondition of the other."

The notion of reverence for life has been embraced by many others. Norman Cousins wrote that "reverence for life is more than solitude or sensitivity for life. It is a sense of the whole, a capacity for wonder, a respect for the intricate universe of individual life. It is the supreme awareness of awareness itself. It is pride in being." Rachel Carson adopted as the basis of her moral philosophy a conviction that "life is a miracle beyond our comprehension, and we should reverence it even where we have to struggle against it."[15] William Hammond, while pointing out that some humanists feel that "reverence is nothing but muddled awe," says we should not let ourselves be turned away from true reverence, for it gives us an appreciative awareness of our creaturehood, and our relatedness to the immediate and ultimate sources of life. Reverence is not something we should make ourselves feel, he claims, but something which we should feel, because feelings of wonder and relatedness are part of the very nature of human nature.[16]

And Edward O. Wilson, 1999 Humanist of the Year, goes so far as to predicate that there is an inborn affinity that human beings have for other forms of life, which he calls *biophilia*. This inborn sense is so strong, he suggests, that it gives us a preference for certain natural environments as places to live; a subconscious kinship with other life forms and the life process, which is embedded in the billions of "bits" of genetic information in even the humblest living creatures. He feels Schweitzer's "reverence for life" will eventually be understood in terms of evolutionary biology and psychology; that the concept of community includes not only the entire contemporary ecosystem but backwards in time to the beginning of evolution. In his opinion:

> The most important implication of an innate biophilia is the foundation it lays for an enduring conservation ethic. If a concern for the rest of life is part of human nature, if part of our culture flows from wild nature, then on that basis alone it is fundamentally wrong to extinguish other life forms. Nature is part of us, as we are part of nature.[17]

If humanism remains stuck in a purely naturalistic "man is the measure of all things" mode; if it cannot embrace the larger concepts of interrelationship and interdependence with nature and grant it worth; if its adherents cannot experience awe and wonder at the inherent marvels of nature and see themselves as only one tiny part of the great universe; then it deserves all the criticism leveled at it. On the other hand, if humanism can open up to the implications of the realities science has shown us, and relate to nature in the ways described in my four (well, last three, actually) models, then it has a legitimate claim to a place at the table where decisions about the future of the planet are being made. Humanists are late-comers, but they have much to offer, and need to be active partici-pants.

As E. O. Wilson said in his address when he accepted the Humanist of the Year award:

> As a biological species we are alone, we will flourish or die as a species together alone, and our reverence is therefore better directed not to tribal gods and iron-age mythologies, which were conceived in the brutal Darwinian past and still carry the stench of arrogance and oppression that made them possible, but to each other, our species, our intellect, our planet, and our future, together.[18]

I close with these words from Brooks Atkinson:

> The purpose of nature is to make adjustments that preserve the variety and onward momentum of life—including the species of man if he can adapt himself to the cosmic scheme. . . . Nature keeps life in balance by continuing the population of the species. No species is permitted to dominate the world indefinitely. Man is one species that so far has succeeded in violating that natural order.[19]

Notes

1. Alan W. Watts, *Nature, Man, and Woman* (New York: Vintage Books, 1970), pp. 27-28.

2. Sarah Oelberg, "The Prairie: From Vast to Vanished," *Religious Humanism* XXXI, 1&2 (1997).

3. Curtis Reese, *The Meaning of Humanism* (Boston: Beacon Press, 1945), p. 8.

4. Lloyd and Mary Morain, *Humanism As the Next Step* (Boston: Beacon Press, 1954), p. 38.

5. John Dietrich, *The Humanist Pulpit* 5 (Minneapolis: First Unitarian Society, 1933), pp. 80f.

6. John Dewey, *Experience and Nature* (New York: Dover, 1958), p. 2a.

7. Roderick Frazier Nash, *The Rights of Nature* (Madison: University of Wisconsin Press, 1989), p. 75.

8. Nash, p. 4.

9. Aldo Leopold, *A Sand County Almanac* (New York: Oxford University Press, 1049), pp. 209-22.

10. Nash, p. 63.

11. Nash, p. 84.

12. Nash, pp. 56-57.

13. Albert Schweitzer, *Out of My Life and Thought: An Autobiography* (New York: Holt, 1933).

14. Nash, pp. 60-61.

15. Rachel Carson, *Silent Spring* (Boston, Houghton Mifflin, 1962), p. 126.

16. William Hammond, *Ecology of the Human Spirit* (Minneapolis: Rising Press, 1996), pp. 15-6.

17. E. O. Wilson, *Naturalist* (Washington D.C.: Island Press, 1994), p. 362.

18. E. O. Wilson, "The Two Hypotheses of Human Meaning: Scientific Empiricism and Religious Transcendentalism," Address, Humanist of the Year Award (1999).

19. Brooks Atkinson, *This Bright Land* (Garden City: Doubleday Natural History Press, 1972), p. 11.

ECOHUMANISM: SOME EXPANSIONS

Robert B. Tapp

In developing and setting upon the topic of ecohumanism for the Adjunct Faculty of The Humanist Institute's 2000 Colloquium, two personal experiences ran through my mind. Before World War II, I had spent many happy weeks with my backpack in the wilderness areas of California's High Sierra and San Gabriel mountains. One of my literary "companions" had been John Muir, and from him I understood a kind of nature mysticism before I even had proper labels for it. In 1946, the destroyer on which I served carried one of the nuclear bombs to Bikini atoll, and I witnessed the first test. As it has turned out, our ship was the only one exposed to serious fallout from that test in the form of a radioactive rain, and the Navy has reluctantly given me the recent title of atomic veteran.

The natural beauties of the mountains remain in my mind's eye. The significant exposure to the gamma radiation, however, was never visible, reminding me to this day that what we call "natural" is sometimes readily perceived, but sometimes very real and not easily perceptible.

Growing up middle-class in California, a car was a constant and year-around companion, and I began to experience a kind of technophilia. The artifactual world of machines was not only real but possessed "feelings," laments over malfunctionings. That not uncommon sentiment of modernity has stayed with me, surely carrying over to the powerful computer with which I write this chapter. Its moods become mine, and this no doubt works both ways.

This blurring of any distinction between the non-human world "outside" of me and a quite-human one was formative. Moreover, the human world, seen more closely, lost much of its luster. Travels in a devastated Germany that had been also a devastator left indelible memories. When I first visited Dachau, it was a NATO base. As I drove inside, having been saluted by an African American U. S. soldier (surely a nightmare for Hitler could he have stayed alive to see it from his prison van!), a fork in the road made one choose: right to the refectory or left to the crematorium! A grim image of the human part of the ecosphere. But a reminder that whatever "nature" was, it was in great need of human interventions and improvements.

During all my years at the University of Minnesota I taught a course in nineteenth-century humanities. For most of those years, this was the only place on campus for students were expected to read the two major books of Charles Darwin.[1] I always conducted a before and after test, using the wording of the Gallup poll, to explore how this reading affected students' religious ideas. Two things remained a constant surprise. The before and after responses, it turned out, changed very little, and the percentage of "creationists" remained about thirty whether the students were Catholic or Protestant. Since this was very little below the national averages, one cynical conclusion might have been that Darwin and evolution were no great threats to people's religions. This was even more curious given the fact that neither Catholics nor most Lutherans came from groups of that denied evolution. Other cynical conclusions might have been that students did not read closely, or listen to their religious mentors very closely. Most probably, the televangelists had become the religious teachers of young America! Underneath all these musings, of course, was the constant question of how to teach more effectively—which comes down to the question of whether it is possible to effect widespread alterations of early childhood conditionings and the effects of a largely media-constricted education which complemented the trivializations and relativizations of the postmodern scene.

I have been teaching and exploring science/religion interactions for fifty years, and it is amazing how strongly nature and ecology have come into a recent focus. Nature, as a category, has always figured in religious discourses, but usually in a quite casual way. Biblical writers urged their audience to imitate ants and doves, but in the case of the latter they had so misperceived the "gentleness" of that species that it was clearly not an area they had seriously observed. In fact, most Western invocations of nature have been similarly romanticized .[2]

Kenneth Boulding once described American cities as drinking the sewage of cities that were upriver. In more contemporary terms should we view this situation as one of pollution or as one of recycling? Or if we use Buckminster Fuller's metaphor of "spaceship earth," each of us in some sense is in contaminating distance of all others.

At the outset, some preliminary definitions are in order. Ecology, although a relatively new academic discipline, already has recognized subdivisions such as "human ecology." For our purposes, we will treat ecology as a scientific discipline engaged in empirical description. Take, for instance, the issue of global warming. Whether this is occurring or how much is due to human activities—these are empirical questions with probabilistic answers. A major study prepared for the failed conference in The Hague showed that the evidence was in. The lead author of its summary,

Kevin Trenberth, stated: "There is increasing evidence from many sources that the signal of human influence on climate has emerged from natural variability, sometime around 1980."[3] One of the most disturbing aspects of recent activisms on this issue has been the divisions among those who otherwise share in a commitment to ecologically sound change. A British scientist-observer said, after the failure of the conference to reach agreement: "When something like this is killed, it is killed by an alliance of those who want too much with those who don't want anything."[4]

How, for instance, global warming can and should be altered—such questions constitute environmentalism. And there are many forms of environmentalism. Some assume the earth should be restored to its pre-human condition. Others assume that "nature" is essentially benign if humans meet certain conditions. Many traditional religions assume that "nature" is beneficent and directed by gods who are friendly to humans.

In recent years ecofeminism, deep ecology, and the Gaia hypothesis have emerged, attracting many followers. These conceptualizations function in a quasi-religious manner, to the extent that religions can be recognized by their commitment to non-falsifiability. We will be looking here at the ecological attitudes of religions, then of liberal religions, and then of nontheistic humanisms; then examining these quasi-religions in this larger context.

The Religions' Track Records

Early in the last century Albert Schweitzer, summarizing the beginnings of what was then called either "comparative religion" or "science of religion," characterized religions as either "world affirming" or "world denying." Schweitzer at that time saw Christianity as a world–affirming religion because of its social ethic. He himself spent much of his life in Lambaréné as a medical doctor in order to atone for the sins of European colonialism.

This contrast is still somewhat useful as a broad classification. Classical Buddhism drew upon one strand of Hinduism to urge the "withdrawal of the senses from their objects" and to preach the transitoriness of all things. The monasticisms of various religions most often originated in a world-withdrawal to achieve an otherwise more difficult self-perfection. The more pragmatic goals of later monasticisms—Benedictine scholasticism, Dominican evangelism, Jesuit power-seeking are later developments. But they are still based on a celibacy which is clearly a form of body/world denial.

Ironically, Schweitzer himself had come to see the "historical Jesus" as an eschatological preacher expecting an imminent ending to this world and the establishment of a totally transforming Kingdom of God. Jesus, he contended, threw his own body on the cross to hasten this turning of the wheel of history. Schweitzer's medical dissertation had valiantly attempted to defend Jesus against charges of insanity that were based upon such ideas about the world. It may be worth noting that toward the end of his life, Schweitzer moved beyond this to sign on with the American Humanist Association.

In many ways, the liberal Protestant Christianity that flourished until of the World War II chose to ignore Schweitzer's Jesus in favor of its own historical reconstruction of a Jesus who was almost a premature political liberal urging his followers to build a Kingdom of God on earth. For better or for worse, that liberalism has essentially disappeared. Certainly the dominant American Protestantism today is deeply eschatological, looking to an end of the world as we know it followed by an establishment of some totally-different, divinely-ruled world. The rather brief appearance of a recent millennial fever should not lull us into thinking that the eschatological expectations of Christians have been transformed, or liberalized, or made naturalistic. The onslaught of books and novels about an alleged "Rapture" testify to this. That theme is more muted in Roman Catholic and Orthodox circles, but it functions—especially within lay circles—to dampen hopes for major social changes.[5]

In their still-neglected study of census information about U.S. believers since 1796,[6] Roger Finke and Rodney Stark have made abundantly clear that a similar kind of evangelical biblicism has been the American Protestant pattern throughout most of our history. American Catholics—whose numbers have grown increasingly since the late 19th century as a result of immigration, large families, and conversions—have never strayed far from this basic eschatological core of Christianity. This may be a Jubilee year for Roman Catholics, but it really is an anticipation of that future when divine rule closes down human history, transforming everything into a Kingdom of God.

What is interesting is the strong continuation of this Irano-Hebrew worldview which has typically been coupled with some kind of messianism. In that view, which clearly pervades Judaism, Christianity, and Islam, the attitude toward this world is summed up perfectly in an Islamic phrase that all three religions have found useful: "This world is a bridge, built not thy house thereon." An erstwhile Secretary of the Interior, James Watt, was guided by this principle when he responded to environmentalists' concerns about the redwood forests with the comment that we really don't know how soon Jesus will be reappearing. Since he and his kind of believers expected that in a brief time everything would be changed anyway, anything they did to the environment would be rendered irrelevant. Remember the ancient Hebrew poet's expectation that the valleys shall be exalted (and the mountains laid low?).

Given this centrality of eschatology in the structures of Western religions, Lynn White's critique becomes even more understand-

able—and the possibilities of any sustained ecological consciousness even slimmer.

Western Religions Eco-records

Western religions became ecologically sensitized with the publication of Lynn White's bombshell article in 1967.[7] Lynn White was
right in an arguing that the doctrine of "dominion" pervaded the environmental attitudes and behaviors of Western religionists. It is
simply that the god had said: This is all yours, in your dominion
(as power over, lordship), to do with as you wish. But when White
suggested that they should turn to Francis of Assisi as the patron
saint of environmentalism, he was recognizing the inevitable his-
toricity of all human movements, including religions. The current
pope recently confused matters further by attributing Francis'
qualities to St. Dominic.

Before discussing the attempts of various religions to affect
policies of the United Nations, we need to reflect on the difficulties
of the very concept "religion." The recent death of Wilfrid Cantwell Smith should remind us of a major contribution this scholar
made to intellectual clarity in an exciting book *The Meaning and
End of Religion*.[8] After showing the many ambiguities of the word
in Western cultures, which stem in part from its dubious etymol-
ogy, Smith contended that we should drop the term completely and
speak only of the various faiths of men and women at various
points in time. Smith was an Islamist, and argued that the things
people believed and did in the name of Islam over time created an
Islamic tradition but that "Islam" itself was an unwarranted reifica-
tion. This, of course, was good social science but Smith contended
that it was also good comparative religion. Another way of putting
this would be to remind ourselves that while the traditions in which
we are born shape us, to a lesser degree we also shape/reshape our
traditions. Appeals to texts or statements of founders will usually

be poorer descriptors of religions than examinations of the lives and values of believers. By the same reasoning, statements of religious officials are poorer indexes than actual practices of living members.

With this in mind, we can look at the efforts of various non-governmental agencies to shape a policy for the United Nations. Although no religions are directly represented there,[9] there has from the beginning been a readiness to recognize the significant role that religions and ideologies play in determining world policies. UN Secretary U Thant named a Canadian businessman, Maurice Strong, to direct the Stockholm conference on the human environment. Strong has remained with the UN to this day, and is presently a senior adviser to the current Secretary General, Kofi Annan. Strenuous efforts were made at that time to have the UN articulate a defense of the environment, but they met with no success. In 1992, Strong was named secretary general of the UN Conference on the Environment and Development, generally known as the Rio Earth Summit.

The Earth Council, headquartered in San Jose, Costa Rica, promoted worldwide consultations to develop an Earth Charter. and their intention was to create a universally acceptable document that could be accepted by the UN General Assembly and provide a form of "soft law." This Charter was envisaged as an "articulation of a spiritual vision that reflex universal spiritual values, including but not limited to ethical values." Professor Steven Rockefeller of Middlebury College was the collector of all these comments. The intention was to draw upon ecology and other contemporary sciences, along with the world's religious and philosophical traditions and "the growing literature on global ethics and ethics of the environment and development."[10]

This process led to two Benchmark Drafts that contained the following values:

respect for Earth and all life, protection and restoration of the diversity, integrity and beauty of the Earth's ecosystems; sustainable production, consumption, and reproduction; a respect for human rights, including the right to an environmental adequate for human dignity and well-being; eradication of poverty; non-violent problem-solving and peace; the equitable sharing of earth's resources; democratic participation in decision making; a gender equality; accountability and transparency in administration; the advancement application of knowledge and technologies that facilitate care for earth; universal education for sustainable living; and a sense of shared responsibility for the well-being of the Earth community and future generations.

This document shows the refining work of many minds. Those critics of the earlier document who had charged it with pantheism might still take umbrage at such phrases as "Earth itself is alive." In fact, the document stands as a brilliant articulation of a global ethic. The phrases have generally stood the test of crosscultural critique.

A somewhat different interreligious effort has emerged from the Religious Consultation on Population, Reproductive Health and Ethics.[11] In many ways this group has been more critical of the religions' pasts. They use such terms as "ecological crisis" and "terricide." Their main position is that religions have been supportive of past positions and will be necessary to most persons for supporting changes. They also take better account of religions diversities.

Another effort to involve religions has come from the International Union for the Conservation of Nature and Natural Resources. The papers from the Ethics Working Group are very helpful in understanding the assimilation of the "sustainable development" concept.[12]

This and other chapters in this volume show that theism is neither univocal or universal. There is a fluid multiplicity in the theism of Hinduism, plus the pronounced nontheism of many forms of

Buddhism, and roles for ancestors in aboriginal religions where godlike qualities are discernible in personifications of nature. The Abrahamic religions tend more toward an ontological rigidity when it comes to God-talk and interreligious dialogue must be sensitive to this.

Jacob Olupona insists that you cannot understand Africa outside the context of its unique exploitation by Europe and America and its postcolonial militarism and mismanagement. Many African nations cannot be called "developing" because they are in worse condition than they were pre-independence.[13]

This consultation takes a more empirical approach to environmentalism, and benefits from a larger-than-Western orientation. It also becomes much more specific in dealing with the human ecology problems of reproductive matters and economics.

The most recent effort to analyze the historical impacts of religions as a basis for future influences of social policies has emerged from the Harvard University's Center for the Study of World Religions. Their excellent volume on Christianity is a must for any balanced assessment of the past and future effects of this religion upon the environment.[14]

The Unitarian Universalist Record

We now turn to the record of the Unitarians and Universalists in ecological matters. These two American denominations, both at the left end of the Protestant spectrum, had been converging for many years and formally merged in 1961 as the Unitarian Universalist Association (UUA). Six study commissions surveyed the past and charted the future of this new denomination. The commission on Theology and the Frontiers of Learning brought together scientists and theologians. They outlined three distinct areas. In the first, knowledge furnished by the contemporary sciences was so indisputably correct that it had been incorporated by almost all religions and theologies. The second area concerned issues in which knowledge was presently more ambiguous, and many turned for guidance to older religions and theologies. The commission noted a third area in which present scientific knowledge gave little guidance. The commission suggested that questions about the size of the human population fell across all three areas. Knowledge area one had helped us reduce the death rate and, in many cultures, reduce the birthrate. In the more ambiguous second area, the maximal population size of the globe was arguable (remember this was 1963). It was in the third area that present science had relatively little to say and therefore answers must come from elsewhere in human experience. Quoting the commission:

> How would the qualities of life be reshaped on a more crowded planet? Could democracy survive? Would human relationships be detrimentally altered? Would our relation to nonhuman life and nature suffer? Would cultural progress be enhanced or stifled? What the implications in developed, as against developing countries? Perhaps the overarching question is: assuming that we have the technology for support, how large a population is compatible with conceivable human values?[15]

Clearly the commission here was referring to values that are as much aesthetic as political or scientific.

In 1966, the UUA appointed a long-range planning committee, the Committee on Goals. In the course of its deliberations, this committee conducted a carefully-sampled survey of the denominations members. They found that 95 percent believed that there had been "progress in the history of human civilization" and that the strongest evidence for this was the "growth of science and knowledge."[16]

The committee did not speak directly of ecology. Instead, it perceived a "new religious liberalism" that was devoted to the "expansion of the quality of life." Where the Unitarians and Universalists had once been liberal Protestant Christians, it was clear by this time that Christian UUs were in the minority, and that there was a center group of post-Christian theists and a large majority of nontheistic humanists.

As it turned out, the UUA did not embark on this essentially humanist vector but instead became involved in a costly struggle over racism that divided UUs and probably had little impact on the world problem. "Black empowerment" struggled against "integration" and won. Only in the 1970s was the UUA able to broaden its action horizons. This time the struggle was over inclusiveness and a Gay-Lesbian-Bisexual-Transgender agenda. The UUA will always be remembered as the first American denomination to have a staff person for "gay affairs" and to seriously prepare congregations to be "welcoming."

Concerned about a stagnation in membership growth when other religious groups were booming, the UUA embarked upon a new program of "pluralism." Officially "creedless" since its founding (and within both founding denominations for many prior decades), the UUA sought to broaden its philosophical/theological boundaries, with the result that caucuses were soon formed for Buddhists, Native Americans, and Pagans. In this process, a seventh principle was added to the bylaws. UU humanists formed a Fellowship of Religious Humanists in 1962 to strengthen their own voice (now the Friends of Religious Humanism).

The Humanists' Eco-record

Although humanists have in recent years become marginalized within the Unitarian Universalist Association (UUA), many humanist UUs had been instrumental in founding the American Humanist Association (AHA) in 1933, and a majority of the signers of the Humanist Manifesto [I] in that year were UUs. In ensuing years many leaders and members of Ethical Societies announced their humanism. By the time of Humanist Manifesto II in 1972, signers came from both organized humanist groups and from unaffiliated individuals, and the religious assumptions of 1933 were considerably toned down. Ecological positions of these documents are discussed elsewhere in this volume.

The Modern Humanist Distinction

Nontheistic humanists have quite consistently argued that reason is the primary screen through which they evaluate possible courses of action. They tend to see reason less as some abstract quality of "mind" and more as a shorthand term to cover the sciences with their enormously successful descriptions and explanations of things and events. The treatment of all religions as human phenomena (comparative religion; philosophy, sociology, and psychology of religions) further describes reasonability for humanists. In contrasting the history and anticipations of such humanists with more traditional religionists, we will also need to look at the sources from which different groups start.

Traditional religions have relied upon texts, intuitions of holy persons, revelations from some god, or simply traditional folkways which have been hallowed by time. The slogan "Scripture, rightly interpreted" describes both the attitudes of fundamentalists and of the most sophisticated modernists.

For naturalistic humanists, such sources are either unreliable or unavailable. Humanists have typically brought to their scientifically-informed understanding of things and events a cluster of ethical judgments, most recently seen as being assessed in terms of their consequences. Probably the easiest way to understand the sources of modern humanism is to look to John Dewey. Humanists clearly are, in the pejorative label of their critics, ethical relativists. They habitually assess the quality of ethical judgments in terms of their situation, their context, their historical development. Often overlooked, especially by many of pragmatism's critics, is the role that aesthetics played for Dewey. In looking at ecohumanism, the ways that humanists have/do/could/should view the environment, we must factor in this aesthetic component.

Modern humanists are also explicitly in the tradition of Darwin, seeing human life as a "glorious accident" rather than the result of any cosmic plan or active cosmic designer. Their naturalism sees the present universe as all that there is, and is nontheistic. Some are atheists who feel godtalk can and should be rejected; others are simply agnostic in regard to the gods, feeling the lacks of any compelling evidence or defensible relevance. This means that many of the assertions of religious environmentalists don't make it into the humanist camp. Humans are neither given dominion over nature nor told to walk gently and leave no traces. There are no guarantees that human life will continue indefinitely. One might call this "intelligent dominion" rather than either "arrogant dominion" or "stewardship."

For Darwinian humanists, natural selection and the struggle for existence are central to any understanding of "nature." The emergence of humans was not guided by any destiny or intelligence; and humans too are involved in an evolutionary competition. Their evolving intelligence, to be sure, gives them many advantages, and the developed process of social evolution (almost unique to humans) gives them an extraordinary advantage. This combination of gene and meme (to use Richard Dawkins' felicitous term)[17] allows them now to understand and control their own evolution as well as the environment in ways heretofore unimaginable. But their situation is fraught with many bedrock dangers. If humanists were composing litanies today, they would have to include:

> Lord god of AIDS, we shall find aid,
> Lord god of fecundity, partnered humans will plan
> their wanted children,
> Lord god of men, we will include the equality of
> women,
> Lord god of rods, we shall spare our children,
> Lord god of kings and dictators, we will shift power to
> people,
> Lord god of battles, we will turn to the ways of peace
> ful negotiations
> Lord god of the poor, we will bless them with better
> economies,
> Lord god of cancers, we are seeking answers,
> Lord god of drudgery, we can create dignified labors,
> Lord god of ignorance, we will establish universal
> education,
> Lord god of genetic defects, we can now alter the
> effects,
> Lord god of dinosaurs, we are grateful for extinctions,
> Lord god of famines, we will improve production and
> distribution of foods,
> Lord god of plagues, we will find cures,
> Lord god of death, we will learn to go with dignity,

Humanity represents the most intelligent and creative species yet to come to our attention. Not exempted from the bedrock struggle for existence, humans have widened their zones of habitability, lengthened their lifespans, controlled many of their present diseases even as they were building cumulative cultures and enormous variability. Humans have consistently redefined inclusiveness and now even articulate "universal human rights." Should we still insist on calling these achievements "progress," we will be remembering that they are human options and not cosmic guarantees. And we will be celebrating the powers of these emerging new values—powers that, in exposing the limitations of existing values, can generate creative revolutions.

Other Alternatives to Ecohumanism

If ecohumanism differs in significant respects from the responses of traditional religions, how does it relate to the quasi-religions of ecofeminism, deep ecology, creation spirituality, and the Gaia hypothesis? To the extent that ecofeminism assumes that there is a different way to do ecology (or any other science, for that matter), most humanists would demur. There surely is a gender-politics pervading many intellectual disciplines, but the best cure is probably making all practitioners of that particular discipline see the limiting effects of such a politics and broaden their horizons. Breast cancer is a good example. Clearly it has until quite recently had a low priority for the predominantly-male medical researchers. To some extent, recent research has been spurred by the presence of more female researchers. But the increase in women's rights has probably been much more determinative. In many ways, there are parallels in the case of race politics and medical research. Sickle-cell anemia was overlooked as long as black citizens remained disenfranchised. In any case, the particular subject of scientific inquiry does not in itself affect what makes for good science.

Any ecofeminism runs the risk of biological determinism. While culture-alone theories have lost out in the nature vs. nurture debates, there remains the thorny issues of allocation along with the intractable questions of in-group variations vs. cross-group variations. For humanists, ecofeminism confuses more issues than it resolves. Feminist correctives of religious ideologies are one thing; feminist critiques of science are quite another. On a purely political level, it would seem disastrous to make better environmental practices a gender issue.[18]

Murray Bookchin has developed a major critique of a "deep ecology" that would restrict human environmental intrusions.[19] Humanists would do well to learn from the transformations of this erstwhile "environmentalist" into a more-balanced and human-centered position.

Another environmentalism with religious rootage is often called "creation spirituality." In examining the statements of traditional religions, creation spirituality has shown much appeal because it posits a benignly-planned universe (and thus a benign planner). Matthew Fox and Thomas Berry have both pushed a Catholic theology in directions suggested by Teilhard de Chardin (incurring the wrath of the more orthodox). A recent volume in this tradition speaks of "a holistic vision sure to expand our awareness of our place and purpose on earth and in the universe."[20]

The fourth quasi-theology is the Gaia hypothesis, the claim that the earth is a wise super-organism. Robert Wright's recent work seems to move in this direction.[21] A more popular version of this tendency is found in "Mother Earth" theories that claim indigenous peoples practice wise environmental policies. A major refutation of such claims can be found in Sam Gill's *Mother Earth*.[22] More recent evidence concerns careful analysis of early human/animal relations which often extinguished whole species (so much for bio-diversity!). William Stevens summarizes the recent contentions of Richard Holdaway:[23]

> With some exceptions, experts say, large-scale extinction of big animals generally coincided with the arrival of early modern humans in places where they had never been.
>
> This did not happen in Africa, they theorize, because people and other animals evolved there together, and African animals were therefore not so naïve about humans.
>
> One of the most rapid extinctions was in North America, where not just big plant-eaters but also the predators that depended on them—including saber-toothed cats, short-faced bears, cheetahs, maned lions and bigger versions of today's wolves—are believed to have vanished in perhaps 400 years.

Three possible causes have been advanced for this extinction episode. Two are related to the blitzkrieg hypothesis: that humans swept across the continent from Siberia in a "killing front" that moved perhaps 100 miles in a decade, and that the animals were killed by diseases carried by people and their dogs from Siberia.

But the fact is, Dr. Holdaway and Dr. Jacomb wrote, "even minimal levels of human hunting pressure caused an irreversible decline in the moa [large ostrich-like animals] population." The results of their study, Dr. Holdaway said, "reinforce the view that people with even the most basic technologies—fire, clubs, snares—can have major environmental effects."

What should one conclude from these religious and quasi-religious revisionings of the non-human environment? Not just that there are always important value issues—this goes without saying. These value issues will never become fully solved by restricting our knowledge to the sciences. True, but there must be a philosophical sophistication if we are to choose between the various proffered alternatives.[24] And it is here that the traditional religions have fallen short, and the quasi-religions have substituted feelings for hard thinking.

The Humanist Advantage

We must now examine the claim that humanism provides a better basis for understanding the full environment in which human life exists than it does either a simple nontheism or deep ecology. Let us examine the conditions for "coming of age ecologically" in terms of what we know about the general development, morally and intellectually, of children. The emergence of a separate "self" is a complex process of interactions between an organism and its environment, recognizing that this environment also includes many other organisms—themselves social. An emerging self reflects these many interactions. That growth, or at least change, is the actuality that is somewhat obscured by the reified term self. Perhaps the best term for this process would be "becoming," Think back on the first steps of the toddler—how important it is that some kind of support and guidance be available. In both cases, the support is physical. Now consider the young child learning to share toys. Here the support issues more from gesture and facial expression on the part of significant others, once a child's attention has been gained. Along with the motor skills of walking, children acquire moral skills. In Freudian terms, additions are being made to the superego. The parental voices (or in this case parental facial gestures) are being seen/heard and interiorized.

An early moral value is responsibility—how young persons learn that they must take responsibility for their environment which includes those around them upon whom they have depended for their growth. This responsibility involves recognizing the existences of, as well the claimable rights belonging to, those others who surround them.

From a humanist standpoint, this involves an acceptance of responsibility for the present and the future of this total environment. As Julian Huxley said, in his presidential address to the founding session of the International Humanist and Ethical Union, once we know the nature of evolution we are responsible for it.[25] This quite easily updates into a commitment to biodiversity. Until we can know quite fully the place of a given species in an ecological niche, we run tremendous risks in trying to alter or eliminate that species. Much as people in Minnesota might like to eliminate mosquitoes, they need to consider the effect upon bird populations and the effects of those bird populations upon other populations before rushing to fulfill their whims and immediate bodily comforts.

It is quite apparent that the only way these goals can be fulfilled is by the acquisition of knowledge, and that the only reliable way to acquire reliable knowledge is through the sciences. How we choose to use that knowledge remains, of course, another matter.

The barriers to knowledge, here as elsewhere, are over-reliance upon the singular, the anecdotal; and then over-reliance upon traditions of knowledge that have not been carefully and critically evaluated.

The humanist stance toward critical intelligence could be termed "eco-accuracy." Before engaging in environmental actions, whether conserving, altering, or restoring some aspect of the biosphere, humanism is concerned with accurate knowledge. Here, as in the sciences, intuitions, feelings, preferences can only serve as starters or motivators for investigations. The humanist will want to know, with some high probability, the alternatives and the consequences of each alternative.

Suppose that the alternative is genetic alteration of agricultural products. Case by case, the costs and benefits need to be assembled. These will range from effects on human health to effects on land and water "health," from effects on producers to effects on delivered prices. There will surely be political, cultural, and religious considerations too, but these may be amenable to change. Since knowledge of future states is always probabilistic, we will continually have to be making best estimates.[26] But in many environmental issues, non-action will not be neutral but the endorsement of a worsening situation.

The main criterion for an ecohumanism will be the effects of situations upon human lives, judged in as global a context as possible. That means taking into account all persons and their descendants as well as the surrounding bio-physico-spheres.[27] First and foremost, the facts. Then the emotional and aesthetic considerations. And only thereafter, the rhetorical and emotional support systems.

Thus, for nontheistic humanists, the starting point is different, the evaluative criteria are different, and therefore the environmental proposals will in all probability also be different. But the focus will always be on the social nature of human life as it affects—and is affected by—the environment. Given that focus, ecohumanists are unable to build upon orientations that respect/restore/renew "Earth." Such slogans too readily lead into an anti-human and anti-scientific posture that separates the needs of humans from putative needs of a separate and non-human sphere. Humanity has progressed too far to return to "life with the bears." The Enlightenment dream of human perfectability ever beckons, ever guides.

Notes

1.   Arthur E. Morgan, in his transition from the TVA to the presidency of Antioch College, argued that the sciences of the past now belonged to the humanities. In those days, history of science had barely emerged as a discipline.

2.   A neglected but useful (1,224 page) anthology has been compiled: Robert M. Torrance, ed., *Encompassing Nature: A Sourcebook* (Washington DC: Counterpoint, 1998).

3.   Andrew C. Revkin, "Scientists Now Acknowledge Role of Humans in Climate Change," *New York Times* (October 26, 1999).

4.   Andrew C. Revkin, "Odd Culprits in Collapse of Climate Talks," *New York Times* (November 29, 1999).

5.   Consider the popularity in holiday cards of the theme of "the peaceable kingdom." Edward Hicks was a very interesting Quaker figure, and his several paintings reveal two common themes: the romantic attribution of moods to animals quite apart from close observation; and the vision that peace required serious and divinely-inspired changes. A California artist once scandalized some of his friends with a Christmas–card version of the scene where each animal could be seen to be contentedly munching on some smaller animal. In the ocean background a shark could even be seen pursuing the human swimmer.

6.   Roger Finke & Rodney Starke, *The Churching of America, 1776-1990* (New Brunswick NJ: Rutgers University Press, 1992).

7.   Lynn White, Jr., "The Historic Roots of Our Ecologic Crisis." *Science* 155 (1967), pp. 1203-7.

326   Ecohumanism

8. Wilfred Cantwell Smith, *The Meaning and End of Religion: A New Approach to the Religious Traditions of Mankind* (New York: New American Library, 1964).

9. For present purposes, ignoring the special status of the Vatican as a "sovereign power."

10. Steven C. Rockefeller, and John C. Elder, eds., *Spirit and Nature: Why the Environment Is a Religious Issue* (Boston: Beacon Press, 1992).

11. Howard Coward & Daniel C. Maguire, eds., *Visions of a New Earth: Religious Perspectives on Population, Consumption, and Ecology* (Albany: SUNY Press, 2000).

12. J. Ronald Engel & Joan Gibb Engel, eds., *Ethics of Environment and Development* (Tucson: University of Arizona Press, 1990).

13. Ibid., p. 12.

14. Dieter T. Hessel & Rosemary Radford Ruether, eds., *Christianity and Ecology* (Cambridge MA: Harvard University Press, 2000). Previous volumes have been Mary Evelyn Tucker & John Berthrong, eds., *Confucianism and Ecology* (1998) Mary Evelyn Tucker & Duncan Ryuken Williams, eds., *Buddhism and Ecology* (1998). Christian Key Chapple & Mary Evelyn Tucker, eds., *Hinduism and Ecology* is to be published in 2000.

15. Unitarian Universalist Association, *The Free Church in a Changing World* (Boston: Unitarian Universalist Association, 1963).

16. Unitarian Universalist Association, *Report of the Committee on Goals* (Boston: Unitarian Universalist Association, 1967).

17. Richard Dawkins, *The Selfish Gene* (New York: Oxford University Press, 1976).

18. From a humanist standpoint, Carol Tavris' treatment of these issues in *The Mismeasure of Woman* (New York: Simon & Schuster, 1992). Similar critiques of the overly-psychologized may be found in Wendy Kaminer, *A Fearful freedom :Women's Flight from Equality* (Reading, MA: Addison-Wesley, 1990). A nuanced sociological position that takes a reasoned account of the biological issues is in Alice Rossi, ed., *Gender and the Life Course* (New York: Aldine, 1985).

19. Murray Bookchin, *Re-Enchanting Humanity: A Defense of the Human Spirit Against Antihumanism, Misanthropy, Mysticism & Primitivism* (London: Cassell, 1995).

20. David Toolan, *At Home in the Cosmos* (New York: Orbis, 2001).

21. Robert Wright, *Nonzero: The Logic of Human Destiny* (New York: Pantheon, 1999).

22. Sam D Gill, *Mother Earth: An American Story* (Chicago: University of Chicago Press, 1987).

23. William K. Stevens, "Suspects in 'Blitzkrieg' Extinctions: Primitive Hunters." *New York Times* (Mar 28, 2000).

24. An excellent examination of these issue may be found in Holmes Rolston III, *Philosophy Gone Wild: Essays in Environmental Ethics* (Buffalo: Prometheus Books, 1986). From the perspective of a Christian process theology, Ian G. Barbour addresses some of the values in and outside of the sciences in "Scientific and Religious Perspectives on Sustainability," Hessel & Ruether, *op. cit.*, pp. 385-401.

25. Julian Huxley, "Presidential Address: Evolutionary Humanism," *Proceedings of the First International Congress on Humanism and Ethical Culture* (Utrecht: Humanistisch Verbond, 1953).

26. Daniel A. Farber, *Eco-Pragmatism: Making Sensible Environmental Decisions in an Uncertain World* (Chicago: University of Chicago Press, 1999).

27. An early book by a close student of the human social scene has been too-often overlooked: Urie Bronfenbrenner, *The Ecology of Human Development* (Cambridge MA: Harvard University Press, 1979).

CONTRIBUTORS

Gwen Whitehead Brewer

Professor (emeritus) of English, Northridge State University, Northridge California; Board, Ventura County League of Women Voters; Board, Ventura County American Civil Liberties Union

Vern L. Bullough

Distinguished Professor and Dean of Natural and Social Sciences (emeritus), SUNY, College at Buffalo; Visiting Professor, University of Southern California; former Co-President, International Humanist & Ethical Union

Kendyl Gibbons

Senior Minister, First Unitarian Society, Minneapolis, Minnesota; President-elect, Unitarian Universalist Ministerial Association

Richard Gilbert

Parish Minister, First Unitarian Church, Rochester, New York

Michael Kami

Business Consultant; former Board, Starr King School for the Ministry; Harley Davidson consultant

Gerald Larue

Professor (emeritus) of Biblical History & Archaeology, Adjunct Professor of Gerontology University of Southern California, Los Angeles; Leader, Ethical Culture Society

Timothy J. Madigan

Editorial Director, University of Rochester Press, New York; Chair, Editorial Board, *Free Inquiry*

Sarah Oelberg

Minister, UU Churches in Hanska & Mankato, Minnesota; Board, Friends of Religious Humanism

Donald F. Page

Electrical Engineer; Former Editor, U.S., International, & Canadian humanist magazines

Howard B. Radest

Former Director, Ethical Culture & Fieldston Schools, New York; Leader, American Ethical Union; Adjunct Professor of Philosophy, University of South Carolina, Beaufort

Philip J. Regal;

Professor of Ecology, Evolution and Behavior, University of Minnesota, Minneapolis

Andreas Rosenberg

Professor (emeritus) of Laboratory Medicine, Pathology, Biochemistry, and Biophysics, University of Minnesota, Minneapolis

Harvey B. Sarles
Professor of Cultural Studies and Comparative Literature, University of Minnesota, Minneapolis

David Schafer
Former Research Physiologist and Developmental Scientist (Molecular Diagnostics), Dept. of Veterans Affairs Medical Center, West Haven, Connecticut

John M. Swomley
Professor (emeritus) of Social Ethics, St. Paul Theological Seminary, Kansas City Missouri; former Executive Director, Fellowship of Reconciliation; former Vice President, American Civil Liberties Union

Robert B. Tapp
Professor (emeritus) of Humanities, Religious Studies, and South Asian Studies, University of Minnesota, Minneapolis; Dean, The Humanist Institute, New York City

Michael Werner
Sales & marketing, hi-tech adhesives; former President, American Humanist Association

Carol Wintermute
Co-President, North American Committee for Humanism/ Humanist Institute, New York City; Vice President, Friends of Religious Humanism; Artist

PREVIOUS ISSUES

Subject to availability, back issues of volumes 1-7 can be purchased for $6.00 each, and volumes 8-13 for $8.00 each.

North American Committee for
Humanism / Humanist Institute
3722 W. 50th St.
P.O. Box 123
Minneapolis, MN 55410

Fax 612/928-9821
Email **palsagay@aol.com**

http://www.humanistinstitute.org